Connected Lives

feminist constructions
Series Editors: Hilde Lindemann Nelson, Sara Ruddick, and Margaret Urban Walker

Feminist Constructions publishes accessible books that send feminist ethics in promising new directions. Feminist ethics has excelled at critique, identifying masculinist bias in social practice and in the moral theory that is used to justify that practice. The series continues the work of critique, but its emphasis falls on construction. Moving beyond critique, the series aims to build a positive body of theory that extends feminist moral understandings.

Gender Struggles: Practical Approaches to Contemporary Feminism
     edited by Constance L. Mui and Julien S. Murphy
"Sympathy and Solidarity" and Other Essays
     by Sandra Lee Bartky
The Subject of Violence: Arendtean Exercises in Understanding
     by Bat-Ami Bar On
How Can I Be Trusted? A Virtue Theory of Trustworthiness
     by Nancy Nyquist Potter
Moral Contexts
     by Margaret Urban Walker
Recognition, Responsibility, and Rights: Feminist Ethics and Social Theory
     edited by Robin N. Fiore and Hilde Lindemann Nelson
The Philosopher Queen: Feminist Essays on War, Love, and Knowledge
     by Chris Cuomo
The Subject of Care: Feminist Perspectives on Dependency
     edited by Eva Feder Kittay and Ellen K. Feder
Pilgrimages/Peregrinajes: Theorizing Coalition against Multiple Oppressions
     by María Lugones
Why Privacy Isn't Everything: Feminist Reflections on Personal Accountability
     by Anita L. Allen
Discovering Feminist Philosophy: Knowledge, Ethics, Politics
     by Robin May Schott
Relational Remembering: Rethinking the Memory Wars
     by Susan Campbell
Varieties of Feminist Liberalism
     by Amy R. Baehr
Connected Lives: Human Nature and an Ethics of Care
     by Ruth E. Groenhout

Connected Lives

Human Nature and an Ethics of Care

Ruth E. Groenhout

ROWMAN & LITTLEFIELD PUBLISHERS, INC.
Lanham • Boulder • New York • Toronto • Oxford

ROWMAN & LITTLEFIELD PUBLISHERS, INC.

Published in the United States of America
by Rowman & Littlefield Publishers, Inc.
A wholly owned subsidiary of The Rowman & Littlefield Publishing Group, Inc.
4501 Forbes Boulevard, Suite 200, Lanham, Maryland 20706
www.rowmanlittlefield.com

PO Box 317
Oxford
OX2 9RU, UK

British Library Cataloguing in Publication Information Available

Library of Congress Cataloging-in-Publication Data

Groenhout, Ruth E., 1962–
  Connected lives : human nature and an ethics of care / Ruth E.
Groenhout.
    p. cm.
  Includes index.
  ISBN 0-7425-1496-X (cloth : alk. paper)—ISBN 0-7425-1497-8 (pbk. :
alk. paper)
  1. Feminist ethics. 2. Caring. I. Title.
  BJ1395.G76 2004
  177'.7—dc22   2003020462

Printed in the United States of America

♾™ The paper used in this publication meets the minimum requirements of American
National Standard for Information Sciences—Permanence of Paper for Printed Library
Materials, ANSI/NISO Z39.48–1992.

This book is dedicated to Todd Groenhout,
who thought it would be more interesting with a superhero.

Contents

Acknowledgments   ix

Introduction   1

Chapter 1   Human Nature and an Ethic of Care   21

Chapter 2   Augustine and Care   52

Chapter 3   Levinas and Care Theory   79

Chapter 4   Human Nature: Is an Ideal Really Necessary?   104

Chapter 5   Care and the New Reproductive Technologies   135

Chapter 6   Care and Cloning   165

Index   189

About the Author   195

Acknowledgments

This book would never have been written without the support and encouragement of a whole network of caring colleagues and friends. The first articulation of the ideas in this book occurred during a National Endowment for the Humanities summer seminar led by Alan Wolfe. I am grateful for his leadership during that seminar, and for his continued encouragement as I worked on this project, as well as for the willingness of other seminar participants, especially the Hamilton Six, to discuss and debate these issues over the course of the seminar.

Calvin College provided me with Calvin Research Scholarships that allowed release time from teaching to work on several chapters of the manuscript. The Calvin Center for Christian Scholarship also provided invaluable support in the form of a grant that provided me with release time to write the chapter on Augustine; it also provided funding for bringing many wonderful care theory speakers to campus for lectures and discussions. Nel Noddings, Joan Tronto, Patricia Hill Collins, Julia Wood, and Wes Jackson all came and lectured in the course of that grant, and the chance to talk with them, and their gracious willingness to meet with the group and discuss projects, are much appreciated. My thanks as well to the other participants in the Care Grant Group, especially Jan Curry and Helen Sterk, co-conveners, and Clarence Joldersma and Simona Goi, collegial critics.

Finally, and most significantly, the Erasmus Institute at the University of Notre Dame supported this project through granting me an entire year's fellowship at the institute. The chance to work without interruption and to experience the intellectual companionship of the other fellows was golden. I could not have finished this manuscript without it. My heartfelt thanks go to Jim Turner and Dianne Phillips for all their academic work and leadership, to Terri O'Bryan for her administrative work, and all the members of the Erasmus Institute for making the year possible and fruitful, and for providing the resources for the completion of this project.

Thanks are due as well to Hilde Lindemann Nelson, Sara Ruddick, and Margaret Urban Walker, series editors of the Feminist Constructions Series at Rowman & Littlefield, for encouragement, constructive criticism, and patience. The manuscript has been improved by their comments and suggestions, and I am grateful.

Introduction

Ethics and politics are not spectator sports.

—Onora O'Neill

Ethical decisions are unavoidable. From the trivial (Should I make a rude gesture at the driver who just cut me off?) to the momentous (Can I, should I, kill myself?), from the intensely personal (Should I get pregnant?) to the maximally public (Should the United States sign an international treaty banning reproductive cloning?) ethical matters structure our lives. Ethical theorists claim to have a certain level of expertise with respect to all of this, and it has become common to hire professors to teach ethics to medical students, business majors, and even the students at the former School of the Americas. In this last case, administrators tell us, a school that became notorious for producing graduates who have been involved in torture, coercion, and the subversion of democratic practices in Latin America should now be trusted because it has hired instructors in ethics and its students will now be taught about human rights. "Yeah," a friend of mine remarked upon hearing this news. "Now its graduates will know which rights they're infringing when they torture someone." My friend was not making light of the crimes committed by graduates of the School of the Americas. He has protested there on numerous occasions. His ironic statement reflects the futility of teaching ethical theory in a context in which there is no commitment to basic moral action.

This raises one central question any writer on the topic of ethics needs to face. Is there any connection between ethical theorizing and being a better person? Is there any important reason for thinking critically and carefully about ethics? I start with a disclaimer. One can study ethical theory in depth without in any way becoming a better person. Because it is possible to split off theoretical reflection from practical deliberation, it is not possible to make someone good by teaching him or her ethical theory.

At the same time, however, theory is not irrelevant for action. The theoretical assumptions citizens hold will structure the political decisions they make. The beliefs we hold about the acceptable range of human actions will have an effect on the choices we make as we structure our lives in personal and social ways. Theory alone cannot make people better, but if people want to be moral, caring agents, theory can provide guidelines for decision making. Unless we think carefully about the ethical assumptions we rely on in our day-to-day decision making, that is, unless we engage in reflective, theoretical critique, we may find ourselves unwittingly choosing social structures that are at odds with the things we value most highly. Theory cannot make us better people, but if we want to be better people, theory can help us think through how the values we hold can be expressed in our individual and citizen lives. Theoretical reflection can also help us avoid making choices that undermine the possibility of a decent moral life. This book directs its attention to theoretical reflection on conceptions about human nature and on what constitutes a good human life. Such reflection about ourselves, our loved ones, and our fellow citizens allows us to construct lives connected to those of others in ways that permit us all to flourish. A central contention throughout is that human flourishing depends on social structures of care that both protect the vulnerable and reflect an accurate understanding of the worth of care. We have laws, for example, that punish parents who neglect their children. But parents who struggle to provide adequate care to their children while working a patchwork of minimum wage, part-time jobs are offered little respect or support by society. If we value care, we need to signal that value using both economic policies and social images that reflect it, and we need to demand public policies that do not subordinate the needs of working families to the economic interests of large corporations.

This book, then, begins with an account of human nature that makes care central, and uses that account to detail what it means for humans to flourish. This language of flourishing, the notion of human nature, the idea of an ethics of care, and a general commitment to ethical theorizing are all suspect, however, in certain sectors of feminist thought. To speak of flourishing requires us to speak about human nature, because the notion of flourishing is inextricably connected to the idea of the well-being of a particular kind of thing. The idea that there is a determinate human nature has been criticized by many thinkers, particularly feminist thinkers, because it seems to deny human freedom. The idea that we can speak of "nature" at all, or of its cognate, "the natural," may seem to fly in the face of a notion of humans as freely determining their own nature and meaning in life. The notion of ethical theorizing is rejected by some thinkers on the grounds that any large-scale theorizing about ethics will necessarily be totalizing and destructive of human lives. The notion of a feminist ethic based on the ideal of care is likewise contentious, since feminists have often been concerned to release women from the requirement that they care for others in ways that destroy their own lives. So before I turn to the question of human nature and an ethic of care, I need to examine these various concepts, and consider why it might make sense for a feminist theorist to hang on to them.

I. Nature and the Natural

Philosophers who argue that we need to examine human nature in order to understand ethics run the risk of being accused of falling into the naturalistic fallacy. The naturalistic fallacy is an error in reasoning that is made, some argue, whenever thinkers try to move from what is (issues of fact, usually assumed to be empirically verifiable) to what ought to be (issues of value). Many thinkers argue that there can be no bridging of this divide: matters of fact are completely and utterly separate from matters of value, and any ethical theory that tries to move from what is to what ought to be demonstrates a failure to understand basic logic. In this view, we can never gain insight into ethical matters, matters of right and wrong, matters of how humans should structure their lives, by examining how humans do live. There is some plausibility to this claim. After all, humans naturally do lots of things they ought not do. Humans lie, cheat, and steal, they murder and rape, and a simplistic assumption that how humans are is how they ought to be would seem to be stuck with affirming all the horrible things they actually do.

But in recent years a number of thinkers have challenged this absolute prohibition on moving from "is" to "ought." Some thinkers, influenced by postmodernism and Kuhnian critiques of the sciences, have argued that the first part of the fact/value split is fallacious because there are no pure facts. Every claim that purports to be a fact comes to us with a host of assumed value presuppositions and observer biases. In its more extreme forms this view rejects any notion that there can be an objective evaluation of anything, and argues instead that all views are utterly and equally subjective. In this view, there can be no fact of the matter, for example, on the question of whether schizophrenia is better treated with medication than with prayer. People who accept the presuppositions of modern medicine will, of course, prefer medication, but some who reject those presuppositions will prefer prayer, and there is no independent, objective truth by which to resolve the question.

Other thinkers have criticized the fact/value split in the other direction. The notion that values float free of the realm of facts, they argue, is nonsense. If I say that a person is courageous (to choose an example made famous by Philippa Foot), I am making a claim that is both factual and evaluative.[1] I can look around for evidence that will show whether or not this person actually is courageous, and can demonstrate that it is either true or false that she is. But I also recognize that terming someone courageous is, all things considered, a positive evaluation of her character. In this case, fact and value cannot be separated, nor should they be. Evaluations of character involve both facts and values, and neither is independent of the other. The facts can make us reconsider values, and values can make us reconsider the facts. This view does not reject the basic notion of objectivity, but it rejects the claim that objectivity is the same thing as being value-neutral, or free from any connection to values.

We can summarize these three basic positions, then, as follows. The first position, held by proponents of the fact/value split, maintains that both facts and values exist, that the former are objective and value neutral, and that the latter are subjective and value laden. The second position accepts this basic distinction, but denies that there are any value-neutral or objective facts. The third view rejects the identity of "objective" with "value-neutral," and argues that there are certain realms of rational inquiry in which objectivity *requires* a certain value orientation. In particular, proponents of the third position argue, when we engage in rational deliberation that is practical in nature, that concerns questions of what actions to perform, we cannot deliberate at all without making assumptions about values (in this they agree with the second position); but that does not mean that our deliberation is a matter of purely subjective opinion. There can be a fact of the matter on certain questions of value.

This debate is particularly important, and hard to deal with, in the context of feminist thought, because each of the three positions seems to offer both promise and peril for the feminist political activist. The first position, for example, allows the feminist to argue that the sexual abuse of women by men is wrong, whatever the facts are about the ubiquity of male aggression in human society. Feminists have often wanted to argue that injustice must cease, regardless of whether or not it is widespread and so, apparently, a "fact of nature." "Let justice be done, though the heavens fall!" they have said, along with Kant, and so have adopted a position that accepts the fundamental split between what is and what ought to be.[2] In this view, the facts are irrelevant to discussions about justice.

But many feminist theorists have not wanted to dispense with the facts, since the facts of women's sexual abuse and male aggression are precisely what they are concerned with. Some feminists have argued that feminist theory itself forces us to the more extreme second position. The very claim that male aggression may be ubiquitous, they argue, is a claim premised on a particular set of value assumptions, such as the assumption that dominance over other groups is advantageous for human life. The claim of advantage is best analyzed, they argue, as a power play on the part of those who defend masculine privilege.[3] We cannot understand the sexual abuse of women without first seeing how masculinity is socially constructed in terms of sexualized violence against women. When we do see that, the claim that male aggression is ubiquitous can be seen as the attempt to define reality in ways that maintain the patriarchal status quo. This view can provide an important critique of purportedly scientific work. When scientists use the sexual behavior of ducks to justify claims that the tendency to rape is genetically determined for some men, it does become fairly obvious that biases about sex are driving the research, rather than the research providing evidence for the conclusions.[4] But while this response allows feminist theorists to identify the biases and lack of objectivity in their opponents' arguments, it precludes any claim feminists might make that their own position is the better one. Since all claims are reflections of particular biases and presuppositions, there are no views that can be shown to be more consistent with the facts. While it can be enormously valuable to analyze the biases that lead a person to a particular conclusion, denial that there is anything beyond biases turns debates over political rights for women into struggles for domination and control between feminist and antifeminist, struggles in which neither side can make any claim to the moral higher ground.

This equation of feminist and antifeminist positions as equally subjective, equally a matter of power rather than truth, is rejected by a third group of feminists. This last group argues that the best feminist response to the claim that male sexual aggression is an essential part of human nature, and vital to human well-being, is to go back and look at the evidence to see if it actually supports that claim. They accept the notion that arguments from human well-being are relevant to ethical deliberation, but they do not automatically accept antifeminist positions on the basis of claims about human well-being.[5]

Instead they argue that a careful examination of the evidence suggests that feminist aims are fully compatible with, or even required for, human flourishing. A human society that is truly good, they argue, will be one that provides for the full development of both men and women as moral agents, and that protects the basic rights and liberties of all its members. This is an argument that is open to refutation by sociological study, and that assumes that there really is some truth of the matter about what counts as human flourishing. In adopting this position it sets itself in opposition to the second view, and does so because it wants to hang on to the notion that there really is a truth of the matter about whether certain practices are harmful to women.

In order for a theorist to accept this third position, however, he or she needs to adopt what philosophers call a teleological view of nature, a view of nature that incorporates an evaluative and goal oriented account of the natural. In adopting this teleological view, proponents of the third position also reject the first position. To call something natural in the teleological sense is to assert that the facts of the case are value laden. This can be obscured because we use the word "nature" or "natural" in at least two different ways, and we often do not distinguish them carefully. The first sense of the term "natural" occurs when we note that an event occurs with fair regularity, as when we say that it is natural for people's eyes to become farsighted as they age. This sense of the term is not evaluative, but observational. But we sometimes use the term "natural" in a more evaluative sense, as when we say that a person needs medical treatment to restore natural functioning, as when they have a broken bone and need it to be set. In this second sense, the term "natural" does not function in a purely observational way, but instead identifies an ideal of functioning. Medical descriptions of health rely very heavily on this second, evaluative sense of "natural." But this sense of "natural" cannot be equated with "what occurs with fair regularity" since it sets itself in opposition to certain regular occurrences. Broken bones do occur with regularity, but that offers us no reason to assume that a broken bone is natural in the second, teleological sense.

A fairly large industry has sprung up in the United States that depends on conflating these two opposing senses of the term "natural." Although vitamin supplements, amino acid supplements, and "natural weight loss" pills are all natural in the first sense, few people would purchase them if they thought that "natural" in this context means "occurs with fair regularity." Instead, the term "natural" is used to advertise these products with the intention of convincing consumers that taking them will restore or maintain natural function, using "natural" in the second sense. Unfortunately for the consumers who purchase these various substances, the two senses of "natural" do not always coincide. Like poison ivy, a fair number of substances that are natural in the first, descriptive, sense are anything but natural in the second, teleological, sense. The evidence for the benefits provided by massive doses of vitamins is underwhelming; most current research suggests that megadoses are of little value at best, and positively harmful in the worst cases, such as massive doses of vitamin A.

The second sense of "natural" is teleological because it assumes that processes and organisms have an internal or inbuilt ideal of functioning, and that the proper functioning of a process or the good of an organism can be partly determined by seeing whether it attains or approximates that ideal. In this view of nature we cannot endorse whatever happens to be, since it frequently happens that things are naturally flawed or unable to function properly. But we also cannot speak of terms such as "health" or "good character," or "properly structured human society" without careful observation of how a particular type of being functions, and of what sorts of internal goals and purposes are demonstrated by that functioning. Without recognizing that eyes serve the purpose of sight, and without a sense of the general range of sight appropriate to a given species, we cannot evaluate whether someone's eyes are healthy or need corrective lenses. Without recognizing that humans naturally exist in affective relationships with other humans, we cannot evaluate a psychopathic person as unable to function properly. We cannot endorse nature tout court, but neither can we ignore nature if we are trying to describe the basic parameters of healthy human life. We find ourselves needing to use judgment to figure out what constitutes naturally healthy functioning. We can get it wrong. We can think that an organism is healthy when it is really not. But without a reliance on some notion of healthy functioning, we cannot engage the question of well-being or flourishing at all.

II. Human Nature and Ethics

But if we are going to endorse the notion that ethical theory has to be grounded in some conception of human nature, we need to face the rather depressing evidence of past theories of human nature, theories that have functioned to propose profoundly unjust social systems and impose them on women. Aristotle, for example, thought that the good human life was a life that only elite male citizens could live. It required that there be "naturally inferior" others, male and female slaves and "free" women, whose proper function was to look after the niggling details of everyday life. Their performing this function freed the "truly human person"—that is, the upper-class male citizen—to live a life of companionship with other upper-class males, to engage in political deliberation, and to engage in the highest of human activities, philosophical contemplation. In Aristotle's picture of the proper ordering of human life, the "naturally inferior others" were both essential, because the good life could not be lived without them, and invisible, because they were not considered fully human, and their exclusion from a full human life merited only a few dismissive comments.

Aristotle's views about the proper shape of human life are found in the works of numerous other philosophers in the Western tradition. This elitist account of human life has not gone unchallenged, however. Those who have been excluded from full humanity by these philosophical definitions have an irritating habit of criticizing the definitions. Slaves, upper- and middle-class women, and others excluded from the ranks of the upper-class male citizenship have argued that they, too, are human. When this argument is made (and it has been made over and over in Western philosophy[6]) those who offer it generally find themselves with two options. They can, on the one hand, accept what dominant voices say about full humanity and argue that they are wrongfully excluded from that category because they have the same characteristics as those who count as "truly human." So women argue that, like men, they are capable of rational deliberation. On the other hand the excluded ones can challenge the very notion of "truly human" and argue that the original thinkers got it wrong in important ways. In the case of women, that is, instead of accepting a male standard of humanity and arguing that women could live up to it, they can instead challenge the very notion that a male standard offers an adequate account of human life.

Traditionally, the first claim has been the easiest to support. We see it operating in Frederick Douglass's antislavery writings, in Mary Wollstonecraft's advocacy of the rights of women, and in countless other discussions of the full humanity of some group that has been legally or socially defined as "inferior." Feminist supporters of this first position have been called equality feminists, and they have been very influential in political battles for legal rights for women. But as women gained basic political rights, they simultaneously began to challenge the implicit assumption that men (upper-class men, that is) should properly define the standard model of humanity. Many humans, one can't help noticing, are not upper-class males, and an account of "human nature" that implicitly excludes the majority of humans from full coverage is an inadequate theory. Sometimes feminist challenges to the "male model" of humanity involve a complete rejection of a masculine model of humanity, replacing it with an alternative female model. This view can be self-defeating, however. If it is morally unacceptable for men to claim full human rights for themselves while denying them to others, presumably the claim that only women are human would be morally unacceptable in the same way and for the same reasons.

A more interesting option involves rejecting a single model of human nature and endorsing, instead, a two-model view, so that flourishing for men is assumed to be different from flourishing for women, because men and women have different natures. Sometimes this second category of feminist theory is termed "difference feminism," because it makes the differences between men and women central to its philosophical account of human nature. But both equality feminism and difference feminism struggle with the difficult task of providing an adequate philosophical account of women's lives in the context of a philosophical tradition that has excluded women from full human existence. Equality feminists argue that women are equal to men, but this implies that the male is the proper standard for measuring humanity, since it is equality with men that makes one count as human. Difference feminist argue that women are different from men, which still assumes that the male is the standard against which difference is measured. So both have been criticized for assuming a male standard against which difference is defined, or in terms of which equality is measured.

If we want to avoid the implicit assumption that elite males are the standard model of humanity, against which all other humans need to be measured, we need to articulate some other vision of what it could mean to be human. Such an account can be found, sometimes more implicit than explicit, in what has come to be called an ethic of care. The Western tradition has generally assumed that the central activity that defines human existence is rationality, and more specifically the sort of theoretical intellectual enterprise represented by philosophical reflection. This is an important part of human existence, of course, but care theorists argue that an adequate picture of human life requires a broader field of activities and capabilities, and a better sense of how rational activity fits into those various activities. Adequate understanding of human life and an ethic appropriate to human existence cannot be attained by limiting one's account of human activities to theoretical reason or philosophical contemplation. Instead, care theorists argue, human life can only be properly understood if we look at the full range of activities and experiences that structure human life and give it meaning. The activities that are essential to the continuance of human life *as human* are particularly important, and these are the activities that involve caring for and educating children, and generally providing for the physical dependencies of human beings—by providing medical care and physical support for those who cannot care for themselves. Further, care theorists argue, we cannot properly understand rationality if we assume it is independent of and unrelated to the contexts of care within which it exists. But the activities of care are largely relegated to the subhuman by the philosophical tradition. Care theorists argue that they are integral to human existence and that their exclusion damages philosophical theorizing.

An adequately complex view of human lives, care theorists argue, leads us to recognize that humans are physical beings who live lives that are inescapably structured in terms of dependence on other humans and on the environment in which they live. Further, because activities such as intellectual reflection require a complex social structure of language, intellectual enquiry, and standards of authority and reasonableness, rationality cannot be understood apart from social context and apart from the social structures that make it possible. Theories that begin with the assumption that rational reflection is an ahistorical process engaged in by an intellect dissociated from any physical life processes simply got rationality wrong, and their mistaken presuppositions created problems in their ethical reasoning as well. To see why this would be, we need to go back to the importance of the notion of what is natural in the teleological sense developed earlier.

Humans are physical beings who live enmeshed in relationships of interdependence. Noting this brings us to an understanding of human nature in the first sense of the term "natural," but not in the second, teleological sense. Theorists in the Western tradition have almost universally noted that humans are physical, embodied beings, but their response to that recognition has been to argue that it is more proper to human life to turn away from the physical and concentrate on the intellectual or spiritual realm. Rational reflection, however, may not be as separate from human physical existence as these theorists have assumed. Without metaphors drawn from physical experience,[7] without social structures that provide the privilege and leisure for some individuals to engage in rational reflection, and without background assumptions about who speaks as an authority and why, rational reflection cannot go on. If this is true, then we should not be so quick to turn away from the embodied nature of human existence. We need to spend some time and effort on the question of what makes physical existence a good existence, one in which physical well-being is supported and sustained. We need to examine how particular types of physical existence affect social relationships and intellectual activity. These are not questions that can be answered in the abstract. We need the perspective of the health sciences, the social sciences, and psychological studies to gain an adequate account of what physical well-being is, how it functions in human life, the relationship between intellectual activity and the physical organization of social life, and the ways in which various social structures can destroy or limit such flourishing.

This question about the relationship between nature and flourishing has affinities with a separate debate, one that rarely makes its way into the philosophical literature: the debate in gardening circles over the use of native versus nonnative plants. There are very vocal proponents of the position that gardeners should use only native plants in their gardens, and their arguments tend to rely heavily on the claim that native plants are natural, while nonnatives are unnatural and so, at some level, wrong, or inappropriate—not to be used. The problem is that there is no neat way to determine which plants are, as a matter of fact, native. I have several varieties of hybrid daylilies growing in my garden. These plants are developed from plants that have grown in the Midwest for centuries, but they themselves are hybrids, not the original strain of tiger lilies that dot roadsides everywhere.

The daylilies I grow have many of the desirable characteristics of native plants; they are hardy and do not need extra watering, heavy fertilization, or other types of special care that make native-plant proponents reject nonnatives. But it is very difficult to argue that the daylilies are native, or even natural, if by "natural" we mean "undeveloped by humans." This suggests that the native/nonnative debate is perhaps wrongly framed. The question is not the biological one of whether a particular plant (historically) grew in a particular region; it is a question more fundamentally of the acceptability of certain practices of gardening. Ultimately the argument is a normative one; gardeners ought to have a certain relationship to the earth that involves using water sparingly, protecting and maintaining topsoil, and avoiding excessive use of fertilizers. The use of plants that are well adapted to local conditions supports this relationship.

The fact/value distinction hovers in the background of this discussion. Although it can be useful to separate the discussion of data from normative claims for certain limited purposes, the attempt to draw a clear distinction between the facts and the values in any discussion is ultimately doomed to failure. Facts are value laden, and values are fact infused. When gardeners argue that nonnative plants should not be used, they are arguing both that certain facts represent important values (protection of water supplies, healthy soil maintenance practices) and that certain values are factually relevant. Discussion of human nature, likewise, cannot proceed in a purely neutral way. Every account of what is "natural" for humans will ultimately depend on normative views about how humans ought to be. But such accounts will also be factual; they will claim at some level that it is true, or a fact, that human lives go better if they follow certain paths of development rather than others.

But the link with environmental concepts is even more direct than this. One central concept in environmental ethics is that of sustainability. An

ecosystem is sustainable when it can survive over time, in the face of changing weather conditions and occasional encroachments by outside forces. It is
worth noting that sustainability does not equate with stasis. A sustainable
system is a dynamic one. The various components of the system change from
time to time, and within the system there is constant reorganization due to
internal and external pressure. But the dynamism of the system does not
equate with unlimited growth. It is generated, instead, by a dynamic balance
between the various components of the system. Unlimited growth is unsustainable. Balance requires that there be both growth and decay, increase and
decrease, in balanced measure.

But sustainability requires more than dynamic balance. It also requires interdependence. A system is sustainable, in part, because the various parts of
the system are interdependent and interconnected. In ecosystems the dependence in question is not intentional, of course; it is generated by seasons
of scarcity and plenty. In human communities, however, since humans are
the sorts of things that can choose whether or not to act in certain ways, and
how to structure societies, interdependence needs to be recognized and supported. This is where characteristics of care enter the picture. Unless a human society incorporates, encourages, and supports the development of caring practices in its citizens, the society cannot sustain itself.

It seems to me, in fact, that societies that reject characteristics of care tend
to follow one or another trajectory. In some cases they reject care in favor of
unlimited growth. Laissez-faire capitalism can proceed along this trajectory,
and when it does, it destroys the social structures a capitalist system requires
to exist, systems such as education and stable political structures. This is not
a successful strategy in the long term. Unlimited growth, like cancer, is
deadly. Seeing the unsustainability of unregulated capitalism has led certain
brands of Marxists to construct societies in which central control is designed
to prevent capitalist excesses. Unfortunately, the most rigid and totalitarian
of such societies are incapable of the flexibility and innovation needed for a
healthy social structure. Further, rigid totalitarianism destroys the social
bonds and relationships needed for a healthy society. A society capable of
sustaining itself for any length of time needs social structures that are pro-
tected from economic attack and from rigid totalitarian control. Among such
social structures are those connected with practices of care, the social structures that allow for the sustaining and education of dependent young, that
provide decent lives for the elderly and those who cannot care for themselves, and the like.

Any healthy society, then, will need to have structures that support and
protect care providers. Societies sometimes relegate the provision of care to

a subset of the population, usually women. In these situations caregivers are usually denigrated and placed in a fairly low socioeconomic position. This state of affairs can perpetuate itself for quite some time, but it is not optimal. In the absence of strong legal or social compulsion, in fact, women eventually opt out of these roles. The United States faces a shortage of in-home nurse's aides, for example, because the women who traditionally held such jobs have found that they can make a better wage elsewhere for less backbreaking work. An editorial in a newspaper some years ago lamented this shortage and blamed it on women's loss of altruism. The author appeared to have no concern for men's lack of altruism, or for the fact that nurse's aides generally do not make enough to live on. But providing in-home care for elderly people and people with disabilities should not be premised on the expectation that women will work long hours at low pay out of altruism. It should, instead, be recognized as an issue that society as a whole should address in ways that are healthy for all. For a society to be able to sustain itself through the various crises that will always appear sooner or later, it needs to ensure that care pervades the society at all levels.

There is a further connection between the concept of sustainability and an ethics of care. Sustainable agriculture requires a respect for local conditions and what Wes Jackson refers to as the wisdom of nature. That is, in order to develop sustainable systems of agriculture one must understand and work within the constraints of an already existing natural ecosystem. In an example that offers insight into how radically different from current practices a sustainable agriculture would have to be, Jackson argues that we should stop paying chemical companies for providing pesticides and herbicides for agricultural use. Instead, he suggests, consider how agricultural practices would change if we paid chemical companies regular fees for the continued health of a particular system, but expected them to pay a fine when the system is thrown out of balance and requires chemical adjustment.[8] That latter picture, he argues, is an example of sustainable thinking. That is, in order to think sustainably, we need to reverse our current economic paradigm, quit offering economic incentives for working against natural ecosystems, and begin to offer economic incentives for working with the ecosystem.

It seems to me that a paradigm shift of this same sort is needed in ethics. Rather than beginning with the question of how we can stop people from being cruel, perhaps we need to begin with the question of when and why people care for each other. If those conditions can be identified and made a social priority, less of society's resources would need to be devoted to incarcerating wrongdoers after the fact. Much of contemporary ethical thought is devoted to the identification of what we ought not to do, with very little attention focused on how we ought to live. To address that second issue, however, a certain conception of what humans ought to be like must be generally accepted and promulgated. Humans must be seen as inherently made to care for others. There are certainly situations in which care cannot or should not be expressed, but the fundamental attitude of one human to another should be seen as one of love, not hatred. Care theory thus needs an articulated account of what counts as a flourishing human life, and such an account can provide new ways of thinking about the proper structuring of human society. Such an account is implicit, I believe, in much of the work done on care. But before I develop and refine that account, a few words about what an ethic of care is, and which theorists have developed it, are in order.

III. A Very Brief History of Care and Its Critics

The origins of care theory can be traced back to work by Carol Gilligan, particularly her early book In a Different Voice, in which she makes the claim that there are two voices in which ethical deliberation can be carried out, a voice of care and a voice of justice. The first, she argues is a voice of responsibility and relationships, while the second is a voice of rights and isolation.[9] She uses the notion of a "voice" to capture the idea that when we articulate moral or ethical reasoning we speak about our experiences or thoughts with a particular set of concepts and assumptions. Her claim is that psychological and sociological research on moral development, particularly that of Lawrence Kohlberg, assumes that only one voice, the voice of rights and justice, really counts as ethical reasoning. The result of excluding the other voice from studies of moral reasoning, Gilligan contends, is to evaluate women as less proficient moral reasoners than men, because women as a group are more likely to articulate their moral concerns in the voice of care and responsibility.

Gilligan's thesis has been both celebrated and criticized,[10] but in terms of the historical development of care theory it is extraordinarily important. The notion that reasoning about ethical issues needs to include women's voices and experiences proved to be enormously powerful, theoretically. In Caring, Nel Noddings argues that mainstream analytic ethical theory, with its focus on impartialist Kantian and utilitarian theories of right and wrong, produces an account of ethics that is inappropriate and falsifying when brought into contact with women's everyday experiences of raising children, caring for loved ones, and going about the day-to-day business of life.[11] Instead of a matter of impartial, absolute principles, Noddings argues, ethical experience is fundamentally a matter of care, an affective response to vulnerability and neediness on the part of a particular other.

Both Noddings and Gilligan explicitly tie their initial discussions to women's experiences. Gilligan speaks of a woman's voice; Noddings develops her account of caring in terms of a maternal caregiver and claims that reflecting on women's experiences in maintaining the basic structures needed for human life (child care, cooking, cleaning) provided the inspiration for her thought about the nature of care. Both revise their stances somewhat in later discussions and argue that what they articulate are the experiences that people socialized as women in our society tend to have. That is, they articulate a perspective that arises from societal expectations and socially constructed experiences, rather than a perspective of some timeless female essence. Despite these qualifications Noddings's and Gilligan's views are often discussed as if they spoke of a uniquely female ethical voice.

At about this same time, Sara Ruddick wrote *Maternal Thinking*, in which she argues that there are epistemological ramifications to engaging in maternal practices.[12] The theory of knowledge she articulates is not neutral with respect to moral values and perspectives, but instead supports, she argues, a politics of peace.[13] The conjunction of these formative books—in addition to an extensive discussion of a "woman's voice," care, and maternal thinking in numerous journal articles and anthologies—seemed to herald an attempt to develop an ethical theory generated by women to respond to the centuries of ethical theorizing done from and for a masculine perspective. This, in turn, generated a heated discussion over the place of mothering in feminist theory.

Some theorists argued that feminist thinking needs to pay attention to the fact that women do the bulk of mothering work in all known societies, and that the work women do is an important resource for moral theorizing. Other theorists argued that women's work in the sphere of child care and private housework is an oppressive social construct and cannot not be the basis for a liberatory account of ethical and political theory.[14] Jean Bethke Elshtain and Mary Dietz, in particular, found themselves at odds over this issue, with Elshtain arguing that women's experiences provide crucial ethical insights into political theory, while Dietz countered that an identification of the self with mothering makes women unfit to participate in civic and public deliberation.[15] The issue of whether the concept of mothering has any role to play in ethical theory became particularly hotly contested, with those who defended theorizing from the concept of mothering branded "essentialists" (since they were accused of assuming or endorsing the view that women's essential nature is defined by mothering), while those who rejected it were dismissed as operating with an implicitly masculine model of the human person.

One of the interesting aspects of these debates is the way they tended to completely ignore the general technique, used, for example, by Sara Ruddick, of using the term "mothering" to refer to the practice of caring for the day-to-day needs of children without regard to the sex of the caregiver. Such a shift should allow an analysis of the practice without automatically assuming an essential feminine nature, but it has proven difficult to separate practice from person, such is the power of cultural understandings of motherhood and, one fears, apple pie.

Meanwhile, in epistemological circles, a similar debate was brewing. In *What Can She Know?* Lorraine Code investigates the epistemological ramifications of the nature of the subject. Standard accounts of epistemology, of the theory of knowledge, tended to assume that the nature of knowledge is determined by what is known, not by who the knowing subject is. Code takes issue with this, arguing that knowledge is relational and situated, so that one cannot evaluate knowledge without taking the situation of the knower, and the sex of the knower, into account.[16] In particular, Code argues, most human knowledge is predicated on relationships with other people, relationships in which power imbalances can affect what can be perceived and by whom.[17] Further, most knowledge relies on trust, warranted or not, and concerns other people rather than the existence or nonexistence of the "mid-sized dry goods" type of object that tended to be the focus of most epistemological theorists.[18] Like Gilligan, Noddings, Ruddick, and Elshtain, Code argues that women's experiences are significant for understanding what can be known, and how, and who has the authority to make knowledge claims.

Virginia Held also contributed to this general development in ethics. Her *Feminist Morality* argues that women's experiences of birthing, caregiving, and mothering provide them with ethical understandings that are clearer and more accurate than the ethical accounts traditionally given by theorists operating from a male-centered perspective.[19] Joan Tronto also entered the debate at this point, arguing that a concern with caregiving, and in particular providing care for the dependent elderly, provides an essential perspective from which to develop a political theory, and from which to articulate a fuller account of public life than those offered to that point.[20]

None of this debate occurred in a philosophical vacuum. In mainstream philosophical circles a generalized debate concerning the relationship between abstract principles and situated ethical reasoning began in the early 1980s. It was framed in terms of a revived interest in Aristotelian virtue ethics, and a concern to analyze human lives and character rather than individual actions, allied with an interest in the historical context of ethical reasoning that could not be reconciled with the ahistorical models offered by Kantian and Utilitarian theories.[21] In psychology there was a fairly strong movement toward a complex view of human identity as irrevocably social, constituted in part by societal beliefs and practices, and situated in a particular historical context, a view that owed a debt to thinkers such as G. H. Mead, and was brought into philosophical circles in the work of Jürgen Habermas.[22] Theorists such as Lawrence Blum investigated the ways in which particular relationships could be an important source of ethical reflection and action.[23]

So care theory is very much in conversation with other philosophical, sociological, and psychological studies. Because of the emphasis among many care theorists on women's experiences and emotions, however, care theory has been categorized as a theory of sex or gender difference by many critics. The criticism contains a grain of truth; care theory does consciously intend to be true to the experiences that characterize many women's lives, and, insofar as these experiences have been excluded from ethical theorizing, it clearly does involve an acknowledgment of women's differences. But including emotions, voices, and experiences that are common to many women is not the same thing as offering a theory of gender difference. Care theory is best interpreted as an account of human life, one that consciously works toward inclusiveness, but not an account of women's lives alone.

Gender differences have always been a double-edged sword for feminist thinkers. Acknowledging gender difference tends to play into the hands of very conservative thinkers, thinkers whose political agendas are often diametrically opposed to those of feminist theorists. If there is a woman's voice in ethics, for example, and if it is a voice that speaks primarily in the language of care and relationships, it would seem to be the case that women are uniquely suited, ethically speaking, to be relegated to the realm of private familial caretaking. Men, with their focus on rights and justice, are suited to function in the public realm of work and politics. It is perhaps not surprising that Gilligan's work (often misinterpreted) became a fairly popular citation in the work of conservative religious groups.

Some theorists thus argued that what Gilligan had identified as a woman's voice is, in reality, the voice of those who are socialized into positions of subordination and powerlessness in society.[24] When social groups are systematically subordinated, some theorists noted, they tend to become responsive, caring, and very attuned to the emotional states of those in power—not because this is morally right, but because it is a necessary technique for survival in a world in which one is dependent on a much more powerful other for economic, social, and sometimes legal standing. The voice of care, then, theorists argued, is not an interesting new ethical perspective, it is instead a reflection of the widespread subordination of women, and needs to be rejected along with a feminist rejection of other oppressive social structures.[25]

This is not a trivial charge. It goes to the heart of feminist theorizing, and is enormously important for any adequate understanding of the human condition, feminist or otherwise. It is one of the central criticisms of care theory that I address in this book. But to address it adequately requires a fuller development of the notion of human nature that is operative in care theory, as well as a detour through the thought of two very disparate thinkers, Saint Augustine and Emmanuel Levinas. Both of these thinkers offer us accounts of the ethical life that arise out of an articulation of a voice of care, or love, but neither generates that account from a woman's perspective. Developing their thought allows us to respond to those who charge that care is not an ethical imperative, but merely a validation of gender oppression. There is a grain of truth to the charge, and I want to recognize that grain, while rejecting the notion that we should dispense with care because it contributes to oppression.

Issues of sex and gender difference are not the only controversial aspects of care theory. Some theorists reject care theory on the basis that the notion of care is simply too vague and fuzzy to provide moral guidance. Care, these critics argue, is nothing more than a generalized "niceness," and they accuse care theorists of falling into the trap of being "nice girls" who lack a robust sense of social justice.[26] This too is a serious charge to level against a feminist ethical theory. Feminism has always insisted on a connection between theory and practice, and on the need to pay attention to the political and social ramifications of one's theoretical activities. No feminist theorist can be comfortable with an ethical theory that might lead to quiescence or to uncritical niceness.

This book articulates an account of human nature in part to respond to this criticism, using the thought of Augustine and Levinas as important resources. But the proof of the fruitfulness of an ethical theory is its usefulness for ethical reflection, so the last two chapters of this book address concrete ethical issues and examine the ways in which the resources of an ethic of care can offer clarity and guidance for our moral reflection.

The first step in this argument, then, is to develop the account of human nature that is operative in care theory. After developing that account and articulating the goals and ideals it presumes for human development, I compare it to the accounts offered by Augustine and Levinas. That comparison serves as a historical detour. After the historical detour I explain how the ideal of human flourishing functions in care theory and how care theory can respond to the criticisms mentioned here. I conclude with an examination of two specific ethical issues, and an examination of how care theory might offer both clarification of the issues and guidance in our reasoning.

Notes

1. Philippa Foot, "Moral Beliefs," in *Virtues and Vices and Other Essays in Moral Philosophy* (Berkeley and Los Angeles: University of California Press, 1978), pp. 110–31.

2. Simone de Beauvoir, it seems to me, ultimately accepts a view of this sort.

3. An excellent collection of essays exploring this debate in feminist theory is Linda J. Nicholson, ed., *Feminism/Postmodernism* (New York: Routledge, 1990).

4. Randy Thornhill and Craig Palmer, *A Natural History of Rape: Biological Bases of Sexual Coercion* (Cambridge, Mass.: MIT Press, 2000).

5. See, for example, Sarah Blaffer Hrdy, *The Woman That Never Evolved* (1981; reprint, Cambridge, Mass: Harvard University Press, 1999); Anne Fausto-Sterling, *Myths of Gender: Biological Theories about Women and Men*, 2nd ed. (New York: Basic Books, 1992); and Natalie Angier, *Woman: An Intimate Geography* (New York: Houghton Mifflin, 1999).

6. See, for example, Lina Lopez McAlister, ed., *Hypatia's Daughters: Fifteen Hundred Years of Women Philosphers* (Indianapolis: Indiana University Press, 1996).

7. For an extended argument about the relationship between embodied experience and reason, see *Philosophy in the Flesh: The Embodied Mind and Its Challenge to Western Thought*, by George Lakoff and Mark Johnson (New York: Basic Books, 1999).

8. Wes Jackson, *Altars of Unhewn Stone* (New York; North Point Press, 1987), pp. 116–17.

9. Carol Gilligan, *In a Different Voice: Psychological Theory and Women's Development* (Cambridge, Mass.: Harvard University Press, 1982), pp. 104–5. Gilligan's work relies, in turn, on work done by theorists such as Nancy Chodorow in *The Reproduction of Motherhood: Psychoanalysis and the Sociology of Gender* (Berkeley and Los Angeles: University of California Press, 1978). But Gilligan's discussion was the first to generate analysis and response in philosophical circles. This sort of lag time in philosophical circles is directly proportional to philosophers' belief that they are the only academics who have the authority to discuss an issue.

10. See, for example, Mary Jeanne Larrabee, ed., *An Ethic of Care: Feminist and Interdisciplinary Perspectives* (New York: Routledge, 1993).

11. Nel Noddings, *Caring: A Feminine Approach to Ethics and Moral Education* (Berkeley and Los Angeles: University of California Press, 1984), pp. 8–9.

12. Sara Ruddick, *Maternal Thinking: Toward a Politics of Peace* (Boston: Beacon, 1989), p. 24.

13. Ruddick, *Maternal Thinking*, chap. 9, "Notes toward a Feminist Maternal Peace Politics."

14. See, for example, Joyce Trebilcott, ed., *Mothering: Essays in Feminist Theory* (Savage, Md.: Rowman & Littlefield, 1983).

15. Mary Dietz, "Citizenship with a Feminist Face: The Problem with Maternal Thinking," *Political Theory* 13, no. 1 (February 1985): 19–37; reprinted in Joan B.

Landes, ed., *Feminism: The Public and the Private* (New York: Oxford University Press, 1998), pp. 45–64. Jean Bethke Elshtain's arguments can be found in *Public Man, Private Woman* (Princeton, N.J.: Princeton University Press, 1981) and in several other essays, among them "Feminism, Family, and Community" *Dissent* 29, no. 4 (fall 1982): 442–49.

16. Lorraine Code, *What Can She Know? Feminist Theory and the Construction of Knowledge* (Ithaca, N.Y.: Cornell University Press, 1991), p. 1.

17. Code, *What Can She Know?* p. 177.

18. Code, *What Can She Know?* p. 99.

19. Virginia Held, *Feminist Morality: Transforming Culture, Society, and Politics* (Chicago: University of Chicago Press, 1993), p. 129

20. Joan Tronto, *Moral Boundaries: A Political Argument for an Ethic of Care* (New York: Routledge, 1994), pp. 153–55.

21. See, for example, Philippa Foot's *Virtues and Vices* (cited earlier), as well as Alasdair MacIntyre, *After Virtue* (Notre Dame: University of Notre Dame Press, 1984); Martha Nussbaum, *The Fragility of Goodness: Luck and Ethics in Greek Tragedy and Philosophy* (New York: Cambridge University Press, 1986); and Charles Taylor, *Sources of the Self: The Making of Modern Identity* (Cambridge, Mass.: Harvard University Press, 1989).

22. Jürgen Habermas, *The Theory of Communicative Action*, vols. 1 and 2, trans. Thomas McCarthy (Boston: Beacon, 1984 and 1987).

23. Lawrence Blum, *Friendship, Altruism, and Morality* (London: Routledge & Kegan Paul, 1980).

24. See, for example, Bill Puka, "The Liberation of Caring: A Different Voice for Gilligan's 'Different Voice,'" in *An Ethic of Care: Feminist and Interdisciplinary Voices*, ed. May Jeanne Larrabee (New York: Routledge, 1993), pp. 215–39; and Patricia Ward Scaltsas, "Do Feminist Ethics Counter Feminist Aims?" in *Explorations in Feminist Ethics: Theory and Practice*, ed. Eve Browning Cole and Susan Coultrap-McQuin (Indianapolis: Indiana University Press, 1992), pp. 15–26.

25. Catharine MacKinnon is one of the strongest proponents of this view. See her *Feminism Unmodified: Discourses on Life and Law* (Cambridge, Mass.: Harvard University Press, 1987), pp. 38–39.

26. Dianne Romaine, "Care and Confusion," in *Explorations in Feminist Ethics*, pp. 27–37; and, more recently, Daryl Koehn's *Rethinking Feminist Ethics: Care, Trust and Empathy* (New York: Routledge, 1998), pp. 30–34.

CHAPTER ONE

Human Nature and an Ethic of Care

An ethic of care must rely, more or less implicitly, on a particular conception of human nature. In the introduction to this book I distinguished between two senses of the term "nature" or its adjectival form, "natural." The first sense of the word is primarily descriptive of what occurs with fair regularity. There is a tendency in some parts of the Western philosophical tradition to also assume that natural in this sense refers to events that occur without conscious human intervention, but this is not implied by my definition; human activities are part of what occurs naturally in this descriptive sense. But we can also use the term nature in a prescriptive sense, in a sense that is teleological because it refers to a trajectory of development and perfection. It is in this second sense that we can speak of care theory having a conception of human nature. Care theorists operate with a sense of what human life should be like and with a strong sense of what sorts of social changes would be necessary to bring contemporary social situations into closer relationship with that ideal.

So when I speak of human nature and an ethic of care, I am not using nature in a purely descriptive sense. At the same time, however, to reiterate a point made in the introduction, the sense in which I use the term cannot be divorced from description, because the sense of nature as an ideal toward which beings develop must be grounded in naturalistic descriptions. The connection here with agricultural metaphors is instructive. Anyone who grows crops knows that there is a sense in which it is natural for a plant to grow into a full and flourishing state, and knows that much of the time, the right thing to do to help the plant is precisely nothing. One needs, most of the time, to get out of the way and, as we say, "let nature take its course." But no one will get a good crop if they always step back and do nothing. It is also natural for disease, insects, or bad weather to make it impossible for a given crop to flourish.

Recognition that the crop is not flourishing is possible because someone with an understanding of that particular sort of plant can recognize both what it looks like when it is healthy, and what it looks like when it suffers from various sorts of unhealthy conditions. Clearly this notion of "knowing what health looks like" is a conception of knowledge that does not fit well with standard philosophical definitions of knowledge. The farmer who knows that her tomato plants are healthy is unlikely to be able to offer necessary and sufficient conditions for health in this case. But she knows what healthy is, nonetheless, and the proof of her knowledge comes with the harvest. This conception of knowledge does fit well with Wittgenstein's notion of recognizing a family resemblance, or of "knowing how to go on," and in a similar way is dependent on paradigm cases. It requires that the knower have certain pictures of what count as healthy plants at various points in their development, and be capable of comparing this ideal of health with what is in front of her. Nor is her knowledge infallible. Debates between farmers devoted to organic methods and those who use chemical fertilizers and pesticides often focus on questions of whether a plant with no visible imperfections is healthier than one with a bit of insect damage.

In debates of this sort, the thinker committed to an account of ethics that does take human nature to be an ideal in some sense cannot point to some transcendent value as the deciding factor that shows one conception of health to be the better one. She must, instead, begin the slow work of seeing what the long-term consequences are of both notions of health. In the case of agriculture, we know how this debate is likely to end. Organic farming and farming techniques that use the minimum of chemical intervention (often called low-impact sustainable agriculture) both are better techniques in the long run because they are, as the name of the second suggests, sustainable. This gives us reason to assume that plants grown by these techniques, though they may look slightly less green and bushy than their chemically enhanced cousins in the next field, may be more healthy in the long run.

An ethic of care is best understood as an ethical theory that assumes that what is true of plants is also true of humans. When we examine human lives we see that some go well and some go badly. The definition of what constitutes a life that "goes well" cannot be determined by pure intellectual activity. We can get a grasp of which lives go well and which go badly only by seeing how humans do, living different lives, under different circumstances.

There are some lives that clearly are not contenders for the "good" category. Lives of drug addiction or lives that involve a constant and unsuccessful fight against severe depression are not good lives. But other lives are good ones to live, and when we begin to reflect on what sorts of beings humans are, and what sorts of needs and capabilities they have, we can recognize that there will be certain commonalities in the structure of any good human life. In the rest of this chapter some of the central commonalities are identified, and the shape they give to human life described.

The chapter ends with a brief description of how these various characteristics might shape our thinking about the structure of human life. This gives us a basis of comparison for thinking about other ways that human life could be structured. Some of the alternatives will be explored in the following chapters, as I turn to Saint Augustine and Emmanuel Levinas. Both thinkers are interesting for my purposes because they adopt a picture of human nature that shares central features of the view developed in this chapter. But, rather as if the care theorist were the organic gardener, and Saint Augustine the farmer who thinks plants are not healthy without chemical fertilizers, they do not agree on their overall picture of how human life should be structured, nor on exactly what should count as a good human life. The differences between them are instructive because in the comparison between them we can see what is at stake in the disparate views.

Care theory does not offer the only possible answer to the question of how we should structure human lives. Seeing what care theory offers, however, can clarify our thinking, allow us to engage others in debate, and allow us to see more clearly how assumptions about the proper shape of human life shape moral reasoning. An examination of care theory, Augustinian thought, and Levinasian philosophical reflection gives us reason to think that certain types of social structures are better suited for flourishing than others. But before such an examination can take place, I need to spend some time describing the account of human nature, and human flourishing, implicit in care theory. I focus on four aspects: care, embodiment, finitude, and the social nature of the self. All of these are connected ideas, and the discussion of one will bleed into the discussion of another. After all, one can hardly be embodied without being finite, and so on. So discussing these aspects as separate categories is merely a matter of organizational convenience.

I. Human Nature and an Ethic of Care

All of the theorists whom I am calling theorists of care, though they may differ on various issues, assume a general account of human nature that structures their ethical concerns. This conception of human nature is significantly different in some aspects from the Western philosophical tradition's view of human nature, and those differences shape a very different perspective on ethical theory. The ideal that structures care theory, though it is not always explicit, is an ideal of human lives as grounded in a web of care with other people, so that each person is able to give care to and receive care from others. The care given aims, in the ideal case, at the full intellectual, emotional, spiritual, and physical well-being of the others cared for, and it occurs in the context of social structures that encourage the development of the capacities to give and receive care in all. The four categories that follow offer a first, rough sketch of the picture of the human person that is integral to an ethic of care.

A. Care

Care is obviously central to an ethic of care. Care theorists argue that what philosophers have often called the affections or the sentiments or the emotions are of central importance in human life. But emotions are not all equally important for human life. Care, the emotion involved in tending to the physical needs of other, dependent humans, holds a central place in ethical theory because of its indispensability for human life. Everyone who reaches adulthood does so because someone else cared for her or him. In Eva Kittay's aptly chosen phrase, everyone is "some mother's child."[1] Without relationships of care, human life would cease to exist. Without carefully developed and nourished relationships of care, human life cannot be lived to the fullest. This centrality of care is not just a matter of human neediness in infancy. It is also a deep feature of human psychology, so that unless we know ourselves to be enmeshed in relationships with others who love and care for us we cannot be psychologically healthy. Nel Noddings speculates that the desire to be cared for may be an empirical universal—there may not be any humans who don't have some level of the desire to be cared for.[2]

This may seem obvious to anyone not trained in Western philosophy. How could humans exist other than in the context of affectional relationships with other humans (and, many times, with other species as well)? The social, communal, and emotional aspects of human life are critical to any surviving society. Moreover, human infants naturally reach out in care and love to others, and while we may outgrow the uncritical trust of infants, we only ever manage to hide the desire for others' care under a thin veneer of sophistication. Advertising campaigns exploit this deep need shamelessly. But this obvious feature of human life has been anything but obvious in the Western philosophical tradition, for several reasons. One reason is the tendency for philosophers to think of humans primarily in terms of a rational intellect. Further, reason has often been defined in terms that exclude the emotions or affections. If reason is the distinguishing feature of the human, then the emotional relationships humans experience are seen as opposed to reason. If they are opposed to reason, then there is no reason to spend time trying to understand them rationally: they are precisely what is not reason. The classic example of this is Plato's portrayal of Socrates' death in the *Phaedo*, in which Socrates calmly engages in rational dialogue about the nature of moral action and the nature of death, while rebuking his wife for her unseemly emotional outbursts.

But the separation of reason from the passions is not the only philosophical trend that has generated an inability to see the centrality of care in human lives. A second reason philosophers have not seen care as primary is that many philosophers lived lives that were characterized by the delegation of care to others. Eva Kittay points out that those who care for dependent others become dependent themselves.[3] But philosophers have tended to define human life in terms of rationality, as mentioned, and further in terms of rational control over the course of one's own life. This ideal of rational control implies that the properly human self is not dependent on others, or vulnerable to the whims of fate. As a matter of fact, of course, we are all dependent on numerous others all the time, but with the proper social organization one can ensure that one never has to recognize one's dependency. Aristotle's account of how life is properly organized, for example, presumes that there will be plenty of women, slaves and free, as well as male slaves and laborers, who will do the work necessary for the philosopher's leisurely intellectual life. Many Western cultures have valued self-control and power very much, and the sorts of people who have the leisure to write philosophical treatises are those who have the social power to delegate dependency care to others. There are clear psychological reasons for such persons to refuse to see the centrality of relationships of care and dependency in human life; if that centrality were acknowledged, their own situation of power and control would be threatened. Not surprisingly, then, we find that most philosophers have ignored care and caring relationships, and those who have mentioned them tend to treat them as subhuman.

The most striking case of this is Hobbes's initial description of the State of Nature, in which, he writes, we are to think of each individual human as at war with all others.[4] From this initial state of total and complete war, he argues, comes the necessity for humans to enter into the social contract. It is clear that his picture of humans is that of relatively equal and self-sufficient adult males. But adult males do not suddenly spring from the earth, fully grown and competent to struggle against each other. If there were not some humans who were not at war, there would be no humans at all. Infants and small children require a very different sort of context for survival and development. Onora O'Neill distinguishes between the abstraction we need for any theorizing and idealization, an abstraction that involves necessarily falsifying assumptions.[5] Hobbes's assumption seems a clear case of an idealization, since the very existence of the individuals who are supposedly at war with all others presupposes that some are not at war, but instead are busy caring for the needs and dependencies of others.

If this is right, then the primary move in human life is toward others, not away. Babies are not born as Hobbesian individuals; they are born reaching out and expecting care, and they continue to expect care even when raised by harsh or negligent parents.[6] The ability to care can be destroyed by sufficiently bad parenting, but it takes active destruction to get rid of it, except in the case of certain specifiable psychological disorders. In any moderately livable set of circumstances humans will care for others as naturally as they learn to speak and walk. More than this, lives in which the ability to care is destroyed are lives that are described as human only in a diminished sense. Sociopaths are only human in an analogous sense—because of their physical humanity they deserve to be treated with a certain measure of respect and care, but in their inability to care or feel any moral emotion they are outside the context of the ethical community. This is why the conscription of child soldiers in the Sudan and Ethiopia is so tragic—turning twelve-year-olds into killing machines destroys their ability to act and feel in ways that are necessary for living a truly human life. So Hobbes's notion of a war of all against all is a notion that gets human interactions wrong from the start. This is not to say that all contract theories are wrongheaded, but instead to point out that Hobbes's version is untenable.

Care theorists side with Hume against Hobbes on this issue.[7] Sympathy (as Hume uses the term) is innate, Hume argues. Hobbes's war of all against all implicitly requires that the Humean sympathy that leads families to care for their neediest members exists first. If humans lacked sympathy, the race would have died out long since, and there would be no one to war against anyone else. I don't want to overstate this point. I am *not* claiming that humans are innately loving and only become aggressive when society corrupts them. Aggression and destruction are also deeply rooted and probably are universal human tendencies. The point I want to make is that these tendencies always occur against a backdrop of sociality and care. Further, care is part of human life, not just women's lives, in the same way that aggression is a part of human life, not just men's lives. Babies reach out for care whether they are male or female, and both men and women have the capacity to respond to the need for care as well as a felt compulsion to do so. Given different cultural expectations, men and women may express their sympathies differently, but that does not negate the basic point.

Humans are social beings, with natural tendencies to offer and receive care from each other. Their existence as social animals with extended childhoods requires this. But is the fact that humans are social beings an important philosophical component of an account of ethics? Care theorists argue that it is. If we are going to offer an adequate account of human lives as they ought to be lived, we must begin with an accurate picture of the basic structure of human interaction, and an unavoidable aspect of that structure is that fact of human affective responses to other humans. When human nature is treated abstractly as a matter of rational self-interested agents, the removal of care is not a legitimate abstraction. It becomes an idealization of a certain (fundamentally false) conception of how humans should conduct their affairs, without care for others with whom they come into contact, treating interactions as contractual agreements entered into without concern for the well-being of another. This picture drives certain aspects of economic reasoning, and has produced seriously flawed research in some areas, but it is even more disastrous when it drives analysis of the relationships among family members, as is the case in some sociobiological accounts of "evolutionary rationality." It then turns into a justification for ridiculous abuses of trust and sociality, as men are encouraged to think of their relationships with women in terms of their own (the men's) "rational interest" in perpetuating their genes, as a matter of exploiting women's willingness to bear children, while women's relationships to their children are defined in terms of "investments" in their own genetic perpetuation.

This is an unsustainable picture of human emotional and sexual relationships. Care for partners and children is deeply falsified in this picture and turned into an economic calculation of genetic benefit. The perniciousness of such theoretical reasoning goes deeper than just misdescribing human relationships. It also is damaging to those relationships, as it encourages people to reject their sense of love and care in favor of an economic picture of who gets what out of the reproductive bargain. When a relationship becomes one of rational calculation rather than one of care, the relationship is no longer sustainable.

Two final notes about care are in order here. One concerns the meaning of the term "care" itself. I have been arguing that care is central in human life, and I have done so without offering a clear and exclusive account of what care is, exactly. To those who are accustomed to analytic philosophy, this will be disturbing. Analytic philosophers tend to assume that one cannot use a term in a philosophical discussion without first providing a definition that sets out the necessary and sufficient conditions for the meaning of the term, or at least the conditions for using it properly. Some care theorists have offered definitions. Joan Tronto, for example, defines caring as "[a] species activity that includes everything that we do to maintain, continue, and repair our 'world' so that we can live in it as well as possible."[8] Her definition is helpful for some purposes, but it is so extensive that it does not provide much specificity in thinking about care. More importantly, this sort of definition does not necessarily enhance the clarity of our thinking about care.

Most of us do use the term "care" without any problem in ordinary discussions about everyday matters. We seem to have a reasonably competent grasp of the meaning of the term, so that we can understand it when others use it, and use it competently ourselves. The attempt to define the term exactly usually puts an end to fruitful discussions rather than enhancing them, since the discussion then begins to focus on the definition, rather than on the concept itself.[9] Further, one of the important issues that I hope to start the reader thinking about is precisely what counts as care, and I don't think there is a final answer to that question. I do think there are clear cases of activities, responses, and social structures that can be seen to be opposed to care, and other cases that clearly demonstrate care. But that is apparent even given the natural language meaning of the term. What I would like, instead, is to keep in mind several paradigm cases of care that can serve as general pictures of what care involves.

I will mention three cases, then, briefly, and we will return to them at various points in the book. The first case of care that has been central to care theory itself is mothering. Mothering is the active tending of infants and children so that they live and grow insofar as that is possible.[10] Some critics argue that fathers do this, too, and so it should be called "parenting," while others prefer the term "mothering" to indicate that this is a job that is primarily done by women, and to give credit, in a sense, where credit is due. Still others reject the term "mothering" precisely because it is so closely identified with women. Rather than enter this debate at this point, I will use both terms, "mothering" and "parenting." A second case that has functioned as a paradigm in care theory is the care offered to aging people by both professional caregivers and relatives. Nel Noddings focuses on this in her analysis of evil in human life, in part because the dependencies of old age are not specific to one sex or the other, though men and women may experience that dependency differently.[11] A final case that functions as paradigmatic for care is that of friendship.[12] Friendship is an important additional relationship because it involves voluntary, reciprocal relationships rather than the involuntary, unequal relationships that are often characteristic of mothering and elder care.

All of these paradigm cases of care share certain features that are central to any adequate concept of care. They all operate with an active notion of care, in that one cannot claim to care for a child, for an elderly dependent, or for a friend if one is not actively involved in the other's life. They all involve a clear commitment to the good of the other. They are all simultaneously intellectual, affective, and physical relationships. In each, the specific identities of the caregiver and care receiver are significant to the nature of the care.

One final note is important here. Care is sometimes described as an ethical attitude that is in opposition to justice. We can see why this might be thought to be the case simply from the paradigm relationships I've just mentioned: all involve relationships of partiality and special interest, and justice is often taken to be opposed to both partiality and special interest. Carol Gilligan's initial description of care as an alternative perspective to justice thinking has given some support to this general assumption.[13] But the assumption that care and justice are opposing ethical values should be rejected. The notion that justice always involves absolute impartiality and so is opposed to partiality is simply false. Justice does require impartiality in certain very specific cases, the most obvious one being the case of the application of laws to citizens. In that context, it is clear that justice rules out partiality. But justice can sometimes require partiality, as when the law stipulates punishments for parents who neglect their children.

Care is not opposed to justice; instead, adequate caring requires a strong sense of justice. As a parent of four children, two of them teenagers, I am constantly reminded of the need to both do and be seen to do justice if I am to be any sort of a caring parent, and the same is true in other relationships of care. But the inverse is true as well. Without room for care, an abstract principle of justice is unlivable. In the absence of a caring concern for the well-being of those affected by principles of justice, the principles become harsh, unforgiving, and frequently misapplied. Although our commonplace picture of the early Puritans has been challenged by recent historical studies, the caricature we have of Puritans (based on the *Scarlet Letter*, in all probability), is one of a society ruled by justice without care, and a cold place it is.

B. Embodiment and Particularity

Care, however, can never be equated with merely having a general emotional attitude of concern for the well-being of another. Care is always connected with an active willingness to reach out to that other in appropriate circumstances. It cannot remain solely at the level of attitude because humans are not simply intellects who interact. Humans are physical beings; they have certain physical resources and limitations, a relatively limited life-span, and they experience their world as it comes to them through their five senses. So the second feature that plays a central role in care theory's account of human nature is embodiment. We understand ethics wrongly if we assume that morality applies to disembodied consciousnesses. Morality arises out of our experiences as bodies in the world, physical selves supported by and in contact with other embodied selves and the rest of material reality. Because of their emphasis on embodiment, many care theorists are willing to consider how the experiences of women, particularly pregnancy, giving birth, and caring for small children, may give women insight into important moral concepts.[14] This emphasis has not been uncontroversial, of course, but it is a natural part of emphasizing the embodied nature of human experience and the moral realm.

The human self is not, and is not experienced as, a disembodied intellectual soul. Humans instead develop a sense of self as a particular physical being in a particular physical context, with all the possibilities and limitations that such embodiment offers. Insofar as we are physical beings, an account of ethics that remains at the level of intellectual considerations without connecting up with concrete physical activities cannot be a full account. Care must involve an actual concern with the physical and psychosocial needs of particular people if it is to provide an adequate account of the moral realm. This is one of the areas in which care theory offers a sharp break from many other theories in the Western tradition. Philosophical thought about ethics has tended to relegate physical concerns to the background of ethical theory, relevant only insofar as the physical needs to be kept under control by the intellect. The physical side of existence for many philosophers, following a long tradition going back to Plato, largely seems to be a hindrance to ethical action, either because physical existence makes the intellectual life more difficult or because physical needs and desires corrupt the intellect.

But if we begin with a clear acceptance that physical existence is properly a part of what it is to be human, and that theory must begin from the embodied self, we are forced to adopt a more complex view of human personality and psychology, a view that recognizes that bodily drives can lead us to do harm to others, but so can intellectual pride; that the intellect can be an important source of moral behavior, but so can the basic bodily affects we have.

We recognize that there is a wisdom of both the mind and the body, so that our physical reactions to a situation can be an important part of our moral reasoning. Again, this is not to substitute gut reactions or bodily intuitions for rational, critical thought, but to strive to integrate the two in a way that recognizes and respects our basic physical being.

Embodied existence is also crucial for an adequate understanding of the developmental nature of humans. Humans are born as infants, grow up as funny little toddlers, stretch into awkward adolescents and vibrant young adults. They experience a period of maturity, and grow old. Along the way, at the many different developmental points of this life, they experience illness, disability, and developmental delays. They die young, or live for years with bodies that don't function well. In developing an ethical theory we cannot automatically assume that all humans are able-bodied, middle-aged adults, capable of self-direction and largely able to support themselves. Instead we need a picture of ethical life that incorporates a respect for the varying ages and abilities of the many stages and types of life we find. Human life must be structured to provide the physical support and care that bodies need, and a social system that relegates this care to the fringes is a social system that is likely to be inhumane and perhaps ultimately unsustainable.

One of the standard criticisms of what are called "contract theories" in ethics derives precisely from this aspect of the theories. Contract theories begin with the assumption that to be human is to be independent and capable of rational deliberation about any issue whatsoever. Given this conception of human nature, ethical rightness or wrongness is determined by whether or not such rational, self-sufficient agents would agree to something, or enter a contract under specific terms. Humans who are incapable of participating in the contract are largely excluded from the ethical community by this definition of human nature. This sets up enormous problems for contract theorists in thinking through issues of the education and socialization of infants and children, since children cannot be contracting agents (they lack the maturity and knowledge), but without education and socialization they will not become capable of participating in the contracts that are fundamental for ethical agency. An expanded account of human existence, one that acknowledges from the start that humans are physical beings, could avoid some of these flaws, since it would need to accommodate humans at many different points in the life trajectory and at many different levels of reasoning, agentic ability.

Embodiment also requires us to take physical harms and benefits seriously as moral issues. In some ways ethical theory has done this—after all, the harms that show up on perennial lists of "wrongs" generally include things such as murder, rape, and mayhem. But Western philosophy has exhibited a tendency to assume that those who can affect the body cannot really affect me if I am a properly trained ethical agent. Harms to the body are often proscribed because of the harm they do to the intellect, not because of the bodily damage itself.

Taking embodiment seriously means recognizing that the harm done in rape, for example, is not just the harm of treating another as an object, or failing to respect her autonomy. Rape also involves the far more serious harm of alienating a person from her own body, so that she no longer feels safe within her own skin. The physical ramifications of such an attack can last for years, preventing even simple enjoyments such as a hug between friends. Because a person is her body, such alienation is a harm that is inscribed on the flesh and must be lived out until such a time as the body manages to heal itself.[15] To the extent that we treat the harm as done to a rational, disembodied substance, we expect it to be curable by rational means, and thus do a second violence to the rape victim. Injuries to the embodied subject have to be lived out, not rationalized away.

Finally, if we are to take embodiment seriously, we need to pay attention to the many ways in which we impose an internalized discipline on the body. As we are educated and grow up in any given society, we are trained, and we train ourselves, to become a proper sort of body for the class, race, and gender roles society provides us.[16] The power of this socialization is quite striking when one travels across various cultures. Voice register, walk, the way one holds one's head or eyes, are all ingrained into us by the culture in which we grow up, and in holding our bodies in this or that way we become certain sorts of people. Since the body and the intellect are not two discrete entities, but two aspects of a single, physical being, the various ways of being a living body bring with them various patterns of reasoning and thought.

Embodiment, then, is a crucial part of the notion of particularity. Each person looks at the world through different eyes, from a vantage point shaped by his or her own physical being and its relationship to other humans and the rest of the physical world. One's particular vantage point is not and cannot be shared by another. (This does not preclude empathetic understanding, of course; it is the ground of the possibility of such understanding. But empathetic understanding gives one insight, not an identical perspective.) When I care for another, I have to be concerned for this particular other who has a certain shape and occupies a certain physical spot. The case of parenting, of course, provides one example of how care requires a focus on the particularity of the individual who is cared for. A parent who tries to treat all children exactly alike is heading for disaster. But we see the same recognition of the importance of particularity in Joan Tronto's discussion of social structures that could provide support for caregiving for the frail and medically needy elderly. A one-size-fits-all policy, she notes, is not ideal, and may not be workable. What we need instead is a system that permits caregivers to provide adequate care within the constraints of the physical needs, cultural understandings, and economic situations of care recipients. Some of the elderly, for example, find being cared for by nonfamily members frightening and demeaning. Others find being cared for by family members threatening to their sense of self. A policy that assumes that family members will provide all the caregiving, in addition to overburdening caregivers, can cause the care recipients to refuse needed care in some cases. Social structures of care need to have built-in mechanisms for flexibility to accommodate the differences among those for whom the care is provided and those who provide the care.

The emphasis that care places on physical existence and particularity also provides a reason for advocating a pluralist democratic social structure. Because the world looks different from different physical vantage points, there are good reasons for making sure that no single voice is allowed to speak for all. When we recognize that bodies matter, we can no longer be content with the assumption that one rational agent can deliberate for all, as Rawls's hypothetical contract suggests, but instead recognize that there is no substitute for deliberative democracy, for the public discussion and debate that is so frustrating and infuriatingly slow, and that does not always reach the conclusions that elite members of the educated classes think it should. We need to recognize as well that there will be no final end to democratic debates, because things will always look different to different people.

Taking physical embodiment seriously requires us to take seriously the differences that embodiment produces in reasoning. At the same time, however, taking our physical nature seriously does not mean that we accept, unthinkingly, the physical constraints that have been traditionally imposed on various types of bodies. To the extent that we take embodiment to be important, we also need to critically examine various ways of training human bodies, recognizing that the way we shape our physical selves affects who and what we are.

C. Finitude and Interdependence

Embodiment is closely connected with a third feature of human nature, the notion that humans are fundamentally interdependent and finite, or limited. Humans are not completely self-sufficient. As embodied beings, they begin life needing extraordinary amounts of care, and, though their needs vary over time, there are no humans who have not spent good portions of their lives dependent on others for one thing or another. This dependence is not just physical. It extends to psychological, emotional, intellectual, and spiritual dimensions as well, so that to be human is to be interdependent on all sorts of other beings for all sorts of things.

Just as is the case with care, the centrality of interdependence in human life has often been ignored by theorists in the Western tradition. As Charles Taylor has argued, the doctrine of atomism has deep affinities with central aspects of contemporary thought, and is difficult to refute in spite of its obvious falsity.[17] The metaphors we use to organize our thinking, the legal assumptions that structure many of our social lives, and even large portions of religious experience reflect a deep-seated assumption of separated individualism in human life. As I write this, the U.S. Supreme Court is debating the legitimacy of the affirmative action program in student admissions at the University of Michigan. The rhetoric used by opponents of affirmative action is strikingly individualistic, emphasizing the extent to which one particular person did or did not experience discrimination in his or her life. The supporters of the program (among whom we find, interestingly enough, the U.S. military and a number of large corporations) tend to use a much more communalistic language, arguing that there are social costs to continued segregation, and that our corporate life as citizens, employers, employees, and soldiers goes better if we have learned to work and cooperate with a diverse population.

When one reflects at any length on lived experience, an extreme separated individualism is clearly at odds with reality. Recent (and some not-so-recent) psychological and social research details the extent to which our perception of reality is determined by others' opinions and experiences, and certainly our sense of self is never independent from what others assume or claim about us.[18] Religious experience is not even possible without a social context that makes intelligible my understanding of the experience as religious (rather than as psychosis, for example). Interdependence is not the same thing as a crude organicism. The interdependence that human beings experience is not a matter of groupthink or mind control, but rather a more nuanced recognition that humans do not exist as singletons. One of the strengths of care theory has been its recognition that humans are essentially social creatures, rather than the solitary individuals of a Hobbesian or Rousseauian State of Nature. Ruddick's discussion of maternal thinking foregrounds the role parenting plays in the development of personhood. Nodding's focus on natural caring as the origin of moral caring is rooted in an account of human development that assumes interdependence and nurturing.

Held's account of feminist ethics describes a lack of connection with and concern for others as a sign of pathology.

If we are seriously dependent on others throughout most of our lives, for emotional and social support, as well as for physical nurture at various times, then our lives as humans can never be understood from a purely individualist perspective. This insight has been widely accepted in sociological circles, but has been slower to move into philosophical circles. It has become almost a truism in sociology that one cannot study one instance of a social animal's behavior—the animal's nature becomes apparent only in the context of a group and of a continued history of group dynamics. The same is true of humans. The responses, reactions, and activities of an isolated individual are not indicative of human nature as it truly is, and the notion of a human who lacks any contact with or dependence on others is hardly conceivable.[19]

Recognition of the interdependent nature of human existence encourages care theorists to move beyond individuals, considered in and of themselves, and to situate any analysis of relationships in a broader social context. To this extent, the reconceptualizing of citizenship in terms of care advocated by Joan Tronto is precisely what is required by the account of human nature at work in care theory. Likewise, Nodding's consistent focus on pedagogical issues places care in the context of social systems of education and development. Each of these analyses, in fact, requires the other for plausibility. Tronto's reconceptualization of citizenship as caring will fail if education does not help children develop the ability and the proclivity to care. But Nodding's education for caring is futile if it occurs in a cultural context in which care is devalued and made irrelevant. In any case, both theorists reflect the natural impetus to address issues of care in a nonindividualistic context.

Further, because care theory recognizes that to exist as a physical being necessarily entails finitude and interdependence, it is able to articulate the value of mutually supportive social structures in ways that are far more difficult for more individualistic theories. We are all dependent on others for both physical and social needs, so it makes no sense to operate with an assumption that, for example, receiving assistance is insulting or demeaning. It may be the case that one lives in a society that defines the person who admits to needing help as diminished, but that definition reflects a faulty organizational structure, not a timeless law of human nature and ethics.

D. Social Selves

In speaking of finitude and interdependence I have already alluded to the fact that humans depend on others for their sense of self and understanding of the world they live in. This brings us to the fourth aspect of human nature asserted in an ethic of care, namely, the notion that human selves are always selves-in-relation. That is, humans become selves, in some sense, in the context of and through relationships with others. These relationships are not opposed to autonomy, as philosophers have sometimes thought, but are instead partly constitutive of it. If humans were not formed partly through relational attachments, but hatched, like cicadas or frogs, as completely isolated beings, human selves and moral relationships would clearly be very different. The relationships and connections that structure human ethical reflection would not be central features of the moral life if we were cicadas, but, since we are not cicadas, we cannot live well without properly supportive relationships, nor can we live well without developing the character traits that allow us to engage in such relationships.

Ethical theorizing that begins with the assumption that humans are essentially isolated individuals, then, has an inherently falsifying starting assumption, rather like a theory in physics that begins with the assumption that there is no gravitational force. Care theorists assume that good caring in most parent-child relationships, for example, involves encouraging the child to grow up to be as healthily self-confident and as capable of entering into close and supportive personal relationships with others as she can be. One cannot make this claim without assuming that healthy self-confidence and the ability to enter close and supportive personal relationships are partially constitutive of the good human life. At the same time, children are not all equally capable of developing these abilities, and part of the care involved in good parenting involves the dual vision of what is good for humans generally and what the specific abilities and disabilities of a particular child are. It is a unique strength of care theory that it rejects a clear dichotomy between the universal and the particular on just this point, developing instead a notion of the need for both a developmental trajectory shaped by a picture of human flourishing and a recognition of how an individual child can best flourish. If either of these is lacking, good parenting becomes impossible. This double vision, bringing together a general ideal and the particular good of the specific other, provides the context for arguing that abusive relationships cannot be paradigms of care, because both people involved in the relationship are prevented from developing into people who can exhibit the characteristics of general human flourishing, and from becoming the particular selves that they are capable of becoming.

But it is not sufficient to simply note that humans are relational. Care theory also requires analysis of the ways that the structure of human social existence either does or does not support ethical relationships. One can give and receive a sort of care within a context in which people's lives are destructively shaped by oppressive social structures. But the care that is given and received is deeply flawed because it cannot be directed fully at the good of the other. Slavery, for example, is a practice that destroys the capacity for a fully developed sense of self, for both the slave (who is defined as inferior by society, and often internalizes that definition) and for the owner (who is defined by society as automatically superior, with all the destructive effects such false superiority produces). Although both slave and owner may say that they care for each other, neither can be completely concerned with the actual good of the other without destroying the relationship as a relationship of slavery.

This provides a theoretical context for understanding why social practices that deny some individuals or groups full social standing are so pernicious. In defining certain ethnic or racial groups as "not fully human," a society sets itself up with deep moral incoherencies, such that those who belong to the dominant group form their identity in terms of a superiority that they know (at some level) to be false and unsustainable, while those who belong to the excluded group are confronted with forming their own identities in terms of cultural values that deny them full worth as persons. Such a context is deeply destructive of the mutual respect required for relationships of care to exist.

Mutual respect as a necessary component of concern for the good of another provides one link between care theory and an ideal of human nature. If I am concerned about the good of another, I need some sense of what that good might be, and I cannot make such a judgment without recognizing what sorts of things are good for beings like this one, human beings. But I also cannot lose sight of the particular being that this one is, whether young or old, talented but undisciplined, or severely handicapped. Unless I am able to keep both of these thoughts in mind at once, any attempts I make to care for this other will run into serious problems. If I cannot see the particularity of this individual, I am likely to interact with her inappropriately, but if I do not know what full and healthy flourishing entails, I also will not know how to help her reach toward it. Care requires that we have a sense of what another can and should become. My reader may shudder at this. It sounds so paternalistic, or perhaps maternalistic. But, paradoxically, if we value independence and autonomy, and so shudder at the thought of determining what another should become, then we are already committed to a particular sense of what that other can and should be. If we did not think that people should be capable of independent thought and critical self-evaluation, we wouldn't find paternalism problematic. But if we value these traits, then it makes no sense to criticize those who encourage their development in others, nor does it make sense to advocate public policy that makes their development difficult or impossible.

The socially embedded nature of human existence is crucial for care theory because of the way it affects how we think about what care is and can be. In Sara Ruddick's account of mothering she lists as one of the tasks of the mothering person the development of traits that will make the cared-for child "acceptable" in her or his culture.[20] She is careful to qualify this, of course, since there are aspects of any given culture that a mothering person may not want to endorse. But her account recognizes that humans exist in a social context, and without a significant degree of the social traits and skills that allow one to fit into that context one is cut off from a central aspect of human existence.

One more thing is worth noting about the recognition that identity is socially constituted. Some liberal theorists have rejected this view because, aware of the deeply entrenched sexism (and racism) of Western cultures, they have wanted to preserve a notion of a freely choosing self that can be its own source of value, independent of the social and cultural messages it may receive. There is a grain of truth to this notion of a free self, in the sense that individuals can and do resist and change social definitions. But if this freedom to resist is overemphasized it can become problematic. Identity is formed in the context of social messages and implicit assumptions about the differential worth of different types of humans. If this were not so, then changing those social messages would not be so important. Overemphasis on individual freedom can lead to dismissal of the need to change social messages. On the other hand, overemphasis on a social-constitution notion of the self poses problems for basic philosophical analyses of things such as ethical responsibility and for the argument that there are resources for change.

We are not going to magically remove sexism from society, however, by simply positing the existence of freedom, or a self beyond social construction. Instead we should recognize that liberation from sexist constructions of the self is going to take place in particular historical contexts and against a particular background, and the same is true for racist conceptions of personal identity. There is no view from nowhere that offers us a completely nonbiased view of human identity from which to critique the views our society currently holds. A postmodern chastening of Enlightenment views of reason forces us to recognize these limitations. What this means is that although (for example) Western feminists have done a good job in identifying some of the ways that sexism affects women's lives, they also may be blind to ways in which their views are constructed in terms of a Western bias, and could use some criticism, in turn, from non-Western feminist thinkers.

An ethic of care is sometimes accused of having no clear way to bootstrap itself out of a social setting in which various biases are present, as if this were a problem unique to care theory. A better way to think about the issue is to accept that this is a problem faced by all theories, that there is no view from nowhere, that any theorizing we do will, at best, illumine a significant part of the human condition, but is unlikely to be the final answer to all of humankind's philosophical puzzles. It is also worth noting that the acceptance of this notion of being socially situated offers us a much better sense of how to react to thinkers from other cultural contexts. Because we are all working from within some cultural context or another, it behooves us to listen to others. It also makes sense for us to be willing to challenge others at times, to point to practices they engage in that look awful to us, and ask why they engage in them. Such questions may lead us to a better understanding of those practices, or they may not. Such questions may also lead others to question their own practices, or to explain to us why they have rejected those practices even though they may be a part of their cultural context. But engaging in a discussion about such issues is far more productive than the two extremes of either condemning others (from our own self-bestowed pedestal of self-righteousness) or defending the practices of others (who may not want the practices in question to be defended).

As so often happens, when we note that the self is socially constituted, we also find ourselves in the paradoxical position of claiming that there is a nonsocially conditioned truth about human nature, namely that humans are all socially conditioned. It would be contradictory to claim that every aspect of human identity, in every dimension, is completely and without remainder a product of social conditioning, since this would generate a logical contradiction to the claim that we can say at least one universal thing about human nature (i.e., that it is socially conditioned). I don't mean to defend the extreme view of social conditioning here. Because, as I've already noted, care theory does begin with, first, the claim that care is universal in human experience, and second, the notion that humans are embodied, providing a further commonality to human nature, I would reject any simplistic claims about the complete and absolute cultural relativity of each human culture. There are clearly common needs and desires that all humans have. At the same time, those commonalities are always filtered through and interpreted in light of a social and cultural set of concepts and assumptions that color them in ways that can be enormously important. Unless we are able to hold together these two thoughts—that humans experience their lives very differently due to social conditioning *and* that humans have deep commonalities—we will not be able to develop an adequate account of ethics.

This preliminary picture of the four aspects of human nature that are found in care theory provides us with a place to begin with our analysis of human nature. It is to that topic that we turn next. The first thing to note about this picture of human nature is that all these features are mutually implicative. We are interdependent because we are embodied, finite beings. Likewise, we care, in part, because of our physical and hormonal makeup. At the same time, our embodiment necessitates a location in space and time, and, in conjunction with our social nature, necessitates particularity. The combination of these various features produces a picture of human nature that is in opposition to the self of traditional Western metaphysics, a self who is an unconnected individual, whose physical being is irrelevant to his identity (though he does seem to be male) and whose emotions, especially the particular attachments he has to kin and family, are antithetical to true rational (i.e., truly human) deliberation. Contrast this latter picture with that of care—humans are social and interdependent, their physical existence is the source and ground of their reasoning and acting, their particular attachments, while not the end of their ethical responsibilities, are certainly the beginning of those responsibilities, and are the training ground for broader moral concerns.

II. How Human Nature Shapes Care

Each of these four characteristics has important ramifications for how we conceptualize care. Interdependence requires a developmental, whole-life view of humans. Theorists who take interdependence seriously begin with the assumption that an account of humans must incorporate the full range of human lives and capacities, from infancy to old age, from developmentally disabled to Olympic athlete, from mentally handicapped to Nobel prize winner. In particular, foregrounding interdependence emphasizes the dependent nature of humans, the way that autonomy is always relative to the support and help of other people,[21] and the extent to which the dependencies that link individuals are relevant to their ethical standing. Giving and accepting help are both integral parts of human life. How the giving and receiving are structured and whether the giving is unfairly demanded of some more than others are important, but no human life exists without its measure of giving and receiving care.

Embodiment points to similar features of human nature as interdependence, such as the recognition that human life follows a physical trajectory from infancy, through childhood, all the way to old age. We interact with other humans from the context of our physical selves, and those selves are relevant to our ethical experiences and knowledge. One of the results of this emphasis is an increased willingness to look at how physical experiences such as pregnancy can shape ethical understanding. Virginia Held, for example, argues that women's capacity for giving birth, and the experience many women have of giving birth, gives them a more life-oriented vantage point than most men.[22] I believe it can be easy to overstate this claim, though Held is careful to avoid such overstatement. But even though women are not universally more life supporting than men, the general principle—that physical experiences are the ground of our ethical life—is an important one.

Embodiment also suggests that our physical relationship with the world is an important part of what it is to be human. It is significant that we experience a world that we can see, touch, hear, and smell. Our ethical experience would be changed if we navigated primarily via echolocation, or if we were completely carnivorous, or if we were capable of independent flight. The physicality of human nature entails that reason itself operates in the context of human physical action, so that we find ourselves dependent in our reasoning on metaphors developed from physical experiences, as is claimed by George Lakoff and Mark Johnson in *Philosophy in the Flesh*.[23] Among other things, this suggests that when the care theorist turns to considering how society should be structured, she or he will not assume that getting ideals right in theory is sufficient. The legal assurance of equal citizenship, for example, is of little use in a society with entrenched racist structures, and unless legal equality is coupled with social structures that protect the basic physical safety and right to an education of minority groups, equality is largely meaningless.

The social construction of the self and cultural embeddedness of meaning also have clear ramifications for how we think about care. We do not operate in a vacuum, with our reason naturally grasping timeless Platonic concepts such as "Justice." We live in the midst of a human society, and the words we learn as children, the conceptual metaphors we use in our reasoning patterns, the concepts we have available for thinking with are all given to us by our society. Human reasoning, in this account, is dependent on a social matrix that provides the material with which we think. Lived experience always occurs against the background of a particular historical and social situation, but that is no reason for thinking it cannot offer resources for a critical examination of that very social context. The most potent social critics usually come from within a tradition, and are able to articulate the ways in which the tradition is destructive of the very values it claims to hold most dear: Martin Luther King Jr.'s articulation of the wrongness of segregation provides a clear and compelling example. If an ethic of care is to be effective politically, if it is to have an impact at the practical level, care theorists need to be able to articulate how the central concerns of care are the concerns shared by wide swaths of people in a given culture. Without this connection to the values people are most concerned about, an ethical theory can never be more than an academic exercise.

Recognizing that all theorizing begins from within a particular social context need not lead to a complete and groundless relativism with respect to the conceptual tools humans use to find their way around in the world. Given the strong emphasis on embodied experience, an ethics of care has good reason for thinking that there will be a high degree of commonality in human experiences, needs, and social structures. The combined features of a recognition of the social construction of meaning and of embodiment provide for an ethical theory that accepts cultural difference as ethically important without making such difference into an absolute. It provides a position from which one can both respect cultural differences and think critically about them, a position that is surely one a feminist theory needs to adopt.

All of these features of human nature, taken together, provide the framework within which care must be defined. Care is embodied concern, focused on the other as another physical being. It is grounded in emotion, though not limited to those cases in which emotions support the expression of care. It is given under specific historical and cultural circumstances. I cannot claim to act in caring ways if I act with complete disregard for the cultural and social context within which I act. But I also cannot claim to care adequately if I do not simultaneously examine the cultural and social context with a critical eye, knowing how often social structures prevent some people from recognizing their own responsibility to care.

Further, theorizing about human life is not a matter of separation from emotions, so that cold, pure rationality can go to work on a series of logical propositions. The very notion of knowledge itself, in this view, is a notion that must incorporate affective connections to the people and issues about which we theorize. In a recent discussion of knowledge in a medical context, for example, Jodi Halpern argues that an adequate account of knowledge requires a recognition that we are emotionally and psychologically attuned to others, and that this "attunement" is not something that makes knowledge more difficult, but rather is an important source of understanding.[24] In order for our emotional attunement to play this role, Halpern argues, we must learn to recognize it for what it is. We are tempted either to identify too strongly with others, so that we cannot give them objective advice, or to cut ourselves off from emotional connections, in which case we cannot offer advice that is appropriate to the particularities of a situation. Halpern argues for a third way, an account of knowledge that acknowledges our emotional empathy with others without letting others' emotional reaction become our own.[25] Further, acknowledging our empathic understanding of another's emotions allows us to provide objectivity to others without abandoning them or separating from them emotionally. If Halpern is correct (and her account of medical reasoning is compelling), then we need to accept the centrality of emotional attunement for any adequate account of knowledge.

III. Implicit Ideals

I have already specified that the concept of human nature at work here is not a merely descriptive one, but a prescriptive one. We can see the sense in which it is prescriptive when we return to the four aspects of care and investigate in each case how the basic conception of human nature also carries with it an implicit ideal. I am going to treat them in a slightly different order than I have so far used because it is clearer how these aspects of human life build on, and presuppose, other aspects if we begin with embodiment and move from there to interdependence and finitude, then to social constitution, and finally to care.

Embodiment offers the clearest and least controversial case of an aspect of human existence that also points us toward an ideal of human flourishing. When we begin with a picture of humans as embodied selves, as physical beings who live in a material world, we can recognize that such things as health, adequate food and clean water, shelter, and protection from physical violence are essential attributes of a fully flourishing life. This provides us with a basis for arguing that any social structures that make it impossible for some people to attain to at least a minimum standard of basic needs also create a society that deserves moral condemnation.[26] Nor can this moral condemnation occur solely within the context of individual nation-states. As Onora O'Neill has argued, the increasing porousness of the boundaries of nation-states implies that ethical evaluation needs to contain a global component, and needs to incorporate a level of concern to work toward social contexts in which no one is denied the possibility of meeting his or her minimal basic needs.[27]

Care theory is sometimes accused of being too attuned to particular relationships, so that it is unable to address global issues of poverty and corruption that destroy the lives of people who are distant from the theorist. But this is a misreading of care theory. If we are developing an account of ethics that respects the embodied physical nature of human beings, then we will also be committed to the notion that there is something deeply wrong with a world in which people starve to death, go without adequate shelter or access to safe drinking water, and are subject to violence and terrorism. There is no reason care theory cannot recognize the wrongness of such a situation. Care theory cannot, of course, solve the situation. No theory can. Theoretical deliberation is not a substitute for concerted political and social action. But unless we are committed theoretically to the notion that living in such a world is wrong, we are unlikely to commit ourselves to action to change it, and at this level care theory does have a contribution to make.

At the same time that embodiment provides us with an ideal of human development, however, it provides us with a clear case of the necessity of the double vision I alluded to earlier. At the same time that parents need a picture of what physical health is in order to raise children properly, they need a sense of what is a reasonable ideal of health for a particular child, and the two will not always coincide. If I am raising a child with disabilities, my notion of what will count as healthy for her will be different from the notion I might have for another child. Even in the case of a child without disabilities, adjustments are regularly made because of individual peculiarities. Physical activity is an important part of health, for example, but faced with a particular child I may decide that isn't of central importance. In such a situation the ideal is still implicitly in place—I still would think that absolute optimality would involve physical activity, but given limits of time and energy, the ideal is set aside in favor of focusing energy on other things. To choose another example, my friendship with another individual may involve ignoring how her smoking is destructive of her health. I want the good for my friend, so I am not blind to the health effects of her habit. But in the context of the friendship we have, constant nagging about the health risks of smoking is likely to destroy other, more important goods of friendship, and so I remain silent.

We find the same double vision when we think more broadly about meeting human needs. Any attempt to address world hunger, for example, faces enormous ethnic and cultural differences. A politically viable attempt to meet needs for food must respect the situation of those who are the recipients, and this is reflected in the ways that nongovernmental organizations have become far more sensitive to culture and gender issues. Again we see the double vision of, on the one hand, optimal physical flourishing for all, and, on the other hand, a reasonable goal for certain people in certain circumstances. Further, in the case of cross-cultural assistance, the recipients themselves have a say in how the ideal is formulated, and so will themselves determine what both the ideal and the reasonable goal might look like. International aid groups that attempt to provide assistance that is not wanted or seen as needed by the recipients are simply not successful at providing aid.

If we return to the case of parenting, we can see that an ideal of health does need to play a role in thinking about what a parent should do. The ideal functions in our reasoning in any number of ways, from allowing us to recognize physical abuse and negligence, to forming the background of our notion of health in a medical context, to providing the frame of reference within which we make decisions about how we will raise a particular child. Although the ideal forms a reference point for our reasoning, it isn't necessarily the goal of all our action. In fact, it may not be the goal for any number of good reasons. We've mentioned the fact that a particular child may never be able to come anywhere close to standard accounts of physical health and motion. In other cases we may have a child whose interests are almost exclusively nonphysical. While it may make sense to encourage a minimal amount of exercise in such a case, vibrant physical fitness may simply not be a reasonable goal—but it nonetheless serves as the reference against which we make judgments about acceptable, unacceptable, and unattainable ideals in this particular case.

Because humans are embodied, as I have argued earlier, they are also interdependent and finite. Interdependence allows us to recognize that lives that claim to achieve complete autonomy are not an adequate ideal for humans. We need an ideal of human existence that endorses and accepts the emotional and psychological and physical support we receive from others. This is an ideal that is hard to articulate, in some ways, because it cuts against some of the central messages our society and Western philosophy together have sent us. But if we set aside images of the Marlboro man for awhile, we recognize that a life without close, nurturing relationships is only minimally a human life, and certainly not one that should be celebrated as an ideal. The lonely gunman on the western plains offers a picture of a miserable existence, not the pinnacle of human life. In the real world, as opposed to the cinematic dreams of Hollywood, humans who lack affiliative bonds are diminished and isolated. The complete lack of affiliative bonds is more likely to be associated with homelessness and mental illness than with any other state. There is some tendency in care theory to associate these affiliative bonds with familial connections, and perhaps this is appropriate as an ideal in many ways. All things being equal, life is better with close, loving, supportive family relationships.

Again, however, the real world intervenes. Families are not always supportive and friendly. Sometimes they are abusive and cold. As feminist theorists have pointed out in numerous discussions, families can be potent sources of harmful pressure and socialization for women and men both. Because of this, Marilyn Friedman's analysis of the value of chosen relationships such as friendships is of central importance in thinking about relationships and the ideal of human existence.[28] So care theory needs first to support and encourage healthy family relationships and second to protect old traditions or develop new ones that sustain the sorts of chosen relationships that are so crucial for a healthy identity.

This discussion sometimes turns into an unhealthy debate in feminist circles, with critics of the family assuming that those who support family relationships are crypto-patriarchalists, while those who pay attention to familial relationships lose sight of the necessity for chosen and nonhierarchical friendships. There is no reason to assume that only one of these is possible, however. A wide range of relationships have their place in the ideal of human life. We should not denigrate familial relationships in a simplistic way. The fact that they can be sources of oppression should not blind us to their essential status. The wrongness of familial relationships that promote oppression lies partly in the fact that they are so central to the development of human personhood—it is their very centrality that makes them so evil when they do go bad. But a focus on the importance of family should not blind us to the centrality of chosen, egalitarian friendships. The lack of either sort of relational web is to be mourned, not celebrated.

The finitude that marks human beings also points to an ideal situation in which support structures are in place to meet the needs and vulnerabilities that are automatically a part of human life. As Joan Tronto has argued, this points an ethic of care in the direction of an analysis of social structures. Humans need care at many different points in their lives, but those needs become particularly acute at certain predictable times. The need for care can be met in worse and better ways, when it is met, either through overburdened caregivers and distant, complex bureaucracies, or through networks of social services and individual caregivers tailored to the particular needs of the situation. Again, it is clear that we have an ideal, against which we measure current social services and find them wanting, but we are also faced with the need to make choices in the world in which we live, a world of finite resources and cultural constraints, and so we do the best we can to arrange decent care that respects both the dignity of the one cared for and the integrity of the caregiver. But in a society that is moving away from the notion of social support networks, even a decent minimum of care for the elderly becomes harder to secure.

Both of these features of human life—finitude and interdependence—point us toward an analysis of social structures. This coincides with the notion that humans develop an identity as a self in the context of social relationships. Individuals thus require support and a social setting in which they can grow, develop, and operate with a reasonable level of success in their projects. Finitude and interdependence take us beyond basic physical needs to a recognition of human needs for social structures with sufficient durability to provide a sense that one's world can be understood and interacted with in meaningful ways. While it is important for the social world within which one moves to be predictable and stable, that is not sufficient for living a rich and fulfilling life. One's life can be diminished if one lives in a context shaped by conceptions of certain humans as incapable of meaningful moral action. Human life should be shaped so that those who are capable of moral agency should not be prevented from exercising that agency by social structures that deny them the basic authority to see themselves as the agents they are. Paul Benson, for example, argues that a social setting that diminishes an agent's sense of moral agency damages the agent's ability to act in morally responsible ways.[29] We need social contexts within which it is possible for all those who are capable of responsible action to see themselves as having value, as capable of autonomous action, as selves with basic human dignity and self-worth.

Finally, the centrality of care in human life also provides an argument for thinking that the socially constituted self needs to be emotionally healthy so that it has the capacity to respond to others in caring ways, and to respond to care that others give in appropriate and nonmanipulative ways. This is one aspect of psychological health, but it is also a requirement for the appropriate use of reason, as I argued earlier, relying on Jodi Halpern's work. This is a notion that comes hard to Western thinkers who are trained to separate reason from the emotions. Some recent work has begun to analyze reason as a combination of emotional connection and moral value. Antonio Damasio's *Descartes' Error*, for example, traces the ways in which ordinary human life becomes impossible for individuals who are not capable of making moral judgments.[30] Martha Nussbaum has also developed an analysis of the necessity for emotional connections and value judgments in anything that approaches adequate reasoning.[31] If emotional connections and moral commitments are integral to knowledge, then the structure of educational institutions, the organization of corporations, and the basic structures of the state need to reflect this. Criticisms of these organizations has often relied, implicitly, on such an ideal. One of the reasons it is problematic to have a political structure composed mainly of white, middle-aged men, for example, is not that such individuals are particularly prone to make evil decisions, but rather that their limited range of experiences will color the issues they see as important, the values they use to weight decision making, and the assumptions they make about how life should be structured. It is almost a cliché for a fifty-year-old man to suddenly awaken to the importance of family and personal relationships. But if he has been unaware of their importance to that point, his contributions to social policy will have been skewed in problematic ways. A diverse body of political representatives is at least more likely to recognize a broader range of issues and matters of importance in its legislation and policy making.

The issue of how we picture the ideal against which we measure and evaluate the current status quo of familial structures, social policies, and the like is returned to in chapter 4. At this point I hope it is clear that we do implicitly rely on such an ideal in our moral reasoning, and that such a reliance assumes a particular picture of what human life should be like, though human life never attains to that ideal.

VI. Conclusion

This discussion has not specified every aspect of the ideal that structures care reasoning. To specify every such aspect would be both boring and futile. There should be an open-endedness to any moral ideal that allows for revisions and new understandings, and care in particular requires such openness. Nonetheless, openness is not the same thing as the lack of such an ideal, and we do need to acknowledge that we are operating with a picture of what human life should be like. Care theory does assume that human physical needs should be met, and that humans should be able to live in the context of supportive and loving families and warm and challenging friendships. The best human societies offer social networks that support these types of relationships, and social services that permit appropriate care to be given when individuals need it. Our social and political activities need to keep one eye on the ideal as we attempt to create lives that are at least livable within the constraints of this particular cultural and historical set of circumstances.

Care theory offers us an account of human nature that is more adequate to lived experience than some of the more rationalistic and individualistic pictures we sometimes find in standard philosophical accounts of the person. But it is an account that has connections to a thread that runs through Western philosophy, surfacing at interesting points in that tradition. It is important to see in what ways care theory fits with, and could perhaps draw on, aspects of the Western tradition, because those connections offer us deeper insight into how this account of human nature can structure ethical deliberation about the issues that most deeply affect us as human beings. So I want to turn in the next two chapters to two nonfeminist, noncare thinkers, both of whom offer important insights into the picture of human nature I have been developing in this chapter—Augustine and Levinas. Both thinkers offer pictures of human life that overlap the picture found in care theory in important ways, but that also diverge from care theory in significant ways. The overlap offers resources for thinking through the aspects of care theory that are common to these disparate thinkers, and for gaining a better sense of the many ways in which the ideals of care can be met. The divergence suggests both dangers that care theory needs to avoid and potentials that care theory has not developed but could—providing, then, a sense of the open-endedness I spoke of earlier.

Notes

1. Eva Feder Kittay, *Love's Labor: Essays on Women, Equality, and Dependency* (New York: Routledge, 1999), p. 25.

2. Nel Noddings, *Starting at Home: Caring and Social Policy* (Berkeley and Los Angeles: University of California Press, 2002), p. 12.

3. Kittay, *Love's Labor*, pp. 40–42.

4. Thomas Hobbes, *Leviathan*, ed. C. B. MacPherson (1651; reprint, London: Penguin Books, 1985), part I, chap. 13.

5. Onora O'Neill, *Bounds of Justice* (Cambridge: Cambridge University Press, 2000), p. 68.

6. Annette Baier, *Moral Prejudices* (Cambridge, Mass.: Harvard University Press, 1994), pp. 106–7.

7. Noddings and Baier make this same point with respect to Kant rather than Hobbes. See Noddings, *Starting at Home*, p. 24. Baier is famous for her argument that Hume offers important resources for feminist theory on precisely this point. See her *Moral Prejudices*, chap. 4, "Hume: The Women's Moral Theorist?"

8. Joan Tronto, *Moral Boundaries: A Political Argument for an Ethic of Care* (New York: Routledge, 1994), p. 103, italics removed.

9. As proof of this point, I offer analytic epistemology in the wake of Chisolm. The literature is marked by an incredibly detailed analysis of various definitions of when a belief is justified, without any real gain in our understanding of what it is to know something.

10. Sara Ruddick, *Maternal Thinking* (Boston: Beacon, 1989), pp. 17, 40.

11. Nel Noddings, *Women and Evil* (Berkeley and Los Angeles: University of California Press, 1989), pp. 91–103.

12. Marilyn Friedman has been a friendly critic of care theory, and her work on the moral resources of friendship is important. See *What Are Friends For? Feminist Perspectives on Personal Relationships and Moral Theory* (Ithaca, N.Y.: Cornell University Press, 1993), chap. 6, "Liberating Care," and chap. 7, "Friendship and Moral Growth."

13. Carol Gilligan, *In a Different Voice: Psychological Theory and Women's Development* (Cambridge, Mass.: Harvard University Press, 1982), p. 167.

14. See, for example, Virginia Held, *Feminist Morality: Transforming Culture, Society, and Politics* (Chicago: University of Chicago Press, 1993).

15. See, for example, Andrea Benton Rushing, "Surviving Rape: A Morning/ Mourning Ritual," in *Feminist Theory and the Body*, ed. Janet Price and Margrit Shildrick (New York: Routledge, 1999), pp. 371–80.

16. See, for example, Iris Marion Young, *Throwing Like a Girl and Other Essays in Feminist Philosophy and Social Theory* (Indianapolis: Indiana University Press, 1990); and Susan Bordo, *Unbearable Weight: Feminism, Western Culture, and the Body* (Berkeley and Los Angeles: University of California Press, 1993).

17. Charles Taylor, *Sources of the Self: The Making of Modern Identity* (Cambridge, Mass.: Harvard University Press, 1989), p. 196.

18. See, for example, Elliot Aronson, *The Social Animal*, 3rd ed. (San Francisco: Freeman, 1980).

19. This is not a particularly new insight, as Aristotle noted that humans are social animals, and that a single human in complete isolation is hardly human. Sociality somehow disappeared from the Western tradition, however, and is still an infrequent visitor in some analytic circles.

20. Ruddick, *Maternal Thinking*, pp. 21–22. See also, in this context, Patricia Hill Collins's discussion of the difficulty African-American mothers face when trying to raise healthy children in a racist society, in "Black Women and Motherhood," in *Justice and Care: Essential Readings in Feminist Ethics*, ed. Virginia Held (Boulder, Colo.: Westview, 1995), pp. 117–35.

21. Our paradigm picture of the autonomous individual, for example, tends to completely obscure the extent to which everyone depends on others. Bill Gates lives in a $75 million mansion—what better example of independence can we think of? And yet he is clearly dependent on a small army of cleaners, cooks, groundskeepers, and the like for his lifestyle. He probably is less able to care for himself on a day-to-day basis than many college students. The management of enormous wealth requires extensive dependence on many others. Gates is conceptualized as autonomous because he can pay to have his needs met. If we begin with the recognition that all humans are interdependent, we are in a better position to recognize that independence or autonomy is always relative to some particular account of dependence. And autonomy will not be the cornerstone of our account of the ethical life.

22. Held, *Feminist Morality*, pp. 136–37.

23. George Lakoff and Mark Johnson, *Philosophy in the Flesh* (New York: Basic Books, 1999), p. 5.

24. Jodi Halpern, *From Detached Concern to Empathy: Humanizing Medical Practice* (New York: Oxford University Press, 2001), p. 10.

25. Halpern, *From Detached Concern*, p. 140.

26. Martha Nussbaum's account of capabilities can provide a framework for this sort of judgment. See, for example, her "Women and Cultural Universals," in *Sex and Social Justice* (Oxford: Oxford University Press, 1999), pp. 29–54.

27. O'Neill, *Bounds of Justice*, pp. 162–67.

28. Marilyn Friedman, *What Are Friends For? Feminist Perspectives on Personal Relationships and Moral Theory* (Ithaca, N.Y.: Cornell University Press, 1993), chap. 8,

"Friendship, Choice, and Change," and chap. 9, "Feminism and Modern Friendship: Dislocating the Community."

29. Paul Benson, "Feeling Crazy: Self-Worth and the Social Character of Responsibility," in *Relational Autonomy: Feminist Perspectives on Autonomy, Agency, and the Social Self*, ed. Catriona Makenzie and Natalie Stoljar (Oxford: Oxford University Press, 2000), pp. 72–93.

30. Antonio Damasio, *Descartes' Error: Emotion, Reason, and the Human Brain* (New York: HarperCollins, 1994).

31. Martha Nussbaum, *The Therapy of Desire* (Princeton, N.J.: Princeton University Press, 1994).

CHAPTER TWO

Augustine and Care

Care theory operates with an implicit account of human nature. It is a conception of human existence that emphasizes the affective, relational aspects of human nature, that makes human embodiment central to human existence, and that takes seriously the extent to which we are social, not solitary, beings. This is a picture of human nature that is not completely foreign to the Western tradition of philosophical thinking, though it has certainly not been a dominant strand. But it is worth seeing how it has functioned in the philosophical thought of theorists far removed from our own cultural context, in order to get a better sense of the strengths and weaknesses of such a view, as well as the degree to which it determines our philosophical reasoning or is open to a variety of different interpretations. So this chapter turns to the thought of Augustine of Hippo. There are a number of important connections between Augustine's account of human existence and that implicit in care theory, and it is worth noting the connections. It is also worth noting the areas in which one might find disagreement rather than agreement, and I will address those as well, after first noting the important areas of agreement.

Augustine does not have a good reputation in feminist circles. He is credited with the antisex and antibody emphasis of large portions of the Western Christian church through the years[1] and he is seen as an important source for an antiwoman bias in the Christian tradition,[2] so it may seem odd to highlight connections between his thought and that of contemporary feminist ethical theory. These criticisms need to be addressed, but they are not the sum total of Augustine. In many ways his philosophical picture of human life offers interesting resources for the feminist thinker. In the first chapter of this book I argued that care is a necessary and inescapable aspect of all good human lives, not just of women's lives. Finding claims about the centrality of love in human life and an interestingly similar picture of human existence in Augustine lends credence to this argument, since Augustine is not writing "in a woman's voice," nor does he intend to offer an account of human life and existence that is particularly woman-friendly. Finding that he nonetheless offers an account of human life that bears significant similarities to an account of ethics that does arise out of listening to women's voices and taking women's experiences into account offers grounds for thinking that perhaps women are human after all, that when women speak out of their experience they are not always making specifically gendered claims, but often have an important perspective on the human condition. Further, it may be significant that women have raised these issues in contemporary life, not because the concerns are uniquely gendered, but because there may be aspects of the way women's lives are arranged that make women more likely to see moral issues. If both Augustine and Levinas, for one reason or another, are able to make these same observations, that may suggest something about which social perspectives make certain sorts of knowledge possible.

A second aspect of Augustine's thought that can be illuminating for feminist theory consists precisely in the differences between Augustine's account and that offered by care theory. These illuminations can take different forms. In some cases Augustine offers important considerations for an ethic of care, and may suggest fruitful considerations for the further development of such an ethical theory. In other cases, Augustine's position may be one that should be rejected, but even then he may prove instructive about dangers that care theorists would do well to avoid. Finally, it is instructive to have a clear illustration of how much thinkers who share certain basic presuppositions can diverge in their thinking from each other. Philosophers trained in the analytic tradition in philosophy tend to assume that shared premises dictate shared conclusions, but ethical thinking is not a mathematical exercise. Theorists can share any number of basic assumptions and still reach importantly different conclusions. It is worthwhile to see where and how such differences appear. Feminist theory encourages awareness of the situatedness and particularity of any vantage point, and of the need for theorists to engage in collaborative and cross-cultural work to avoid parochialism. Feminist pedagogy emphasizes the way that philosophy and critical thinking both improve when understood as dialogue rather than monologue. It is worth our while to spend some time in discussion with a figure as significant to the Western tradition as Augustine, working within a very different cultural, historical, and social context, but with important areas of overlap in how he describes human existence.

Before we can examine how and why these differences arise, however, we need to think about whether it can be claimed that Augustine offers a picture of human existence resembling that offered by an ethic of care. We can see this resemblance if we return to the four features I emphasized in the first chapter.

I. Augustine, Human Nature, and Contemporary Feminist Thought

Augustine is a complex thinker. He wrote prolifically, and his writing is aimed at a number of different audiences, from treatises intended to convince pagan audiences of the truth of Christianity, to theological investigations and sermons intended for a primarily Christian audience, to practical life rules for communities of monastics. Given the sheer quantity of his writings, it is not surprising that different readers find different Augustines. In what follows I focus on the *Confessions*, with occasional sorties into other works. Though I emphasize central features of Augustine's thought, they are not always put together in quite the way I suggest here. I begin with the feature that first prompted me to draw comparisons between Augustine and care theory, namely the centrality of love in Augustine's thought, analogous to the centrality of care in care theory.

A. Care and Love

According to care theorists, care is at the center of human life. Without it we could never exist; without sharing in care, both giving and receiving, human life is a mere shadow of what it ought to be. In Augustine we find a very similar view of the place of love in human life. We are created, he believes, to love. The heart naturally strives to find an attachment to other things and other people to meet its central need for connectedness. Further, the things our hearts long for are good, Augustine says, because they are the creations of a good God. Since God is the origin of all that exists, and God is wholly good, created things are likewise all good. This view sets up the problem of evil for Augustine, of course, since it seems to entail that either evil does not really exist, or that a good God can be the source of evil. Augustine resolves this problem by grasping the first horn of the dilemma, in a sense—he denies that evil has an independent existence and argues that it is always a corruption or perversion of the good, and only possible in the case of beings created free.[3] I return to this topic in the discussion on embodiment; at this point what I want to emphasize is that Augustine believes that since created things are good, our love for them is appropriate. It goes wrong when they are loved in the wrong way, but the love itself is the correct response to the goodness and beauty of creation.

It is an open question, of course, whether what Augustine means by the word translated "love" is exactly the same concept as what care theorists call "care." But the two concepts are obviously very close. Both are connected with the affective part of humans, not in opposition to rationality, but in conjunction with it. Both care and love are oriented toward a non-self-centered good, and both involve active striving rather than mere intellectual appreciation. The major difference between Augustine's love and care is that Augustine's love is properly directed first and foremost to God, while care is defined as emotional attachment to others, and most care theorists do not work within a theological framework. I return to the issue of Augustine's discussion of God in a later section, but I want to set this to the side for the moment to focus on the role of love/care in Augustine's account of human existence.

If humans are innately loving, then at a fundamental level connection is more primary than separation. Humans start from a response of reaching out in trust toward others, and given love will naturally return it, though both of these tendencies can be destroyed. Separation is an important part of human life, but it cannot be the most fundamental aspect of our moral thought. We are, Augustine thinks, created to love, and our lives can be understood only in the context of that constant affectional, emotional reaching out toward others. Augustine, then, sides with care theory against theorists, such as Hobbes, who make separation primary in human life. Ethical theories that begin from the assumption that the only, or the most important, part of ethics is the protection of the rights of one against the intrusions of another miss out on essential and ineliminable aspects of human life. Among other aspects of this relational view, then, is a willingness to consider familial bonds and friendships important parts of human life rather than marks of immaturity that fully adult humans give up.

We can hear echoes of this view in Carol Gilligan's *In a Different Voice*. She argues that psychology, particularly the standard psychology of child development, operates with a faulty picture of human life, insofar as it defines maturity and adulthood in terms of absolute separation and autonomy. Absolute separation, she argues, is a mark not of maturity, but of pathology. Describing the developmental models of Daniel Levinson and George Vaillant, she notes that both researchers developed psychological studies of moral maturity that "convey a view of adulthood where relationships are subordinated to the ongoing process of individuation and achievement."[4] Gilligan goes on to note, "among those men whose lives have served as the model for adult development, the capacity for relationships is in some sense diminished and the men are constricted in their emotional expression. Relationships often are cast in the language of achievement . . . and impoverished in their affective range."[5] Gilligan's concern in this section is to note the exclusion of women from these studies, and the concomitant oversimplification of the developmental model as a trajectory from separation to attachment (an attachment, she notes, that never occurs in these men's lives). What she does not emphasize, though it runs through her discussion as a subtext, is the failure of the researchers she cites, Levinson and Vaillant, to notice that the subjects they chose as models of maturity were clearly living bizarrely isolated lives. This type of blindness arises from the presupposition of separation and disconnection as the normal or default mode of human life. Augustine, like the care theorists, would reject such a proposition as fundamentally falsifying.

Not surprisingly, when we turn to Augustine's description of his own life in the *Confessions*, we find a picture of a person deeply enmeshed in relationships. Augustine's relationship with his mother, Monica, was famously close, and he devotes large portions of the *Confessions* to her.[6] Considering the context within which he wrote, this focus on an uneducated woman is remarkable, and Augustine clearly intends her portrait to serve as a model for the faithful Christian life. Other personal relationships are also central to Augustine's self-portrait; chapter after chapter of the *Confessions* can be characterized by the friends Augustine lists as determining his life at different periods.[7] Accustomed to modern biographies, we may miss the significance of these figures in Augustine's life, but we need to remember that the *Confessions* is a spiritual biography, and could have been composed as a story with only two characters, Augustine and God. Instead it is the story of a life lived in community with others, and a life in which important choices and changes are always experienced in the company of family or friends. Likewise, in the *City of God*, Augustine emphasizes the corporate nature of our human existence, the way we live as members of communities rather than as isolated individuals, and how the desirable human life is necessarily social.[8] In part, of course, this emphasis on relationships is common to writers prior to the ascendancy of twentieth-century metaethics. Friendship plays a central role in the thought of Aristotle, many of the Roman thinkers, and many of the medievals as well. But unlike a thinker such as Aristotle, Augustine does not limit close relationships to those who are of the same social status and sex. Instead, in the radical turn that characterizes one aspect of Christian thought, he argues that every human bears the image of God and is thus properly an object of love.

Augustine argues that humans are created to love God and their neighbors. All created things are good, but humans command our love in ways other things cannot. Instead, Augustine believes that the other humans with whom I am in contact are the most central focus of my love because they bear the image of God. In an interesting precursor to contemporary discussions of the nonunitary nature of the human self, he focuses on how the Trinitarian nature of God is discovered in human existence.[9] This means that when I am in the presence of another I cannot treat that other as an object to be dismissed or destroyed, but must respond to her or him with love.[10] It is significant in this respect that, though Augustine did eventually accede to the use of state power to coerce heretics (a charge that frequently comes up in discussions of his views), he resisted the use of such power strenuously, and only acquiesced when the religious sect involved began trying to carry out assassination plots against the leaders of the church. Even at that point, it is worth noting, Augustine continued to oppose the imposition of death on such heretics, arguing that a response of love could never be to sentence someone to eternal damnation.[11]

The relevance of this account of the centrality of human relationships of love to an ethic of care is fairly clear. Noddings has been criticized, unfairly, I think, for arguing that there are circles of care that begin with those most closely connected with us,[12] and for asserting that, while we can care for animals, the relationship is never fully exemplary of care because of the lack of reciprocity in such relationships.[13] Both of these claims arise naturally from Augustine's perspective. As Augustine would see it, those who are closest to me are the neighbors in whom I see the image of God reflected. I am both inclined and obligated to reach out in care or love to those who have been put in proximity to me by God's creative ordering of the world; they are the proper focus of my love.[14] But, like Noddings, Augustine does not wish to make this notion of proximity an excuse for exclusion. I cannot claim to have no obligations to those who are farther from me because of the exclusive quality of my relationships to those who are close. Proximity is used by both Noddings and Augustine as the occasion for care, but not an excuse for failing to care more broadly. In a similar way, responses to animals, in both Noddings's and Augustine's accounts, are seen as significantly different from responses to other humans. This means not that one cannot have moral obligations to animals, but that such obligations operate at a different level and are voluntary in ways that human relationships are not. As Noddings puts it, "[A] philosophical position that has difficulty distinguishing between our obligation to human infants and, say, pigs is in some difficulty straight off. It violates our most deeply cherished feelings about human goodness."[15] Augustine might justify this view using language Noddings would not choose, namely the language of the image of God in the other, but they would most certainly agree on the basic principle.

But this poses a problem. How can one affirm that all other humans manifest the image of God, and yet hold that one's primary moral obligations are to one's neighbors, those in close proximity to oneself? Isn't any such move an illegitimate preference for certain individuals to the exclusion of others? For both Noddings and Augustine, such a question is itself somewhat misguided. Care for those others who are nearest to me should never be the occasion for excluding others from moral concern. But unless and until I engage in loving care for others who are close I will never be capable of loving those who are farther out. Care begins with the particular. So we find in Gerald Schlabach's development of Augustine's thought an argument for what Schlabach calls Augustine's "immanent teleology," the notion that the relationship between love of neighbor and love of God must find expression in love of particular others. He writes,

> In Augustine's first attempt to explain the relationship between the two loves, in chapter 26 of the *Morals of the Catholic Church*, he could think of "no surer step [*gradus*] toward the love of God than" the love of one human being for another. Alternately, he continued, perhaps love of neighbor was "a sort of cradle [*quasi cunabula*] of our love of God."[16]

This love cannot be divorced from the particularities of the neighbor, which brings us to our second theme, embodiment.

B. Embodiment and Particularity

Embodiment might seem a strange place to find parallels between care theory and Augustinian thought. Many feminist thinkers trace much of the suspicion of the body that is found in Western Christian thought back to Augustine and accuse him of being one of the great sources of a generally Platonic turn away from the flesh toward the spirit.[17] This criticism does have a grain of truth to it, but it also represents a profound misunderstanding of an important aspect of Augustine's thought. The grain of truth has to do with Augustine's concerns about bodily desires as a cause of sin, concerns that were overemphasized by Augustine himself, and overemphasized even more in the tradition that followed him. Those concerns need to be situated in the context of Augustine's creational ontology, an ontology that leads him to reject a Manichean equation of the material realm with evil. Instead, Augustine affirms the basic goodness of the material world, and this feature of his thought is largely missed in contemporary feminist criticisms.

Augustine explicitly rejects the division of human nature into impure body and pure spirit. In a superficial reading of the *Confessions* this is easy to miss, since he frequently speaks of the "will of the flesh" as opposed to the "will of the spirit," and occasionally drops the phrase "will of" to speak simply of the flesh and the spirit. But for Augustine, both spirit and flesh are matters of the will. The will of the flesh is that part of our being that turns away from God and true goodness in order to pursue other, lesser goods. The flesh can draw us to intellectual sins as easily as to bodily sins, and the pre-eminent sin of the flesh is pride—wanting to be greater than God.[18] Further, Augustine, in a fascinating passage of the *Confessions*, discusses the irony of the fact that he can command his physical body to do just about anything, and it will obey. But when he commands the "will of the flesh" it will not obey him—and it draws him into evil activities. Clearly this passage makes no sense if we try to interpret "the will of the flesh" as the physical body, since it is here opposed to the physical body.[19] For Augustine the will is the true source of evil, not the physical body.

In accordance with scripture Augustine recognizes that human physical existence is a part of God's good creation. Human physical existence is first of all good. It is part of the created order, part of how things ought to be, and for that reason is not inherently evil, but rather created good. "The life which we live in this world," he writes, "has its attractiveness because of a certain measure in its beauty and its harmony with all these inferior objects that are beautiful. Human friendship is also a nest of love and gentleness because of the unity it brings about between many souls."[20] Augustine's appreciation for the beauty and goodness of the created world are evident throughout the *Confessions*, as well as throughout the *City of God*.[21] From angels to the least of inanimate objects, Augustine argues, all things are created good.

Many of the things that humans tend to consider evils, he notes, are not evil in and of themselves, but are only perceived to be evil by us because we experience them as conflicting with our own desires and plans. So biting flies, earthquakes, storms, and wild beasts are considered by him to be good in and of themselves, because they originate in the creative activity of a good God, though they can be harmful to us as finite individuals.[22] This is hardly the reaction of an other-worldly ascetic, but is instead a perspective from which it might be possible to develop a theistic, nonanthropomorphic account of respect for the nonhuman world and its integrity.

Augustine's affirmation of the goodness of physical, embodied creation leads him to affirm and respect a developmental account of human existence. The *Confessions* begins with infancy and adolescence, both because it is a biographical account of Augustine's journey to faith and because Augustine thinks that such a developmental account of human subjectivity is necessary. If we do not see ourselves as beginning as helpless infants, unable to exist autonomously, if we do not see ourselves as having lives structured in part by the adolescent friendships we develop, we will make mistaken assumptions, Augustine thinks, about what it is to exist as humans in a physical world. Augustine never assumes that all humans are adult, independent, fully rational beings, but rather assumes that humans exist as embodied beings, developing in ways that require constant contact with other people.

One cannot stop here, however. Augustine also thinks that the body is particularly apt to draw one away from the love of God, and his development of this idea does lead him to a harsh assessment of physical desires at times. This is the grain of truth in the criticisms of Augustine as ascetic. For Augustine, all of life involves a struggle of one love against another. The human condition is one of constant temptation to love wrongly—to love finite things as if they were infinite. He continues the passage I quoted above in this way: "Yet sin is committed for the sake of all these things and other of this kind when, in consequence of an immoderate urge towards these things which are at the bottom end of the scale of good we abandon the higher and supreme goods, that is you, Lord God, and your truth and your law."[23] Bodily desires, because they are so immediate and so powerful, are particularly tempting for us. Here, of course, Augustine is speaking from his own experience. He had a long battle with sexual desire that preceded his conversion to Christianity, and knew how powerfully physical desires could control one's life. He writes, as well, at a time when a life of devotion, for both Christians and pagans, was assumed to require an ascetic rejection of physical pleasures.[24]

Augustine's diatribes against physical pleasures occur within a historical and social context in which they would have been both expected and seen as normal. When we read them today we do not encounter them in that context, but instead read them against the background of a consumer society that validates and glorifies satisfaction of desires regardless of any other considerations. Given our current situation, reading a thinker who cautions us about the dangers of physical desires is not always a bad thing.

But there is more to Augustine than simply a counter-cultural influence. He also respects the embodied nature of humans in a way that we may need to grapple with. Insofar as we are embodied and physical beings, we do need to be aware of how powerfully our physical existence can control us, sometimes in ways that are quite harmful. To take one example, one that is pertinent to care theory, mothers have extremely powerful urges to protect and defend their children, urges that sociobiologists want to attribute to physical, genetically determined drives. A drive to protect one's child is good, presumably, but it can become pathological when a parent begins to ignore other moral demands, such as the demand for justice. I may love and protect my child, but not when she is harming others. Then I need to set aside my "natural urges" and make her quit. Augustine reminds us of how powerful these urges can be, and how subtly they can influence us to rationalize wrong actions. Though he uses a language to express this that is foreign to our ears today, it is not a concept that we should forget. Because feminist theorists often need to rescue women's experiences and emotions from the denigration of masculinist theorists, they are sometimes tempted to the opposite extreme, to a glorification of whatever emotions women feel. But Augustine reminds us that good natural processes can be turned toward evil ends.

Augustine himself was aware that he tended toward too much asceticism. In a fascinating passage on the delights of the ear, and music in particular, he writes:

> Sometimes, however, by taking excessive safeguards against being led astray, I err on the side of too much severity. I have sometimes gone so far as to wish to banish all the melodies and sweet chants commonly used for David's psalter from ears and from the church as well. . . . Nevertheless, when I remember the tears which I poured out at the time when I was first recovering my faith, and that now I am moved not by the chant but by the words being sung, when they are sung with a clear voice and entirely appropriate modulation, then again I recognize the great utility of music in worship.
>
> Thus I fluctuate between the danger of pleasure and the experience of the beneficent effect, and I am more led to put forward the opinion (not as an irrevocable view) that the custom of singing in the Church is to be approved.[25]

This passage may ring a bit harsh to modern ears, but in the context of the extremely ascetic church of which Augustine was a part it is fairly moderate. It also demonstrates his basic principle that evaluation of desires requires contextualization. If physical pleasures lead one to sin, to loving in wrong and harmful ways, then those pleasures must be foregone. But if those pleasures become means for loving rightly, then they are a proper and delightful part of human life. This general teleological framework for the evaluation of pleasures and their place in human life does not seem out of place in an account of care.

C. Finitude and Interdependence

Augustine also recognizes the finitude and dependence that mark human existence. He rejects any sense that humans are independent and self-sufficient beings. The *Confessions* emphasizes from beginning to end that humans are not able to care for themselves, that humans cannot take full responsibility for themselves, and that human knowledge is unavoidably dependent on human relationships. Augustine assumes that belief or trust is a prerequisite for knowledge. In his discussion of infancy in the *Confessions* Augustine makes a point of noting that his own knowledge of his origins and early years comes from the testimony of others. Those others whose testimony he relies on are primarily women. Clearly, he thinks, these are not reliable witnesses, and this reliance on unreliable witnesses is an indication of his own finitude, particularly in comparison to an omniscient God.[26] While we might deplore the deep misogyny that infuses this comment, it is perceptive nonetheless. We have only questionable evidence for many of the pieces of knowledge that are most important for our very identity. It is hubristic and self-deceiving to presume that we can establish all truth for ourselves. We depend on others for all sorts of things, and knowledge is among those things.

The dependent nature of all human knowledge is an important feature of Augustine's thought. It indicates a respect for the limitations of human reason that tends to disappear in more modern thinkers, but reappears in some feminist and postmodern thinkers. For Augustine, reason is an important and powerful tool for acquiring knowledge, but it is never the absolutely reliable mechanism for acquiring truth that it becomes for later thinkers of the modern era. Reason, instead, depends on other things—on the words of other people, on the evidence of our senses, and on the grace of God—and so is never independently reliable in the way that it seems to be for Descartes.

The epistemological ramifications of this finitude and dependence are quite important for Augustine. The human situation is always one of particularity and situated judgment. While God does not change, and while human nature retains certain commonalities, Augustine is very much aware of the ways in which human lives, social circumstances, and historical conditions are variable. Discussing the lives of the Old Testament patriarchs, and the fact that they seemed to be held to different moral rules than those of the culture in which he himself lives, he comments that "the moral customs of different regions and periods were adapted to their places and times, while [God's absolute] law itself remains unaltered everywhere and always."[27]

There are moral absolutes, Augustine believes, but they are expressed in different ways in different times. "An act allowed or commanded in one corner is forbidden and subject to punishment if done on an adjacent corner. Does that mean that justice is 'liable to variation and change?' No. The times which it rules over are not identical, for the simple reason that they are times."[28] The historical and social context within which we live affects the way right and wrong actions can and ought to be expressed. Within the church, in fact, Augustine advocated cultural diversity, with the proviso that such diversity should not hinder worship.[29]

This is a clear example of situatedness without absolute relativity—right and wrong still exist, and we are still required to act justly, but what justice consists in is partly determined by the times in which we live. Moral considerations are not the only ones affected by one's situation and the particularities of the events with which one is confronted. Reason as well functions within a situated context. Augustine is famous, of course, for his recognition that what can be known is partly a function of what we love; knowledge is partly grounded in the heart. But knowledge is also partly a function of our conceptual apparatus. Augustine's conversion to Christianity is made possible by his reading of the neo-Platonists, and he recognizes that he could not have seen the truth of Christianity without the conceptual apparatus of a Platonic metaphysics.[30] I don't want to endorse his Platonism here—I think it is problematic in a number of ways, and at odds with both his endorsement of the goodness of the created world and a traditional understanding of the incarnation—but his insight that we cannot see certain truths except from certain perspectives is a powerful one, and one that fits well with the account of human knowledge and subjectivity found in many contemporary feminist ethics discussions.

D. Social Nature of the Self

Dependence is largely a matter of human finitude. Augustine is very aware that humans are not infinite or independently autonomous. They begin life as helpless infants. They have no desire, frequently, to learn the things they need to know to survive in life; they are not able to direct themselves or care for themselves. Humans are not born independent and fully rational, and a large part of their growth and development is completely outside their own control.[31] Augustine supplements this notion of finitude with a recognition of how opaque our own motives can be to us, so that we can think we are searching for knowledge when what we really want is the respect and awe of other people.[32] Taken together, these functions of Augustine's psychology—dependence, finitude, and self-deception—lead to a complex and subtle view of the search for knowledge as a corporate activity. Even the words we use to grasp various concepts, he notes, come to us from our parents, our teachers, and the others around us.[33] We are profoundly dependent on a social support network for every aspect of our lives.

Again, this recognition of our dependence on socialization resonates strongly with feminist critiques of certain strands of contemporary ethical thought. It is commonplace for feminists to criticize the unrealistic individualism of contemporary liberalism by pointing to the sorts of features that Augustine focuses on in these passages.[34] Humans do not spring full grown into the social contract. They are socialized into humanity by family, peers, and society; their abilities and knowledge are partially determined by these socializing forces; and their conscious motives are often different from what seems, to an outside observer, to be the real focus of their pursuits.

If humans are finite and dependent, then thinking of them as absolutely self-determinative and self-creating makes no sense. If human existence is one of embodied particularity in the context of matrixes of care—matrixes that provide needed resources for developing a sense of self—then the self exists in relation to others; depends on others for care, information, and the like; and is porous and non-self-transparent. This is particularly clear in Augustine's discussion of his own infancy. He sees human life as enmeshed in relationships that are often unchosen, and he sees human subjectivity as developed, in part, through interactions with all the others who surround one.

Relationships can determine central parts of our lives, and yet we cannot always see the ways they form us, the ways in which they structure our own understanding of ourselves or others. This leads Augustine to offer a fairly complex psychology, in which our desires and drives are often not directed by our rational intellect, and in which we frequently find ourselves strangers to ourselves.[35] Again, this picture of the complexity of human subjectivity finds echoes in contemporary care theory and related discussions. For example, the essays in *Relational Autonomy*, a collection edited by Catriona Mackenzie and Natalie Stoljar, explore the many ways in which a relational view of the self requires a shift in the philosophical understanding of autonomy. In particular, Paul Benson's essay details the complex ways in which moral responsibility connects to socially constituted aspects of subjectivity. "Social relationships," he writes, "modify the kinds of moral dialogue that are possible among people, and in doing so, influence the terms of moral responsibility that are possible between them."[36] Benson, however, takes this concept much farther than does Augustine, arguing that recognition of the social constitution of the self may make moral demands on us to fight systems of oppression. Recognizing that subjectivity is partly constituted by social relations, we also should see that destructive and oppressive social relations constitute a particularly evil sort of structure, since they affect essential aspects of the persons whose identities are formed within that structure.

I think it is not unreasonable, then, to claim that there are certain interesting similarities between basic features of Augustine's account of human nature and the picture implicit in care theory. But the presence of these similarities does not imply absolute agreement. There are significant differences between Augustine's thought and care theory's account of how human life should be organized, and these are illuminating for our project as well.

II. Dissimilarities

Three aspects of Augustine's understanding of human existence represent central dissimilarities from the account found in contemporary care theory. One is Augustine's account of the relationship between humans and God, and his account of the meaning and nature of the transcendent. The second is Augustine's treatment of hierarchy, with its concomitant notion of the great chain of being. The third issue, already mentioned, is Augustine's assessment of the place of physical pleasures in the properly ordered human life. In each of these cases Augustine offers us significant food for thought, even when he goes wrong—as, I will argue, in his discussion of hierarchy. Thinkers can often teach us as much with their spectacular failures as with their more pedestrian successes, and so it is worth thinking through how and why they end up where they do.

A. Transcendence

Augustine develops an account of the human condition that begins with a creator God, and continuously points back to the divine in whom all things have their beginning and their true end.[37] This provides the framework for Augustine's teleology, since all things are properly ordered, he believes, when they are directed to God in a way appropriate to their nature. For nonrational beings, this is largely a matter of glorifying God simply by existing; for beings with an intellectual nature and freedom, humans and angels, this is a matter of choosing to love God as each was created to do. Augustine believes that the most central relationship a human should have is with God, not with other humans. Our relationships with other humans are important, there is no doubt about that, but it is the relationship with God that truly constitutes our identity. "Our hearts are restless," Augustine writes in one of the more famous lines from the *Confessions*, "until they rest in Thee."[38] We are created to be in a proper relationship with God, and apart from that relationship nothing in our lives can ever make any sense.

The reason Augustine thinks this is that God is the ultimate good. God is the source of everything good, and the goodness of all created things is a reflection of their relationship with God.[39] Since God is a good beyond all created goods, none of the created things should be loved to the exclusion of God.[40] All loves should be ordered, Augustine thinks, by reference to the ultimate source of all goodness, and we should not love lesser things more than greater things. There is clearly a rigid hierarchy at work here, a hierarchy that drives much of Augustine's reasoning on any number of subjects, and I examine it in more depth a bit later. But I want to focus first on this notion of God as ultimate, transcendent good, and the claim to ultimate loyalty Augustine thinks this requires.

It is important to note, first, that Augustine's claim that God is properly the ultimate focus of our love does not mean that we cannot love the things, and more important the people, of the created world. The goodness of God provides the framework for Augustine to analyze the many ways in which we can properly love the things of this world—as the creations of a good God, they are properly loved, and are a delight to us. All things, Augustine thinks, should be loved insofar as they point to their creator, and loved in and through our love for their creator. Other humans, in particular, are the image of God to us, and so they are always to be treated with a recognition of their reflected holiness. When human relationships are in good order they involve each person loving the other as the self, each concerned about the good of each.[41] The image of all of creation engaged in loving response to its maker and to the other created things is a beautiful one. The central notion that human life is situated in the context of a relationship to the transcendent, to something that goes beyond the confines of the present world and that endows life with a deeper and richer meaning, is important. Augustine's ontological sense of the source of all that exists as good and loving provides a context within which human morality makes sense in a way that it does not always make sense in the context of other ontological schemas.

Augustine's ontology offers a challenge to feminist thought that is worth taking seriously. The challenge is this. In an Augustinian picture of human life, only God deserves absolute loyalty, and any other human love needs to be held in a relationship proportional to that one ultimate loyalty. This raises the question of whether feminism requires exclusive loyalty, or whether it is possible to be a feminist, but to have other "loves" as well. There is a tendency for political movements to make exclusive claims to their members' loyalty, and feminism can fall prey to this temptation. So the question of whether one can be a limited feminist is worth asking. Asking the question sheds light on some feminist debates, since the vigor with which they are conducted and the deep feelings they evoke seem sometimes the result of religious fervor. My own sense is that feminism should be a political movement, not a religion. It should not enforce a set dogma, nor should it involve the forced excommunication of heretics. It should be a movement compatible with a wide range of other commitments, so that one could legitimately claim to be a feminist while having other aspects of one's identity determined by other commitments. I believe that for the most part feminism has accomplished this, and has had room for a wide range of views and even differing interpretations of what feminism is. At the same time, it is always tempting to try to define orthodoxy, and to achieve the sense of power that comes from defining one's self as in and another as out of acceptable opinion, and this tendency is occasionally evident in feminist thought.

So Augustine does offer a cautionary note to feminism as a political movement. His notion that only God is worthy of ultimate and exclusive worship and the concomitant claim that human institutions and structures should never claim more than a limited sort of authority or loyalty are worth hanging onto, whether one is a theist or not. The attempt to turn any human belief structure into a god is always a mistake, and a particularly problematic mistake if one is an atheist. Augustine's notion of a transcendent God allows him to identify the demand for unqualified obedience on the part of any human construct as a form of idolatry.

On the other hand, there is a tendency for Augustine to focus so strongly on the transcendence and infinite "beyondness" of God that the things of this world pale into insignificance. The sharp dichotomy he sometimes draws between loving the things of the world and loving their creator reflects this focus. On this issue I think Augustine is not entirely consistent. While acknowledging that physical existence is a good, and that it is not incompatible with the absolute goodness of God to become incarnate in the flesh of the man Jesus, Augustine is never completely comfortable with this affirmation of the physical. On this point, feminist criticisms of Augustine's treatment of physical desires and drives have some justification. He consistently advocates discipline and control of our physical desires, out of a concern that those desires will come to take the place of the love we should reserve for God alone. While we might concur with the claim that discipline and control of the physical are worth developing, this need not lead us to a rejection of the basic goodness of those drives and desires, nor should it have led Augustine to that conclusion.

One other aspect of Augustine's account of the relationship between humans and God is worth noting, and that is his account of sin. Unlike the Platonic account of error being a result of ignorance, Augustine's account of sin puts the free will at the center of the picture. Sin occurs when the will chooses perversely, when it chooses a lesser good in preference to a greater good. Pride is the central and original sin, in Augustine's account, because the first sin involves using one's freedom to reject God's will in favor of one's own, inferior will.[42] Because the relationship we should have with God is broken by sin, according to Augustine, we cannot restore our lives to wholeness just by our own efforts.[43] Further, sin pervades our lives, so that even when we intend to act rightly, we nonetheless pursue the wrong goals, choose the wrong methods, and often misrepresent our own motives to ourselves and others. One of the virtues of this account of sin is that it led Augustine to develop a far more complex psychology than most philosophical systems had developed before him. Unlike the Socrates we find portrayed in the dialogues of Plato, for example, Augustine never thinks that knowledge can produce virtue. Because the seat of sin is the will, not the intellect, sin and evil are a matter of choosing wrongly, not of ignorance.

This account of sin as radical and pervasive is an element that is lacking in contemporary discussions of an ethics of care. It assumes a picture of humans as radically flawed, and accounts for both the evil that humans do, and the sense that things should be otherwise, in this way. To date care theorists have not offered an alternative account of why evil is as pervasive in human life as it patently is. Nel Noddings offers a phenomenology of evil in women's lives, and she describes the reality of the experience of evil and its effects.[44] She does not, however, offer an explanation for why evil exists and flourishes the way it does. Without an understanding of why evil exists and what it is, it is difficult to know how to confront it adequately.

Care theory needs an account of the source and nature of evil. Because it is an ethical theory that emphasizes the depth of care, moral attitudes, and sympathies in human life, it runs the danger of offering a one-sided, overly rosy picture of human nature. We do care, we do naturally reach out in love to others, but we also respond to others with swords, spears, and smart bombs. Further, even our deep tendency to care for others can be the source of evil actions and desires. Augustine's notion that sin involves the will in turning away from the truly good and toward lesser goods out of self-love helps to remind us that every human emotional attachment can be turned to destructive ends. No matter how good the fundamental attitude of care may be, it can still lead to evil if it is wrongly directed. If, for example, I am motivated by care for my own family to create social structures that protect us, but leave other families unable to meet even their most basic needs, then care is directed toward evil.

This analysis of sin, if taken seriously, has two implications for care theory. The first implication is that, although care is the fundamental moral motivator, actions that are accurately described as arising out of care are not always morally right or commendable. While care is a necessary component of ethical character and ethical action, it is not a sufficient component. Ethical character must incorporate care, but that care must be turned to ends that are themselves morally worthwhile. This means that even when actions flow out of caring attitudes, the actions still need to be evaluated in terms of whether the care that motivates them is properly directed at the true good of the other, and at a just set of social structures. The second implication of Augustine's account of sin, in the context of care theory, is that no system of ethical thought, and no political or social structure, will ever be completely perfect. If Augustine is right about the pervasiveness of sin, then theorists need to recognize a certain level of fallibility in their theorizing and in their prescriptions for social change.

This can be a valuable counterweight to a tendency to utopianism. From an Augustinian perspective, social change can be beneficial, and can ameliorate various injustices and evils, but what it cannot do is bring about absolute peace and justice. From the perspective of absolute justice, Augustine argues, all human structures are unjust.[45] This doesn't mean that some aren't better than others, but it does mean that none is perfect. If we take Augustine seriously on this point, then we will advocate social structures that are revisable, that can be challenged and changed. We will also adopt a chastened view of what social changes can accomplish. Social change can be intended for good and result in harm. Or social change that addresses one set of evils can itself produce a new set of problems and harms. Augustine encourages us to ask, about any proposal for social change, "What will we lose if we win?" Social change is necessary, and feminists should continue to fight for an end to sexist and patriarchal practices. But for any given proposal, we need to look carefully at the costs involved in winning: If we ban the sale of pornographic materials, will feminist literature fall under the category of "pornographic" and be banned?[46] How can we structure divorce and custody laws so that they are fair for most women and men most of the time? The problem of unforeseen side effects is not a reason to give up on social activism, but it does provide a reason for being realistic about the improvement any particular change can actually make.

B. Hierarchy

In terms of the place of transcendence and of human relationships with the divine, Augustine offers some important resources to a feminist ethic of care. When we move to the place of hierarchy in Augustine's thought, we find that the opposite is true. This is a subject on which feminist theory offers an important critique of Augustinian thought. Care theory begins from a recognition of power differences. The call to care comes from the vulnerable, and calls to those with the ability and resources to care. While we can't make sense of human life without recognizing that people are differentially vulnerable, and that some people must use their power and resources to care for others, we also need to be very clear about the dangers involved in accepting these differentials as a justification for entrenched hierarchy. On this topic, then, Augustine will serve as a cautionary note rather than as a model. I would like to focus on his application of a conception of hierarchy to sex differences and their place in human life. The problems that appear in this part of Augustine's thought reappear in other parts, such as his failure to offer adequate criticisms of other societal structures of his day.

When discussing sex differences, Augustine starts off well. He asserts that both men and women are fully made in the image of God and so both are called to live in relationship and faithfulness with God. If he had stopped there the history of the church might have been radically different from what it was. But he goes on to assert:

> As in [the human] soul there is one element which deliberates and aspires to domination, and another element which is submissive and obedient, so in the bodily realm woman is made for man. In mental power she has an equal capacity of rational intelligence, but by the sex of her body she is submissive to the masculine sex. This is analogous to the way in which the impulse for action is subordinate to the rational mind's prudent concern that the act is right.[47]

This was his considered opinion. He reiterates this basic analysis in *The Trinity*[48] and never questions the conflict generated by the assertion of both equality of being and absolute inequality in terms of social order and legal status.

In the context of our culture today, a culture that, at least in theory, assumes the equality of men and women, Augustine's views read as nothing more than a non sequitur. Augustine asserts in these discussions that women have exactly the same rational capacities that justify self-rule in the case of men, but that an additional feature of their physical bodies, namely their sexual difference from men, makes their rational abilities somehow not properly ordered to play the very role they were created for. The lack of logical connections is glaring. But in Augustine's culture, and for his predominantly male readers, this apparently seemed to make good sense. Women are made to submit, men are made to dominate, and this is a part of the good created order.

Cultural forces and assumptions are obviously at work here, and we should not ignore the extent to which cultural presuppositions create the framework within which logic functions. But there is more going on in Augustine's discussion of sexual difference than an unthinking advocacy of social assumptions about the proper roles of men and women. Augustine lived at a time when chaos threatened to overtake every social structure extant. The Roman Empire was crumbling, and many of Augustine's contemporaries blamed that dissolution on the abandonment of the traditional Roman religions in favor of Christianity, a new and rather radical offshoot of Judaism. The *City of God* is written to respond to these charges. Along with the shifting political scene, and the violence and warfare that accompanied the collapse of the Roman legal and social structure, Christianity itself seemed to many believers to offer an excuse for anarchy. Christian teachings seemed to support a radical egalitarianism, a rejection of traditional social roles for men and women, and even the rejection of the authoritative structures set up by the Church hierarchy to ensure order and orthodoxy.

In this context, Augustine's advocacy of traditional authority structures makes sense. (Which is not to say that it is commendable.) He was a bishop of the church, facing violent attacks by splinter sects on congregations under his authority,[49] he faced a society in the process of falling apart, with authority structures increasingly unable to maintain any sort of peace and order, and he faced calls within his own church to accept politically radical movements that would have made the church's institutional structure unable to function.[50] It is not surprising that in this context Augustine defended a strongly hierarchical and traditional apportioning of authority and power. As is so often the case, he framed the issue in terms of order or chaos, a stark either/or. Order, he assumed, required an absolute chain of command, while chaos would result from any change in authority structures.

There is, however, another alternative to these two. Authority and hierarchy are not evil in and of themselves. Augustine was right to think some form of authority structure essential for any sort of peaceful life. But we can acknowledge that some form of authority is necessary without assuming that the power of authority must be absolute, or that those subordinate to that power should submit to it completely. Augustine's own notion of transcendence, a notion that Augustine was committed to by his Christian principles, provides us with a way to think about authority and hierarchy that offers an alternative to power exercised as domination and control.

Augustine himself recognizes that God is characterized by a love that expresses itself in servanthood, and that divine power is properly expressed in creation and empowerment. The incarnation and death of Christ are both in conflict with any simplistic assumption that domination is a necessary aspect of created order. The incarnation subverts domination in multiple ways. First, it demonstrates that the helplessness and neediness of infancy are not opposed to God's power and majesty (in the way evil *would* be opposed to God's goodness). Further, that God came into the world through a woman demonstrates that social value does not correlate with God's valuation of people. Christ's coming in order to serve (a comment that he repeats throughout his ministry) indicates that service, care, and humility are essential components of God's nature. While this is a hierarchy, it is a most unusual one. Christ's death is the clearest case of the divine destruction of a "natural order of domination," since it demonstrates God's transcendence precisely through a giving up of power over others and a willingness to suffer with others that are directly opposed to power exercised as domination.[51]

Augustine occasionally recognizes that domination is not the same thing as properly exercised power. In the *City of God*, for example, he begins his discussion of the differences between earthly systems of power and those driven by a love of God by pointing out that the church has functioned as a place of refuge for Christians and pagans alike, and this, he claims, is partly what allows it to be identified as a system driven by a love of God.[52] He has the resources in his philosophical thought to recognize that power can be expressed as either protective sanctuary or oppressive domination, but that recognition is only patchy and partial. Further, given Augustine's account of the pervasiveness of sin, and of the tendency for sin to express itself through self-aggrandizement at the expense of others, he should have recognized a need for structures of authority that build in accountability for those who rule, structures that require that authority be validated by those for whom the authority is wielded.

This is a theme that one finds over and over in the literature on an ethics of care. Virginia Held notes that imbalances in power are an unavoidable part of nurturing relationships, but she does not conclude that these relationships are therefore relationships of authority exercised as domination (although they certainly can be). Instead she argues that in the mothering relationship we see a model of power exercised to promote the autonomy of the other.[53] The limitations on the power of the caregiver are not generated by a Hobbesian fear of an equal other, but rather by care for the one cared for, and by concern to sustain relationships of care and trust. Power is thus not exercised for purposes of maintaining rigid hierarchical structures, but is used to diminish power differences. Theorists of care offer a needed corrective to Augustine's own thought.

Augustine's account of sin is not the only resource he had available. The doctrine of the Trinity, for example, a doctrine he defended staunchly, breaks open his rigid hierarchical structure and presents us with a picture of mutual love and service that is offered equally to all persons of the Trinity without diminishing the capacity to love the rest of creation. Further, Augustine's development of Trinitarian doctrine begins with the establishment of the equality of the three persons of the Trinity, not the hierarchical nature of their relationship. Likewise, God's example of love for creation shows that love for created things is fully compatible with love for their creator. The love demonstrated within the Godhead is a love that overflows boundlessly, so that love for Godself becomes the impetus for the creation of more and more things, including beings with the freedom to love in return. But Augustine's resources for an alternative picture of love went unused, and instead he started the church down a path of asceticism and sexual domination that it still struggles with today.

Before we leave this topic, one more lesson can be drawn from Augustine's account of authority and hierarchy. I have argued that his acceptance of authority as absolute domination follows partly from the social context in which he found himself, a context in which many shared his perception that all of life was flying toward chaos, that the loss of traditional social values was leading to irretrievable anarchy, with all of the destruction and injustice that anarchy breeds. If someone thinks that the only two options are a somewhat unjust authoritarianism and a violently unjust anarchy, it is not surprising that he would choose authoritarianism as the lesser of two evils. This is an important consideration for contemporary feminist ethical theorists, because there is a common perception among some sectors of society today that we live in times that are chaotic and heading toward anarchy. Fear of chaos leads almost inevitably toward acceptance of strongly authoritarian leadership, because people feel such authority is the only safeguard against such chaos.

Feminists are rightly seen as advocates of change. They appear to nonfeminists as agents of chaos, since they aim to change traditional structures of authority. Feminist theorists who hope to generate widespread social support for their policies need to articulate the ways in which their proposals can be implemented, and change can be brought about, without the threat of chaos looming in the background. This is both possible and good political practice. If a social system cannot generate a certain level of stability, it is not going to bring about improvements in people's lives, no matter how theoretically appealing it may be. Feminist political advocacy is much more effective when it offers a positive vision of a flourishing life, rather than offering a negative critique of the status quo without a clear alternative. Augustine's errors serve as a useful reminder that proposals for social change must be realistic enough to represent an alternative to both rigid hierarchy and anarchy.

III. Conclusion

For Augustine, what makes sense of the notion that humans are created to be in loving relationships with others—embodied relationships with other fleshly human beings—is the fact that all humans are created by a good, loving creator, and created in the image of that creator. This basic conviction provides the grounding for Augustine's affirmation of love for several reasons. First, it allows love to be more than self-interest or rational calculation. Ultimately, reaching out in love is prior to and deeper than reason, though not contrary to reason. Further, love is not a simple technique for getting what one thinks is in one's self-interest—that is a pathological perversion of love. Finally, the reason other humans are the focus of love is a sacredness or a transcendence that is experienced in other humans. They are more than simply the furniture we find in the world around us. Instead, they are unique and irreplaceable others, beings who confront us as both mystery and promise of response. In other humans, even at their most vulnerable, we are confronted with the image of God, and we thus experience them as deserving, and calling for, care.

When we come into contact with another, we are not confronted with another self. Instead we find ourselves faced with something more mysterious yet—another who is not like me, who does not think the same thoughts as I do, who has experiences I can never have, who is conscious like me, but unlike me is conscious of thoughts I can never have. This mystery of the other person offers me a glimpse of something that transcends ordinary experience, and that calls me out of my own thoughts and beliefs to be in communication with another. In this way other humans image God to me. They offer a glimpse of the sacred and unknowable that calls us to a relationship of love.

Further, as Augustine develops his doctrine of creation, God is not only the one who calls us to a relationship of love, but also the creator of all that is, one who orders the world in ways that may be incomprehensible, but can be trusted as good. This makes our reaching out in relationship to others and our love and care for the creation around us in accord with reason. The attitude of care and trust is not grounded in reason. Reason itself must start with trust, so it cannot be the basis of trust. But trust is not contrary to reason, either, as trust is ultimately based on a view of life as meaningful and suited to human flourishing.

It is worthwhile thinking through these themes in the context of a contemporary ethics of care. Most care theorists to date have noted that care is a basic and necessary attitude of human life. Noddings argues persuasively that the moral imperative to care would not and could not arise if there were not a basic emotional response of caring to begin from. In opposition to Kant she argues that reason alone cannot provide the motivating force for a moral response to the other, though reason can certainly work with an already present attitude of care to allow for a moral response.[54] But the origins of that initial and basic caring response are left largely obscure. It simply is a fact about humans that we find them to be this way, and we can then theorize from that starting point.

An Augustinian picture of the fundamental goodness of creation, however, offers an explanation for why humans are naturally created to care. It is not simply a brute fact about the world, nor is it a contingent matter that could have been otherwise. More than this, a theistic framework makes sense of care itself. For Noddings, it becomes necessary to say that we care because we care, we choose to act in morally right ways because morality matters to us. We could choose otherwise, however, and part of the human existential experience is that sense that we could choose otherwise. I don't deny the truth of Noddings's insight here, but there seems to be something deeper than mere choice in the realm of moral caring. That something more is given a very different articulation than Augustine's in the thought of Emmanuel Levinas.

Levinas, like Augustine, engaged in philosophical enquiry within a theological tradition, the Jewish tradition rather than Augustine's Christianity. His life, like Augustine's, involved a search for an understanding of evil in the context of a fundamentally good creation. Several of the themes I have noted in Augustine's thought can be found in Levinas's philosophy, as well as some new formulations that cast light on issues of importance for an understanding of human nature that can ground an ethics of care, and some themes that are problematic and need to be challenged. After working through Levinas's discussion of the ethical structure of human existence, I draw some conclusions about how we should think about human nature and an ideal structure for human life.

Notes

1. See, for example, Susan Bordo's "Anorexia Nervosa: Psychopathology as the Crystallization of Culture," in *Women, Knowledge, and Reality: Explorations in Feminist Philosophy*, 2nd ed., ed. Ann Garry and Marilyn Pearsall (New York: Routledge, 1996), pp. 394–95.

2. See, for example, Nancy Tuana, *The Less Noble Sex: Scientific, Religious, and Philosophical Conceptions of Women's Nature* (Indianapolis: Indiana University Press, 1993), pp. 11–12.

3. Saint Augustine, *Confessions*, trans. Henry Chadwick (Oxford: Oxford University Press, 1998), 7.11–13.

4. Carol Gilligan, *In a Different Voice: Psychological Theory and Women's Development* (Cambridge, Mass: Harvard University Press, 1982), p. 154.

5. Gilligan, *In a Different Voice*, p. 154.

6. See, for example, *Confessions*, 1.11, 3.11–12, 5.8–9, 6.1–2, 9.8–13.

7. Consider, for example, his famous unnamed friend from *Confessions*, 4:iv, as well as the importance of Alypius and Nebridius at key points in Augustine's life (in *Confessions*, 4, 8, and 9).

8. Saint Augustine, *City of God*, trans. Marcus Dodds (New York: Modern Library, 1999), 12.27; 19.5, 12.

9. Saint Augustine, *The Trinity*, trans. Edmund Hill (Brooklyn, N.Y.: New City Press, 1991).

10. In the *Confessions*, 1.18, for example, Augustine criticizes lawyers who are more concerned with their professional status than with the death or life of the individual they defend.

11. For a more detailed discussion of Augustine and the heretics, see John Von Heyking, *Augustine and Politics as Longing in the World* (Columbia: University of Missouri Press, 2001), chap. 7, "The Coercion of Heretics."

12. Nel Noddings, *Caring: A Feminine Approach to Ethics and Moral Education* (Berkeley and Los Angeles: University of California Press, 1984), pp. 46–48.

13. Noddings, *Caring*, pp. 86–87.

14. Augustine, *City of God*, 19.14.

15. Noddings, *Caring*, p. 87.

16. Gerald Schlabach, *For the Joy Set before Us: Augustine and Self-Denying Love* (Notre Dame, Ind.: University of Notre Dame Press, 2001), p. 37.

17. Nancy Tuana, for example, treats Augustine and Aquinas together as exemplars of the Platonic rejection of the body in *The Less Noble Sex*. See pp. 11–12, 58–59.

18. Augustine, *Confessions*, 2.6.

19. Augustine, *Confessions*, 8.8–9.

20. Augustine, *Confessions*, 2.5.

21. See, for example, *City of God*, 9.21, 22, 26; 12.1, 3, 4.

22. Augustine, *Confessions*, 7.13.

23. Augustine, *Confessions*, 2.5.

24. See, on this topic, Aline Rouselle, *Porneia: On Desire and the Body in Antiquity*, trans. Felicia Pheasant (New York: Barnes & Noble, 1996); and Peter Brown, *The Body and Society: Men, Women, and Sexual Renunciation in Early Christianity* (New York: Columbia University Press, 1988).

25. Augustine, *Confessions*, 10.33.

26. Augustine, *Confessions*, 1.6.

27. Augustine, *Confessions*, 3.7.

28. Augustine, *Confessions*, 3.7.

29. Augustine, *City of God*, 19.17, 19.

30. Augustine, *Confessions*, 7.10.

31. Augustine, *Confessions*, 1.11.

32. Augustine, *Confessions*, 1.12.

33. Augustine, *Confessions*, 1.8.

34. See, for example, Susan Heckman's comparison of Gilligan's and Lawrence Kohlberg's conception of the moral self in *Moral Voices, Moral Selves: Carol Gilligan and Feminist Moral Theory* (University Park: Pennsylvania State University Press, 1995), chap. 1: "The Different Voice."

35. The most famous example of this, of course, is the conversion scene from *Confessions*, 8.

36. Paul Benson, "Self-Worth and the Social Character of Responsibility," in *Relational Autonomy: Feminist Perspectives on Autonomy, Agency, and the Social Self*, ed. Catriona Mackenzie and Natalie Stoljar (Oxford: Oxford University Press, 2000), p. 83.

37. Augustine, *Confessions*, 1.1.

38. Augustine, *Confessions*, 1.1.

39. Augustine, *The Trinity*, 8.2.

40. Augustine, *Confessions*, 2.5–6.

41. Augustine, *The Trinity*, 8.5.

42. Augustine, *The Trinity*, 4.4.

43. Augustine, *Confessions*, 8.9.

44. Nel Noddings, *Women and Evil* (Berkeley and Los Angeles: University of California Press, 1989).

45. Augustine, *City of God*, 11.25–27.

46. Catherine MacKinnon's proposed ordinance banning material that portrays "the sexually explicit subordination of women" was thought by many jurists to cover some of the writing of Andrea Dworkin, MacKinnon's colleague in her fight against pornography.

47. Augustine, *Confessions*, 13.32.

48. Augustine, *The Trinity*, 3.10.

49. See Heyking's *Augustine and Politics*, pp. 229–33, for a description of the violence endemic among the Donatists, Augustine's main concern at this time.

50. Peter Brown discusses the political and social situation that played a role in shaping Augustine's thought on sexual difference and authority in *The Body and So-*

ciety: Men, Women, and Sexual Renunciation in Early Christianity (New York: Columbia University Press, 1988), pp. 396–408.

51. These same strands can be seen in the theology of that deeply Augustinian theologian, Martin Luther. And, like Augustine, Luther ignored them in his political thought. For a discussion of these strands in Luther's theology, see Mary Solberg, *Compelling Knowledge: A Feminist Proposal for an Epistemology of the Cross* (Albany: State University of New York Press, 1997).

52. Augustine, *City of God*, 1.4–7.

53. Virginia Held, *Feminist Morality: Transforming Culture, Society, and Politics* (Chicago: University of Chicago Press, 1993), pp. 211–12.

54. Noddings, *Caring*, 49–51.

CHAPTER THREE

Levinas and Care Theory

To the extravagant generosity of the for-the-other is superimposed a reasonable order, ancillary or angelic, of justice through knowledge, and philosophy here is a measure brought to the infinity of the being-for-the-other of peace and proximity, and is like the wisdom of love.

—Emmanuel Levinas

We have looked in some detail at the connections (and sometimes disjunctions) between care theory and Augustine's account of human nature. I would like to turn now to a very different thinker, Emmanuel Levinas. Like Augustine, Levinas is not a feminist thinker, nor is he interested in developing what might be considered a "feminist-friendly" account of ethics. Levinas also uses language and ideas that the contemporary feminist may find problematic. But his philosophical analysis of the ethical is acute, and the similarities between his account of ethics and that given by care theory are too important to dismiss out of hand. While we may not want to follow his thought in every particular, it is nonetheless worthwhile to understand it.

Again as in the case of Augustine, it is worth noting that Levinas's account of ethics, an account very close in a number of ways to that given by care theory, is not derived from women's experiences or moral reasoning. While this is in one sense a problem that must be dealt with, it is at the same time evidence that care theory is not applicable only to women, nor is it derivable only from women's experience. Instead, the similarities between Levinas's account of ethics and that offered by care theory suggest that careful philosophical investigation into lived human experience generates just this type of ethical theory. That is, claims by thinkers such as Nel Noddings and others that care theory speaks to the human condition are supported by finding a similar account of ethics offered by thinkers who are not feminist.

I. Levinas and Human Being

So, let us begin with those aspects of Levinas's account of the human condition that resonate with contemporary care theory. I emphasize features that are important from a care perspective, as I did with Augustine's account—namely, features of a relational self, embodiment, and the particularity of the other person.

A. Relational Existence

As with Augustine, one central area of resonance in Levinas's thought is the notion that human existence is fundamentally relational. Levinas places himself in opposition to the philosophical tradition, particularly as developed by Heidegger, in which an understanding of human existence begins with ontology. Human existence is not, first, a sort of individualized way of being in the world, Levinas argues, but instead is a profoundly relational existence.[1] To be human is to find myself always already in relationships I do not define or control with others who, while like me in their humanity, are fundamentally (or, to use Levinas's term, "infinitely") other than me. I can neither define them nor experience what they experience.

Like Augustine, Levinas uses the language of the image of God in the other.[2] Unlike Augustine, however, he resists the notion that the relationship with God comes first and is then recognized as reflected in another.[3] For Levinas, we encounter transcendence only in other persons, never in the abstract. To begin where Augustine does, with the concept of an infinite all-powerful being, one who is ontologically prior to the personal relationships in which one stands, is to risk using an idea to justify the denigration of, or to deny the transcendent reality of, the individual with whom I am faced. If I begin with the notion that I can have an unmediated relationship with God, I risk doing damage to this person in the name of God. Instead, Levinas argues, I only ever recognize the trace of God in the face of this other person who stands before me. In Levinas's words:

I do not want to define anything through God because it is the human that I know. It is God I can define through human relations, and not the inverse. The notion of God—God knows, I'm not opposed to it! But when I have to say something about God it is always beginning from human relations. The inadmissible abstraction is God; it is in terms of the relationship with the Other (*Autrui*) that I speak of God.[4]

So, unlike Augustine, Levinas begins with an account of the transcendent that never permits the divine to take the place of one's ethical responsibility to other humans.

But then what is the relationship between one human and another, and how does this notion of the divine come into it? Levinas argues that in every relationship with another one finds oneself in a relationship to something that can only be captured by the language of infinity. The nature of that relationship, he argues, is determinative for human experience. So he writes:

We think that the idea-of-the-Infinite-in-me—or my relation to God—comes to me in the concreteness of my relation to the other man in the sociality which is my responsibility to the neighbor. Here is found a responsibility that I contracted in no "experience," but of which the face of the other, through its alterity and through its strangeness, states the command that came *from who knows where*.[5]

A number of aspects of this complex quote resonate in important ways with features of care theory. I would like to concentrate on four of them. First, Levinas emphasizes the extent to which we are relational beings. Second, the relations in which we find ourselves are physical relationships, because we are embodied beings. We are called to moral responsibility by the concrete physical presence of others. It is not an abstract duty generated by the presence of rationality, but is experienced as a direct result of finding oneself in the physical presence of another. Third is the idea that the basic relationship with the other is an ethical one, a normatively oriented relationship, not what we might call the normatively neutral relationship of simple physical proximity. Fourth, the other to whom I have an ethical responsibility is other, strange (a concept Levinas regularly uses the term "alterity" to indicate). That is, the other I respond to cannot be defined or known prior to experience, nor can she or he be assumed to be identical to me. I would like to deal with each of these in turn, though, because they are interrelated, each will implicate the others.

For Levinas, the relation with other humans is not a relationship with an abstract ideal of human nature, nor is it a theoretical idea generated by some abstract concept such as rationality. It is, instead, a concrete, embodied relationship with a particular other.[6] Levinas uses the notion of the face to develop this idea. When I am confronted with the face of the other, he writes, the nakedness and vulnerability of that face call me to an infinite responsibility. This notion of the face is Levinas's shorthand for the way we recognize that we are in the presence of another person and find ourselves in a responsive state prior to any rational calculation of relationships.

I sometimes use an anecdote I have heard attributed to Wittgenstein to make this point to my students. If you are walking along a path and see two trees, a person, and another tree, your response is something along the lines of mentally registering the first two as "tree," "tree," and then switching to response mode to say "Hi!"—then resuming registration mode for the final "tree." That is, when faced with humans we are in a different mode of existence in the world than we are when simply moving about amid objects. To use another example, most people who live in large cities for any length of time learn to avoid the eyes of those they pass on the sidewalks, in order to avoid being overwhelmed by the press of humanity in that setting. But it is only other humans one has to learn to avoid being conscious of. Trees, cars, buildings, and hedges do not require us to develop techniques to tune them out. Levinas's point is that we find ourselves in relation to other humans, a relationship that is irreducibly communicative and unchosen. We develop all sorts of behavioral techniques to allow us to tune this relationship out, but those techniques would not be necessary if the relationship were not basic.

The similarity between this account of how we exist as humans in relation with other humans and the account given in care theory of our basic predisposition toward others is striking. In both cases the basic picture of human existence is one that is irreducibly relational, and one in which to fail to be in relation is to fail to exist as a human. This account of human existence has important ramifications for how we assess practices and social institutions, since practices and institutions that either assume separated, isolated agents or place enormous barriers to existence in relation require ethical criticism.

B. Embodiment

There is a second feature of the quote we are unpacking that is worth our consideration. The relational existence we humans experience is one of physical encounter. Humans are neither disembodied intellects nor rational calculators. Again, this is an aspect of Levinas's thought that resonates with care theory. In a phrase Levinas repeats over and over, the other is the poor, the widow, the orphan. The others who call me into human relationship are others who have physical and emotional needs, and toward whom I have responsibilities. This is important because it means that responding to the ethical call of the other is always a matter of responding to a physical being with concrete needs. I cannot respond ethically by (simply) having the right attitude, or by "caring about," to use Joan Tronto's phrase. I must care for—that is, I must respond, and I must respond as an embodied being to another embodied being.

Further, embodiment for Levinas is not a matter of experiencing the self as an intellect that finds itself in a rather distant relationship to a physical body. It is not a Cartesian dualism in any sense. Levinas uses the term "enjoyment" to capture the sense of physical existence that humans experience, and connects it with the notion of play. Our existence is a physical presence in a world that is a matter of delight.[7] This does not mean, of course, that physical existence cannot be experienced as a burden, as excruciating pain, or as misery. But if we did not start from a recognition of the basic goodness and existential priority of physical experience, these conditions could not be recognized as evils that require a response. Although Levinas never uses the language of a good creation, one finds echoes here of Augustine's notion that the physical realm is first good, though susceptible of becoming destructive and twisted into something evil. So human existence is an existence of enjoyment, of embodied experience in a world of which we are one physical part.

This basic affirmation of both embodiment and the goodness of the physical is echoed in care theory. The notion that taking delight in embodied existence is not something to be rationalized away, but an important part of human life, underlies central concepts in care theory such as the joy that Noddings notes can accompany receptivity to the sensible and the affective.[8] Likewise, Sara Ruddick's description of human flesh from the perspective of natality is riddled with words such as "play," "enjoyment," "celebration," and "pleasure."[9] None of this should suggest a romanticized account of human embodiment. Neither Levinas nor the theorists of care are in any way unrecognizant of the pain, suffering, and death that accompany human existence. But all start with a recognition of the fundamentally positive aspect of being in the world.

Levinas, like care theorists, sees human existence as fundamentally embodied and relational. These embodied relationships, furthermore, are irreducibly moral. Levinas does not offer us a contract ethics, in which initially isolated individuals contract together so that each, individually, can preserve a sphere of liberty for himself or herself. Nor, in Levinas's world, are people defined as human in terms of a particular essence or quality that inheres in the individual. Instead, human existence at its most originary (or basic) is in physical, embodied relation to others. That relationship to others is one of responsibility. This brings us, then, to the third aspect of the quote we've been examining, namely the nature of the relationship in which I stand to the other. It is fundamentally a relationship oriented toward the Good, or God.[10] The trace of God is apparent in the other, Levinas says, in the vulnerability of the other that forbids murder. The other confronts me as a being who can be killed or destroyed. But that very vulnerability is the source of my responsibility to the other, and my recognition of the other as a unique, irreplaceable existent immediately places me in a moral or ethical relationship with the other.

I can, of course, reject that moral relationship and choose to harm or kill the other. But in a way that is certainly different from my relationship with, say, rocks, I cannot choose to make the relationship a nonmoral one. When I am confronted with a rock, I face no moral demand that can be obeyed or ignored. My freedom is not in any way limited by the rock's existence. In Levinas's own words, "things have no face."[11] But when I am confronted with another person, I can't choose to be in the same nonmoral relationship I experience with the rock. I can choose to do some really terrible things. I can enslave the other, and do my best to turn him into an object that I use. But, Levinas notes, even in slavery, I have to (first) recognize the humanity of the other and the ethical demands that humanity makes on me, in order to deny those demands to the other. This is borne out by the practices that grew up in slavery, such as forbidding slaves to look directly at their masters or speak before being spoken to. One doesn't have to forbid a rock or a berry bush to look at one, because in neither case does an ethical relationship already exist.[12] But in the case of other humans, the relationship is there; it is the very basis of our existence as humans, and so, paradoxically, it has to be denied in order for me to pretend, in my actions, that the other is not human.

Thus, for Levinas, as for Augustine, there is a deep incoherence or irrationality at the heart of immorality.[13] However, the incoherence that Levinas notes is not the Augustinian incoherence of choosing a lesser good in preference to a greater, but instead the more Kantian incoherence of affirming and denying another's humanity simultaneously. When I treat the other as an object, I affirm and deny her humanity at one and the same time. If she were not human I would not be attacking, enslaving, or lying to her, but in order to attack, enslave, or lie, I must deny her humanity. Levinas is conscious of this Kantian strand to his thought, but rejects Kant's emphasis on rationality as the origin of our respect for the other. The response to the other, in Levinas's account, is quite simply what makes us humans; it arises in relationship and is in some sense prior to any onto-logical account of "what humans are."

C. Particularity and Otherness

Finally, the other who confronts me is infinitely other. That is, I am con-fronted with something in the other that escapes my rational or intellectual grasp. This ineffability undergirds communication, leading Levinas to distin-guish between what he calls the saying and the said. When we speak to each other, the words and the phrasing we use constitute the said. Those same words can be repeated, analyzed, recorded, or ignored. They have an inde-pendent, objective existence of some sort. But the saying of those words is not repeatable. The particular discursive event in which you (a "you" I can-not completely define or grasp) broke into my self-awareness and caught my consciousness, and in which I opened myself up to you in turn, responding to you as to an other, not an object, is an event that is unrepeatable and that eludes any conceptual definition. Language *is* ethics, Levinas says, and by this he means not that ethics is best thought of in terms of linguistic concepts, but rather that the communicative relation toward another is necessarily an ethical relation of responsiveness.

In communication the other comes to me as the infinite, as that which es-capes the boundaries of concepts, categories, and ideas. I can define an idea in terms of necessary and sufficient conditions, but no set of necessary and sufficient conditions will capture what it is to *be* you. Levinas regularly in-vokes the name of Descartes in his discussions of this point, endorsing Descartes's recognition that the notion of the infinite breaks in on my con-sciousness from without, associated with the image of God. Levinas rejects, however, Descartes's argumentative move to attribute this infinity to an ab-stract idea of an all-perfect being, and instead locates infinity in the en-counter with the other person.[14]

Again this aspect of Levinas's thought resembles aspects of care theory in important ways. Levinas emphasizes the particularity of the other, the ways in which the other cannot be defined in advance, and the ways in which I discover what it is to be human when I open myself up to another who challenges my assumptions about the world and about how things ought to be. Compare this, for example, with Ruddick's account of how practices of mothering can result in ways of knowing. In the case of both thinkers, we find that human existence is not properly thought of as a matter of getting my concepts rightly aligned with objects in the world, but instead is a matter of being in relationship to others with whom I en-gage in human life.

II. Self-Sacrifice and Justice

It is not difficult to note that there are important areas of similarity between Levinas's work and care theory. We also find that Levinas's approach to certain central ethical problems—namely, the related problems of self-sacrifice and justice—resembles the approach to those problems found in care theory. Once the other is described as infinite, and my relationship to the other as one of moral responsibility, the demands that morality makes on me seem to become infinite as well, requiring absolute self-sacrifice. This is a problem that reoccurs in care theory, so it is important to address it here. In a description of the nature of subjectivity, Levinas writes, "The truth of the will lies in its coming under judgment; but its coming under judgment lies in a new orientation of the inner life, called to infinite responsibilities."[15] In individual relationships, for Levinas (as for care theorists), my responsibility for the other is boundless. I never reach a point at which I can say that I have done enough for the other; instead, I find myself always guilty of doing too little.[16] Here, then, a difference from Kant appears. Kant believes that we have duties both to ourselves and to others, and implies that our duties to ourselves must be discharged first—they take priority over our duties to assist others. But for Levinas, the other's call to me is a call to give up everything. It is infinite. This is the dark side, so to speak, of the infinity that I encounter in the other. Since the call to ethical responsibility is primordial, I am "always already guilty," Levinas says, called to an infinite ethical responsibility to the other that I cannot fulfill and that requires more of me than can be given. We hear echoes of this language in Noddings. "Can I be free of guilt?" she asks rhetorically. Her answer: "I do not think it is possible. Paul Tillich describes the anxiety of guilt as ontological. It transcends the subjective and the objective. . . . I want to care, but I do not. I feel that I ought to behave as though I care, but I do not want to do this."[17]

Not surprisingly, then, Levinas's account of the ethical life has been criticized, as has care theory, for requiring far too much in the way of self-sacrifice of the individual. The call of the other is infinite, Levinas notes, and I am always already guilty and can never meet my responsibilities. But, as critics have pointed out, this infinite responsibility seems to require too much from me. I would like, at times, to live my own life, not to be continually at the service of the other. The notion of a realm of privacy, of individual freedom prior to responsibility to the other, is a deeply entrenched notion in our contemporary liberal society. The same criticism has been made of care; if care for the other is the basic human attitude, then there seems no space left for restricting care, for limiting my responsibilities to others in order to go about my own life in ways that would allow me to flourish.

Because this criticism is made of both Levinas and care theorists, it is important to see how Levinas responds to it and to consider whether this is an adequate response for an ethics of care. Levinas's solution to the problem of infinite self-sacrifice is found in his discussion of the notion of justice. While Levinas does argue for an infinite responsibility to the other encountered in the flesh, he also recognizes that I never encounter only one other. There are lots of others, people all around me, and if I devote myself to meeting the infinite call of one other, I run the risk of neglecting, or even destroying, the many others who are excluded by my focus on this one. So Levinas sets up a second layer of ethical thought, the realm of justice.

My initial relationship to the other is one of infinite responsibility to this particular other, and this being-in-relation is what it is to be human. But all humans are beings-in-relation, each one facing unavoidable first-person responsibilities to others. Confronted with a multitude of others I must consider how their competing ethical demands fit with one another, and how all of us can construct a human world in which we can meet one another in ethical responsibility. Concerns about how we structure our lives together, Levinas argues, are concerns about justice, politics, and happiness. Justice concerns the competing demands others place on me, and on each other, and so the third party, the one who is also present in encounters between myself and the other, is always connected with the concept of justice.[18] Levinas is sometimes misunderstood on this point. He should not be taken to be arguing for the rather silly view that I have an infinite responsibility to an individual as long as he is the only one in the room, but if a third person enters we immediately enter a different set of relationships. Instead, Levinas writes,

> It is not that the entry of a third party would be an empirical fact, and that my responsibility for the other finds itself constrained to a calculus by the "forces of things." In the proximity of the other, all the others than the other obsess me, and already this obsession cries out for justice, demands measure and knowing, is consciousness.[19]

Justice is not a separate, alternative stage of ethical responsibility. It is, instead, an entailment of the primordial ethical relationship. Faced with another who places moral demands on me by her very existence, I also find myself commanded to work toward social systems that protect the rights and permit the moral duties of all. Justice and the moral "for-the-other" relationship are not identical; Levinas speaks of them as, respectively, politics and religion,[20] but they are mutually implicative.

Again, there are striking similarities between this picture of human life and that offered by care theorists. Joan Tronto, for example, argues that while care must involve concrete practices of caring for particular others, it also requires a careful analysis of the political structures and institutions that permit caregiving, require it, or make it impossible. Selma Sevenhuijsen has offered a similar analysis of public policy in the Netherlands and its relationship to how private caregiving is carried out. In a way that fits well with Levinas's overall picture of the relationship between individual caring and social structures, Tronto and Sevenhuijsen argue that caring requires both individual responsiveness and political structures that enable adequate care.[21] One weakness of Levinas's account here is that he fails to do what Tronto and Sevenhuijsen do, that is, he fails to offer concrete suggestions as to what political structures and institutions can support ethical relationships, or an analysis of how particular structures destroy such relationships.

A strength of Levinas's account of the profoundly ethical nature of human existence, however, is the way it rings true with much of what we experience in our ethical lives. As Annette Baier has pointed out, we do find ourselves in the midst of responsibilities that are not always chosen; we find ourselves duty bound to meet the needs of others with whom no contract was ever (or could be) written.[22] To this extent, phenomenologically, Levinas's account of ethics does seem to capture some central features of human experience.

Further, the notion that we exist always already in the realm of ethical responsibility, specifically the responsibility to respond to the other, fits well with care theory's notion that care is a fundamental aspect of human experience. In fact, without this basic orientation of being-for-the-other it is unclear how any ethical requirements could ever get a hold on us. Like Levinas, Noddings grounds ethical caring in natural caring. Both are feelings, she argues, but the former could not exist without the latter.[23] In the same passage, while considering how a theorist might philosophically justify the claim that an individual has moral responsibilities, she argues that the moral viewpoint is prior to any justification. "We are not 'justified'—we are *obligated*—to do what is required to maintain and enhance caring," she writes.[24] (That the language sounds Levinasian is certainly no accident. Martin Buber is regularly quoted in *Caring*, and Buber is one of the major influences on Levinas's work.) After all, if I do not begin with an obligation to the other, how could such an obligation ever be generated, whether by the force of abstract reason or divine law? Unless obligation is a primordial, there is a sense in which it can never generate its demands on me. To put this another way, if my basic existence is one of being for myself, there seems no way to make the leap to an absolutely binding moral obligation. Any moral obligations will have to take second place to my first obligation to myself, and if and when they conflict with such an obligation they must necessarily give way.

Levinas's account of ethics prior to ontology, then, does make phenomenological sense of the nonvoluntary nature of the moral demand on us. But is this an adequate response to the charge of unacceptable self-sacrifice? Here I think two points need to be made. The first is that every ethical theory faces the problem of whether to start from a response to the other or from self-interest, from duties to the self. In either case, it is difficult to limit the starting duty sufficiently to generate the second set of duties. If I exist for the other, it is difficult to protect the self from the infinite responsibility to the other. If I exist first for myself, however, it is difficult to reach the point at which the other can make moral demands on me, particularly demands for positive assistance. Both cases face a similar difficulty, and both, it seems to me, are in a similar theoretical position with respect to the nature of ethical demands, since each has trouble with a central and important aspect of the moral life. We can see this difficulty worked out in any number of ethical theories. Utilitarian theories, for example, are regularly criticized because the rule that everyone should count for one, and no one more than one, poses problems for the special concern individuals have for themselves. Contract ethics, with its starting point in the self-interested rational agent, has difficulty generating sufficiently robust accounts of our duties to others. Virtue ethics begins with the responsibility the agent has to become a good human being, and so has difficulty generating sufficiently robust concern for others.

Clearly any account of the ethical life must generate both concern for the self and concern for others if it is to be adequate to our moral experience. Just as clearly, one or the other set of concerns will be theoretically prior. So the interesting question for our purposes is not whether a theory faces the problem of making either other- or self-oriented duties primordial—every theory must begin with one or the other. The first interesting question concerns which starting point generates a more satisfactory, less strained, account of our ethical experience. I have already indicated that I think Levinas's account of ethics does a fairly good job of mapping onto our ethical experience. A second interesting question concerns how well the theory bridges the gap between first and second duties. Does Levinas's account have an adequate explanation of how one can have duties to the self if one begins by "being for the other"? Since this is a central criticism of care theory as well, this is a particularly important question for our purposes.

Humans naturally care about their own good. Levinas notes this—he describes the "originary hedonism" of the individual's existence, when one's life is experienced as a matter of needs that are met and desires that are fulfilled, and when no other appears on the horizon to call one to responsibility. For

Levinas, this state does not deserve negative moral judgment, since it exists in a realm in which the ethical does not appear. But at the same time, he argues, it is a realm that is not fully human. We experience life as *human* life when we are called into responsibility by the appearance of the other and recognize that we do not exist solely for our own sake. But this originary hedonism reappears, for Levinas, when we enter the realm of justice and politics. In that context happiness reenters the philosophical picture. No longer do we find that Levinas's language operates in terms of duty and responsibility alone. When we begin to speak about social and political life, social structures that protect human rights and enable decent lives are invoked. So we find Levinas writing,

> Finally, the distance that separates happiness from desire separates politics from religion. Politics tends toward reciprocal recognition, that is, toward equality; it ensures happiness. And political law concludes and sanctions the struggle for recognition. Religion is Desire and not struggle for recognition. It is the surplus possible in a society of equals, that of glorious humility, responsibility, and sacrifice which are the conditions for equality itself.[25]

So political protection of equality and the human right to demand recognition from others is what ensures the possibility of happiness for each. Protection of the self occurs at this level. But note that Levinas also argues in this quote that the first ethical command, of being for the other, is made possible by a political structure that protects equality. Conversely, being for the other is the precondition of equality. In other words, ethics and just political structures, while not the same thing, are mutually implicative. Levinas develops this idea further in "Peace and Proximity," in which he argues that the political order must be founded on respect for the other rather than on abstract truth claims. The latter always carry with them, he thinks, the potential for violence and the destruction of the other in the name of truth.[26]

So Levinas's solution to the issue of self-care is grounding it in a just social order. Care for the self becomes possible in a social order in which all people find themselves with basic rights and protection. This solution to the issue of responsibilities to the self bears a strong resemblance to the view developed by contemporary Augustinians, such as Paul Ramsey, who also return to care for the self by way of first developing how ethical responsibilities to a particular other always generate demands of justice toward all, so that ethics and political theory are mutually implicative.[27]

III. Contrasts between Levinas and Care Theory

I have argued that there are strong similarities between Levinas's account of the ethical and that offered by care theory. Both fit, phenomenologically, with human experience; they offer similar accounts of human existence as both embodied and relational; and both begin from the ethical response to the other. Having said this, however, it is worth noting that there are important differences between Levinas's account of the ethical and that offered by care theory, and the differences indicate, perhaps, why care theory arises from feminist thinkers and why it offers an important corrective to the views offered by Levinas. Two important differences come to mind. The first is the peripheral role the political plays in much of Levinas's theorizing, and the second is the more nuanced and acceptable account of gender and ethics found in an ethics of care. But before I turn to these issues I'd like to make a brief detour past a third potential difference, because it has been the source of some feminist criticism of Levinas. I call it "potential" because I think that on this issue Levinas is misread.

A. The Abstract Other

Some critics have charged that Levinas's account of the other emphasizes the unknowability of the other excessively. The infinite other, Levinas argues, cannot be grasped or rationally comprehended by me, and trying to grasp the totality of the other intellectually is always the first step toward the annihilation of the other's being.[28] This seems to place an unbridgeable distance between myself and the other, and to negate the commonalities emphasized by care, commonalities of physical embodiment, neediness, emotional openness, and the like. In particular, Cynthia Willett argues, Levinas's "transcendent face" is an abstract nudity, one that may forbid murder, but that does not forbid, for example, the specific violations of women's bodies that have gone on throughout the ages.[29] The problem, as Willett sees it, is that the very infinity or transcendence of the face in Levinas's thought removes the other from the realm of concrete particularity to the realm of abstraction. John Caputo, in a similar manner, takes Levinas to task for his use of the language of the absolute other, though he is not specifically concerned about gender issues in this passage.[30]

But I think the critics who have raised these charges against Levinas mistake his point. When Levinas uses the language of infinity he is not attempting to describe the abstractness of another person. Interpreting him this way runs against the grain of far too much of his focus. His discussion of themes I have already mentioned—themes of embodiment, neediness, and the call of the other—would make no sense if the other were a disembodied infinity. Instead, what Levinas calls our attention to is what he calls the element of transcendence in our encounter with others. When I meet another person, I certainly meet her as another physical human being, one who eats, sleeps, and has perhaps given birth to children, as I have. But simultaneously I am confronted by a consciousness who looks at me out of eyes I can never see through, whose thoughts I can never fully enter into, and whose life is her own. Levinas uses any number of words to try to capture this experience. "Infinity" is a term he frequently uses, but he also speaks of "transcendence," "height," "God in the other," and "the sacred." All of these are appropriate, and yet all fail to capture fully what he is trying to gesture at, precisely because he is trying to point at what cannot be captured with words. If it could be said, the other would not be truly unique, but describable in universal terms. It is precisely the otherness and irreplaceableness of the other that Levinas gestures at with these terms. Rather than charging him with being too abstract, then, we might argue that he provides a language to describe a significant part of care. What it is in the other that calls for particular sorts of responses from me is not definable in advance because the other is, ultimately, her own self. She cannot be captured by a definable universal, and the language of transcendence seems crucial for capturing the importance and moral inviolability of the other as a particular and unique person.

In fact, Levinas, argues, the irreducible otherness of individuals is phenomenologically necessary for human existence as experienced. If humans were all, ultimately, manifestations of some universal form—say, of reason—then any differences between them would be flaws, failures of reason to come to full expression. But Levinas rejects this totalizing picture of human existence precisely because it is untrue to our experience of the call to responsibility that confronts us in the face of a particular other.[31] Again, the connections here with care theory are striking. Levinas refuses to predefine the individuality of the other person in the same way that care theorists have emphasized the necessity of the particularity of care. Care, properly speaking, is directed at the particular good of another, not at the general, universalizable good of an abstract concept such as reason.

B. The Political

This emphasis on the infinite individuality of the other leads directly to the problem of the political, however. To the extent that the relation to the other is a relation to a particular other, are we not prohibited from developing any political structures? After all, political structures seem to require that we make assumptions about a common human nature, that we treat all like cases alike (to use the hoary old formula offered by Aristotle), and that we assume not the particularity, but the equality, of all. It appears that Levinas's strong emphasis on the ethical makes any concern for the political impossible. Worse, it looks as though this impossibility of the political vitiates Levinas's ethical thought, since the call to individual responsibility to particular others seems to offer nothing in the way of serious political critique of structures of oppression and violence. If what Levinas offers us lacks an adequate standpoint from which to critique social structures of oppression, it seems worthless (or worse) from a feminist point of view and disturbing as a model for an ethics of care.

Appearances can be deceiving, however, and it would be a mistake to think that Levinas has nothing to say in the political realm. I have discussed above the ways in which he thinks that justice and the ethical are related. It is, though, a fair criticism of Levinas to charge him with inadequate development of the political side of his thought. Very few of his philosophical writings deal directly with political structures, legal systems, institutional matters, or the like. In this way, interestingly enough, he fits rather well with a theorist like Noddings, who emphasizes personal moral responsibility and has only recently addressed issues having to do with national-level politics. But Levinas does address the issue of political structure tangentially in several essays, and those remarks, while insufficient, are worth attending to.

In "Peace and Proximity"[32] Levinas analyzes the notion of peace, relating it to the disillusionment experienced by those who saw European ideals of justice and rationality function as ideological weapons of destruction in the twentieth century. Hegelian visions of the triumphant march of reason can too easily function to rationalize wars of destruction: what are a few million deaths when one is trying to bring about the ideally rational state? Ideals of justice too easily turn into ideals of absolute sameness that justify the genocide of all who are defined as different, hence disruptive, hence to be destroyed. Against this misuse of justice Levinas reemphasizes the primacy of the particular other and the illegitimacy of any system or structure that reduces particular others to predefined quantities. Peace, then, should not be understood as complete unity, and instead must be thought of as "incessant watch over this alterity and unicity."[33] Peace requires social structures that guard the irreducible uniqueness of the individual. Justice is a matter of rights that are grounded in the ethical relationship of the one to the other—such as the moral prohibition on killing that commands me in the face of the other—not abstract rights based on an individual's status as a rational being. The egalitarian and just state, Levinas concludes, is not founded on the war of all against all but rather on the ethical responsibility of the one for the other. In *Totality and Infinity* he addresses the notion of justice a bit more, working out an account of justice as fraternity, reliant on the paired concepts of brotherhood and a common fatherhood.[34] I will return to the gendered nature of these notions shortly, but first it is worth noting what Levinas himself means by these terms. The notion of fraternity, or brotherhood, Levinas argues, contains both the requisite notion of commonality (a common father) and the notion of individuality that is not reducible to some abstract universal. In the same way that we hold commonality and difference together in the concept of brotherhood, we should hold together mutuality and responsibility in justice.

These are suggestive remarks, but they are also incomplete. While Levinas has offered very general comments about the foundations of justice, equality, and peace, and has offered important theoretical considerations for how these concepts ought to be understood, he offers very little in terms of concrete discussions of how social structures can protect the uniqueness and integrity of the other. Levinas fails to offer a contentful account of the structures of justice, or even a more detailed account of human rights. The notion of fraternity may help us to understand what justice is not, but it is not clear that it provides sufficient theoretical specificity to help us in developing just social structures or egalitarian institutions. Levinas is correct to call our attention to the ways in which abstract accounts of justice can fail to protect particular individuals, and can, in the worst cases, be used to destroy individuals. But pointing out the failures of particular specifications of justice offers little guidance for thinking about how corporate human life ought to be structured.

While this lack in Levinas's theoretical thinking is problematic, however, it is also indicative of a danger that care theory, like Levinas's thought, needs to avoid. Both theories are correct in emphasizing the uniqueness of the other individual, and in recognizing the extent to which abstract theories of justice can run roughshod over the very individuals they are supposed to protect. But any theory that emphasizes uniqueness and alterity runs the risk of having too little to say about what structures of justice should look like. Care theorists such as Tronto and Held have done much more than Levinas to develop an account of social structures and institutions that can provide a framework within which care becomes possible, and in this way care ethics offers a further theoretical development than Levinas's ethics. Noddings also addresses these issues in her most recent book, *Starting at Home: Caring and Social Policy*, and what is striking about the book is that it begins to develop a picture of what it means for humans to flourish. Noddings discusses embodiment (with concomitant notions of health and physical flourishing),[35] family structures (with ideals of familial functioning that allow imaginations to flourish and that respect both physical and intellectual work),[36] and social structures, specifically for facilitating care, meeting the housing and other needs of the homeless, and treating those defined by social norms as deviants, particularly drug abusers.[37] While she rejects utopianism, Noddings is clearly driven in this discussion by a vision of what it would be like to construct a life together in which humans could develop their various potentialities and flourish as individuals without barriers imposed by poverty, rampant homelessness, and the like. This type of analysis is lacking in Levinas.

C. Levinas and the Feminine

Levinas's ethical thought also uses the notion of the feminine in problematic ways. As I mentioned earlier, he uses the terms "fraternity" and "fatherhood" in developing his account of justice. The terms are not incidental in Levinas's thought. He is not using them as synonyms for "human siblings" or "parenthood," as is sometimes (at least nominally) the case with thinkers from an earlier period. Levinas is very clear that he is speaking as a man here. For example, in *Totality and Infinity* he spends a fair amount of time developing the importance of the paternal relation, a relation he finds significant because it involves both identity (this child is my child) and absolute difference (this child is a stranger to me). Part of what creates the absolute difference in the case of paternity is that the child appears through a relation with the feminine.

When Levinas does speak of the feminine, it is in the problematic context of his development of the idea of hospitality. The feminine represents hospitality to Levinas. Women provide a comforting, quiet refuge; they provide food and drink; and women make a house a home.[38] This may seem a positive role for the feminine to play in an ethical theory, since the feminine, for Levinas, is associated with the welcome extended to the other, that is, with the ethical. Unfortunately it is a role that seems to mirror traditional gender roles, particularly in the way that women and the feminine are invoked to suggest warm feelings about the welcoming home, without any clear indication of the reciprocal call to a man to welcome and provide for the physical needs of women. The feminine plays a background service role, for Levinas, and it disappears when he moves to a discussion of work and labor, of exteriority and the relation with the social. Luce Irigaray argues that women are effaced in Levinas, that they disappear in the way that women so often have in patriarchal systems.[39]

The one other place women do appear in Levinas's account of the ethical life is as part of the trio of needy others—the widow, the orphan, and the stranger—to whom the greatest ethical debt is owed. But this seems largely an artifact of the biblical language Levinas adopts, rather than a deliberate focus on moral responsibility to women. When he moves to a consideration of particular others to whom the moral debt is owed, Levinas clearly pictures the other as a man—hence the language of fraternity mentioned above as the highest expression of life together.[40] Women thus seem to serve as background for Levinas's conception of the world of ethics, a world populated by men and their (masculine/Father) God, relating to each other as brothers, sons, and fathers, and leaving the care of basic needs to invisible, faceless women. Levinas may speak of taking the bread out of his mouth to give to the hungry, but perhaps he is not fully cognizant of the humanity of the woman who is supposed to cook and serve that bread.

But perhaps he is. A careful reading of Levinas's discussion of the phenomenology of eros and even his discussion of paternity suggest that he is attempting the difficult task of speaking as a man about mutuality between men and women.[41] While he speaks of paternity, he also links paternity with the encounter with the other as feminine, and as the Beloved. It is precisely the relationship with the Beloved that contains the possibility of fecundity and others/children that grounds an understanding of human existence as multiple, an understanding of difference as real difference rather than sameness, and an openness to others as truly unique.[42] So sexual difference in Levinas is not simply a matter of reiterating standard sexist tropes. While some of his thought does exactly that (the identification of the feminine and hospitality, for example), other aspects hint at an attempt to incorporate difference into ethics.

Gender issues are, in any case, a deeply problematic thread in Levinas's thought. Having noted the problematic nature of Levinas's treatment of gender, however, it is worth making three further points about it. The first is a reminder of how glaring blind spots can be from other perspectives. The role gender plays in Levinas's thought gives rise to a deep incoherence, evident in his seeing the widow as one of the prime exemplars of the other, coupled with his use of the notion of fraternity as the highest human political ideal. As Irigaray notes, Levinas succeeds in effacing females from his world.[43] To destroy or fail to see the face of another is, as Levinas uses the term, murder. Irigaray goes on to note, it is in the effacing of the feminine, with its connotations of the bodily, the physical, and the natural, that Levinas moves away from the direct encounter with the physical, embodied other to focus on an abstract (totalized?) other in the brother or son.

In a deeply ethical thinker like Levinas, this moral blind spot is problematic. But it is instructive for feminist thinkers to reflect on the ease with which deeply ingrained cultural assumptions can create such blind spots in our thinking. Cynthia Willett argues that care can be developed as a morally acceptable ethical ideal only if the care to be given is endorsed by the cared for, and she is correct when we are speaking of relations between people who are all capable of such responsiveness. Levinas's widow needs to be given a voice and a place in Levinas's moral community, and an adequate ethics of care needs to structure its social situations so that those who are on the receiving end of care are allowed to critique, change, and define practices of care. Feminist discussions of communicative ethics[44] and Helen Longino's account of intersubjective objectivity in scientific practice[45] both offer models that theorists of care need to incorporate into their account of care. As we saw in the case of Augustine, and as we see in the case of Levinas, it is very easy for those in authority to assume they know what is best for those under their authority, and for this easy assumption to generate serious contradictions within an ethical theory. Care, then, can be conceptualized as care only when those who are cared for can endorse the choices made by others for their sake.

There are cases, however, in which the one who receives care cannot endorse the care given. These cases run along a spectrum, from infants and young children, who are too immature to endorse or criticize the care they receive; to the elderly suffering from senility, who are unable to respond; to those with severe mental retardation; to the irreversibly comatose. In such cases the notion of intersubjectivity is problematic, because of the irreducible asymmetry of such relationships. This is an issue I return to in the last chapters of this book, since it has important ramifications for the analysis of medical techniques such as infertility treatments and public policy debates about cloning. In both of these cases there are "voiceless others" who will bear many of the costs of individual and social decisions without being in a position to respond to those decisions. The presence of these voiceless others, however, should never be used as a justification for failing to incorporate intersubjective responses into those relationships in which the others are not voiceless.

One of the strengths of Levinas's account of ethics, however, and an important similarity with care theory, is its capacity to recognize even these asymmetrical relationships as ethical without relying on some capacity such as rationality or moral autonomy in the other. For Levinas, the other's ethical demand on me is generated by the fragility and neediness of the other, and those who have cared for people with severe dementia or profound mental retardation can recognize the force of this command.

While there are problematic aspects of Levinas's account of the feminine, his views are interesting from a feminist perspective because Levinas articulates the requirement of altruism from a masculine perspective as a moral requirement for men. In Levinas's account, the moral agent is always guilty, always falls short of true responsibility to the other, and the moral life is one marked by the constant attempt to overcome egoism and truly love the other, or the image of God in the other. An ethics of care has been criticized for entrenching female self-sacrifice. Levinas's account of ethical responsibility may offer a needed corrective in its call to absolute self-sacrifice on the part of men. His account also suggests that the call to care as an ethical primordial is not gendered—it is a feature of human life. The call to care is a feature of human life that disappears if we fail to begin our analysis from the embodied relation within which humans exist. It is only when we begin our theorizing from concrete human relationships that we can see that human lives exist in networks of communicative responses to others.

Levinas thus offers an alternative to the dichotomy posed by the libertarian/communitarian debate. Like many feminist thinkers he offers a position that keeps its distance from both atomism and organicism in its account of human life. Humans are not atomistic, completely self-sufficient individuals (the parody of liberal thought often criticized by communitarians), nor are they completely defined and created by the communities and traditions of which they are a part. Levinas over and over resists the move to make morality and the moral life a matter of abstract rules that apply to all agents in exactly the same way. He emphasizes the extent to which I find myself uniquely responsible. It is through finding myself uniquely called to moral responsibility that I become human. This preserves the truths that both liberals and communitarians are concerned to point out. Communitarians are correct to note that we are not human in isolation; we do not exist as unconnected atoms in a universe of unrelated particles. Levinas notes that we are called into humanness by the other—to be human is to exist in community. But liberal thinkers are also correct to note that we bear responsibility as individuals. We cannot use the fact of our social existence to avoid or evade the call that each of us faces individually to respond to others morally. Further, the call to moral response cannot be evaded by falling back on traditional limits on responsibility. Levinas's reminder that it is the stranger for whom we are morally responsible avoids the communitarian danger of limiting the scope of our moral responsibility to those who are like us. So while Levinas's account of the feminine is problematic, his account of human life and its ethical core offers resources for feminist thinkers.

IV. Conclusion

So what does Levinas have to offer an ethics of care? His account of the ethical life, first, corresponds to and supplements Noddings's claim that emotional caring is basic to human existence. The ethical response to the other is basic to being human, whether the other is my own child or the stranger at the gate. Levinas's account of how we are called to humanity by the ethical demand of the other offers an alternative to the separation Noddings posits in *Caring* between natural and ethical caring. Noddings argues that the emotional response of care is first premoral and then becomes moral when the agent deliberately chooses to endorse the care. This leads her to describe emotional caring as not yet moral.[46] Levinas, in contrast, recognizes that the call to care is ethical from the start, and that there is no fully human experience that does not involve moving in the midst of ethical responsibilities. But Noddings and Levinas are both right to note how easily I can turn away from that deep impulse, and how evil it can be to do so.

Second, Levinas offers a careful articulation of the nature of our relationship to the other, and the alterity, or irreducible otherness, of those for whom we are called to care. This is a feature care theorists should take seriously, since the reliance on the mothering paradigm can make it very easy to assume that the other is like me—flesh of my flesh, so to speak. Care theorists have also emphasized the particularity of the other, of course, but Levinas develops this account more fully. When faced with another, Levinas reminds us, we cannot define that other completely in our own terms. Recognition of this temptation provides impetus for care thinkers to build responsiveness into the theory (as I think many have done) to prevent care from becoming smothering. But it also requires that responsiveness and intersubjectivity be placed within the context of particular relationships and particular lives. In cases in which the other cannot respond due to inability or incapacity, the requirement that we care is not obviated, but the care given does need to aim at different sorts of ends. As was mentioned earlier, this inclusion of those who cannot respond within the purview of care is an important feature of Levinas's theory.

Further, Levinas articulates this notion of the otherness of the other in terms of the sacred. This adds a dimension to the call to care that is, I think, missing in contemporary care theory (though Noddings emphasizes sacredness in her discussion of evil).[47] I have discussed the sacredness of the other as well in conjunction with Augustine. This is an important aspect of Levinas's thought for contemporary feminist ethics. The language of the sacred has been misused in the past, but it can be properly used, as in identifying the recognition of an other who calls me into an ethical relationship. It is also properly used when it functions as a barrier against making any human structure or ideology into an absolute value. Like Augustine, Levinas cautions us against absolutizing the relative.

Levinas also, like Augustine, offers an account of the ethical life that emphasizes men's call to moral altruism, and the responsibility men have to feel with and hear the voice of the other. I do not think that the ethical life should be thought of primarily in terms of sexual categories, so ultimately I think both Levinas and Augustine should be criticized for their blindness to women's full moral agency. But in the context of an ethics of care, an ethics that has frequently been charged with placing a heavier moral responsibility to care on women, these two thinkers offer resources for arguing that moral responsiveness is a part of the human condition, and part of human moral responsibility, and is not limited to either men or women.

I have looked, then, at the resources for care theory in the thought of Levinas and Augustine. But now I need to address another issue. In what ways does the account of human nature I have been giving up to this point actually provide a structure for thinking about what care is? Even more important, in the context of a theory that emphasizes particularity and uniqueness, can any parameters be set for determining which responses to another are legitimately caring, and which are illegitimate manipulation? In the next chapter, I turn to this question and begin to develop in some detail an analysis of the nature of care in light of the account of human nature and human flourishing I have been developing up to this point.

Notes

1. See, for example, Emmanuel Levinas, *Totality and Infinity* (Pittsburgh, Pa.: Duquesne University Press, 1961), pp. 38–9, 197, 201; and *Otherwise Than Being* (Pittsburgh, Pa.: Duquesne University Press, 1997), pp. 13–14, 75–81. See also "Is Ontology Fundamental?" in *Emmanuel Levinas: Basic Philosophical Writings*, ed. Adrian Peperzak, Simon Critchley, and Robert Bernasconi (Indianapolis: Indiana University Press, 1996), pp. 1–10. Here and in the rest of this essay I am doing some damage to Levinas's thought in presenting it in a too-simple way. In particular, I am speaking in ontological terms (what it is to be human), while Levinas argues that ethics is prior to ontology, that humans find themselves first called into ethical relationships and can speak in ontological terms only against the background or horizon of already being in an ethical relationship. Levinas himself is very difficult to read because he is trying to say something that to some extent cannot be captured in the lim-

ited categories of ideas and concepts; much of his philosophical writing strains against the constraints of what can be said.

2. Levinas, *Totality and Infinity*, p. 211. See also Emmanuel Levinas, *Ethics and Infinity: Conversations with Philippe Nemo* (Pittsburgh, Pa.: Duquesne University Press, 1985), p. 92.

3. See especially Levinas's discussion in *Otherwise Than Being*, pp. 94–96, as well as "Transcendence and Height" in *Basic Philosophical Writings*, p. 29. Levinas rejects the more Augustinian notion that we can begin with God's nature and being in our philosophical thought. To begin there is to assume what needs to be recognized as fundamental, namely the experience of transcendence in the encounter with the other. Levinas discusses this issue at some length in *Of God Who Comes to Mind* (Stanford, Calif.: Stanford University Press, 1998), pp. 62–65.

4. Levinas, "Transcendence and Height," p. 29.

5. Levinas, *Of God Who Comes to Mind*, p. xiv.

6. Embodiment is a central notion for Levinas. Because of its centrality he frequently moves back and forth between language of vision (the face to face) and language of tactile encounter (the caress). In fact he sometimes criticizes the language of vision for being too Platonic, for entailing too much the notion of intellectual grasping from a distance (see, for example, *Totality and Infinity*, p. 194).

7. Levinas, *Totality and Infinity*, pp. 130–34.

8. Nel Noddings, *Caring: A Feminine Approach to Ethics and Moral Education* (Berkeley and Los Angeles: University of California Press, 1984), pp. 144–47.

9. Sara Ruddick, *Maternal Thinking* (Boston: Beacon, 1989), pp. 205–17.

10. Levinas, *Otherwise Than Being*, p. 123.

11. Levinas, *Totality and Infinity*, p. 140.

12. The extent to which we have moral responsibilities to natural objects in a Levinasian context is an open debate. Levinas himself, in a very Kantian sort of way, does not see our ethical responsibilities as extending beyond the realm of the human. But John Llewellyn argues that excluding animals categorically from the realm of the ethical may be more problematic than Levinas realizes; it may make the responsibility to the other human so rarified and divorced from the physical and concrete nature of the other human that it becomes vacuous ("Am I Obsessed by Bobby? Humanism of the Other Animal," in *Re-reading Levinas*, ed. Robert Bernasconi and Simon Critchley (Bloomington: Indiana University Press, 1991), pp. 234–45.

13. Levinas, *Totality and Infinity*, pp. 198–99.

14. Levinas, *Totality and Infinity*, pp. 210–11.

15. Levinas, *Totality and Infinity*, p. 246.

16. Levinas, *Otherwise Than Being*, p. 150; and "Substitution," in *Basic Philosophical Writings*, p. 91.

17. Noddings, *Caring*, p. 38.

18. Levinas, *Totality and Infinity*, p. 213.

19. Levinas, *Otherwise Than Being*, p. 158.

20. Levinas, *Totality and Infinity*, p. 64.

21. Joan Tronto, *Moral Boundaries: A Political Argument for an Ethic of Care* (New York: Routledge, 1994); and Selma Sevenhuijsen, *Citizenship and the Ethics of Care: Feminist Considerations on Justice, Morality, and Politics* (New York: Routledge, 1998).

22. See, for example, Annette Baier, "The Need for More Than Justice," in *Justice and Care: Essential Readings in Feminist Ethics*, ed. Virginia Held (Boulder, Colo.: Westview, 1995), p. 55.

23. Noddings, *Caring*, pp. 79–80.

24. Noddings, *Caring*, pp. 82–83.

25. Levinas, *Totality and Infinity*, p. 64.

26. Emmanuel Levinas, "Peace and Proximity," in *Basic Philosophical Writings*, pp. 160–69.

27. Paul Ramsey, *Basic Christian Ethics* (1950; reprint, Louisville, Ky.: Westminster/John Knox Press, 1993), p. 189.

28. Levinas, *Totality and Infinity* p. 39.

29. Cynthia Willett, *Maternal Ethics and Other Slave Moralities* (New York: Routledge, 1995), p. 82.

30. John Caputo, *Against Ethics* (Indianapolis: Indiana University Press, 1993), pp. 80–81.

31. Levinas, *Totality and Infinity*, p. 218.

32. Levinas, "Peace and Proximity," pp. 160–69.

33. Levinas, "Peace and Proximity," p. 166.

34. Levinas, *Totality and Infinity*, p. 214.

35. Nel Noddings, *Starting at Home: Caring and Social Policy* (Berkeley and Los Angeles: University of California Press, 2002), pp. 126–48.

36. Noddings, *Starting at Home*, pp. 121–25.

37. Noddings, *Starting at Home*, pp. 248–70.

38. Levinas, *Totality and Infinity*, p. 155.

39. Luce Irigaray, "Questions to Emmanuel Levinas: On the Divinity of Love," trans. Margaret Whitford, in *Re-reading Levinas*, ed. Robert Bernasconi and Simon Critchley (Bloomington: Indiana University Press, 1991), pp. 109–18.

40. This brief account of the place of gender in Levinas's thought does not do full justice to the complexity of the issue. For more in-depth analyses, see Luce Irigaray's "Questions to Emmanuel Levinas"; Catherine Chalier's "Ethics and the Feminine," and Tina Chanter's "Antigone's Dilemma," all in *Re-reading Levinas*, ed. Robert Bernasconi and Simon Critchley (Bloomington: Indiana University Press, 1991).

41. These issues are addressed in Claire Katz's "'For Love Is as Strong as Death': Taking Another Look at Levinas on Love," *Philosophy Today* 45, no. 5:124–32.

42. Levinas, *Totality and Infinity*, p. 269.

43. An alternative interpretation of Levinas on the feminine can be found in Jeffrey Dudiak's discussion in *The Intrigue of Ethics: A Reading of the Ideal of Discourse in the Thought of Emmanuel Levinas* (New York: Fordham University Press, 2001), pp. 134–38. But even in Dudiak's account, an account that is far more positive than Iri-

garay's, there is an essential asymmetry between the masculine subject and the welcoming, feminine other who provides a home.

44. See, for example, Daryl Koehn's *Rethinking Feminist Ethics* (New York: Routledge, 1998). Koehn argues that an ethics of care should be replaced by a communicative ethics, while I would argue that a care ethics should incorporate communicative concepts without losing its grounding in care.

45. Helen Longino, "Essential Tensions—Phase Two: Feminist, Philosophical, and Social Studies of Science," in *A Mind of One's Own: Feminist Essays on Reason and Objectivity*, ed. Louise M. Antony and Charlotte Witt (Boulder, Colo.: Westview, 1993), pp. 257–72.

46. Noddings, *Caring*, p. 83.

47. Nel Noddings, *Women and Evil* (Berkeley and Los Angeles: University of California Press, 1989), p. 243.

CHAPTER FOUR

Human Nature: Is an Ideal Really Necessary?

In the first chapter of this book I argued that a particular conception of what the good human life looks like is implicitly assumed in contemporary care theory. In the second and third chapters, I argued that it is a conception of human nature that bears certain important resemblances to the conceptions operative in the philosophical systems of Augustine and Levinas. But although I have offered some details as to what this picture of human nature is like, I haven't yet given an argument for the necessity of such an account. Even if the claims of the preceding chapters are compelling, even if it is true that care theorists have implicitly operated with an account of human nature, and the account resembles a picture found in certain strands of the Western tradition, it still might not be the case that care theory needs to articulate and examine this ideal. Instead, a critic might argue, what care theory needs to do is to purge itself of this reliance on a particular ideal of human life. An examination of this criticism permits us to see what is at stake in adopting or rejecting the notion of an ideal of human flourishing; it also allows us to see more clearly how different ideals affect the ethical theories that rely on them.

The skeptic who thinks care should not have or rely on an ideal conception of human life has some important reasons for her skepticism. The first is a general suspicion about claims about human nature. Such a suspicion is found in many parts of feminist theory these days, and it is rooted in feminist critiques of the Western philosophical tradition and the way thinkers in that tradition have used theories of human nature to justify treating women as second-class citizens.[1] But there are also concerns that are more specific to care theory. In particular, our skeptic might want to ask the following sorts of questions: Why can't care theory function properly without any picture of human nature? Isn't it possible to simply react from a caring attitude (say) or develop the character traits of care in one's own person, and thus become caring? Why is an entire account of human nature needed, and what exactly does one gain by developing this account?

We can, in fact, strengthen the skeptic's argument here. In the first place, care theory would seem to be inimical to any development of an account of human nature because of its emphasis on particularity and uniqueness. Shouldn't it be diametrically opposed to any attempt to spell out what human nature is and how that might figure in our thinking about human flourishing? Further, some care theorists, most notably Noddings, develop care theory in opposition to principle-based theories in ethics. Principles, Noddings argues, can get in the way of care, especially when they require absolute impartiality and universality.[2] It seems a short step from a rejection of absolute principles to a rejection of some timeless absolute ideal of human nature. Further, advocating a particular view of human life as an ideal seems to rule out respect for otherness, and seems to support the sort of moral imperialism that so many feminist theorists have identified and rejected.

So this chapter examines why care theory cannot function without an ideal of human nature, and why the skeptic who rejects any account of human nature is making a mistake. The role of a picture of human nature and an ideal of human life in care theory can be seen most clearly in response to two specific criticisms of care theory, criticisms that have led some theorists to reject care theory and others to argue that care theory is antithetical to feminist concerns.

I. Critics of Care

Two criticisms of care theory appear regularly in both feminist and nonfeminist discussions. The first is that care theory is incapable of self-reflective critique because all it really offers in terms of ethical content is a vague command to be caring. If, according to an ethic of care, all I am required to do is to act as my heart dictates, then care seems to be nothing more than a sentimental relativism. Worse, if my emotions and feelings have been shaped in a sexist or racist culture, what I will find is that my heart dictates behavior in keeping with sexist or racist assumptions. Further, I will not feel the need to critique those assumptions because I will be assured by my heart and my emotions that what I have done is "the caring thing." Critics of care ethics charge that it cannot engage in systemic critique because its validation of caring emotions makes it incapable of a critical examination of the formation of those emotions. If people are simply told to act in caring ways, they are not asked to reflect in a critical way on whether their caring emotions may have been generated by deeply racist or sexist social structures. If this were true, then care theory would, it seems, be forced to endorse those parents who deny their daughters an education out of a firm and loving conviction that educated women are doomed to a miserable existence because they are flouting God's plan for their lives. If care theory simply advocates certain emotions and feelings, then it can offer no resources for thinking through how emotions and feelings can themselves be ethically problematic.

Diemut Bubeck offers a variant of this criticism, aimed primarily at Noddings, arguing that Noddings privileges care at the expense of justice. Bubeck argues that, because of the role emotional attachment plays in Noddings's thought, a person who acts, as Noddings advocates, in caring ways is likely to do unjust things. The specific case she uses as an example, one we'll call the example of the barricades, involves the experience of Ms. A, who hears a classmate, Jim, describe his experiences of racist oppression. Jim ends his description with a plea for a revolution, for an armed uprising against all those who hold and perpetuate racist views. Ms. A's heart is with Jim, but then she stops to think of members of her own family who are blatantly racist: her father and her aunt, both of whom have raised her with love and consistent care, and both of whom are bigoted. These are people I love, Ms. A thinks, and if they were threatened with death I would fight to the death to protect them. But in so doing I'd find myself on the wrong side of the barricades.[3] Bubeck cites this as an example of a case in which Noddings's care theory fails to live up to the demands of justice because it relies on emotional responses to the other rather than obedience to abstract principles of justice.[4] Worse, Bubeck charges, this lack of respect for the principles of justice leads women to accede to unjust, exploitive relationships that perpetuate sexism, racism, and other morally evil social structures. If care theory really does advocate a situationalism in which any action generated by caring emotions is morally right, then it should be rejected by feminist theorists. Such a simplistic situationalism is not an acceptable account of the moral life, particularly for a feminist theorist.

But before answering this charge of situationalism it is worth examining a second criticism implicit in Bubeck's discussion, namely the charge that care theory entrenches rather than fights oppressive sex-role stereotypes. In the example of the barricades, Bubeck examines Noddings's ability to criticize unjust racial structures, but the example could as easily involve unjust patterns of sexual discrimination. If an ethic of care cannot recognize, criticize, and offer an alternative to socially entrenched sexism, it is clearly not a theory worthy of the title "feminist." A number of feminist critics of care claim that all of these charges are true, and they tend to focus on those care theorists who use the role of mothering as a central part of their theory.[5] These critics charge that the notion of mothering, first, illegitimately endorses cultural stereotypes of all women as mothers; second, entrenches cultural stereotypes of women as "naturally" suited to service work of the sort involved in mothering; and third, produces a theory that cannot critique culturally oppressive gender roles. (In this third aspect of the critique we see it converge with the antisituationalist critique, and it is only this third that Bubeck endorses. She does not offer the other two.)

If care theory merely advocated acting in a caring way, if it were a situationalist ethic, all of these critiques would be accurate. If care theorists merely advocated acting in a caring way, then care theory would be unable to generate a substantive critique of oppressive cultural stereotypes. If acting in a caring way were all it took to make actions and choices morally right, then individuals who perpetuated racism and sexism, but did so out of caring attitudes, would be doing what care theorists advocated, and care theory would find itself in opposition to justice. Further, care theorists do note that women's experiences in caregiving roles such as mothering produce an increased ability and willingness to care. It is hard to see how care theorists could criticize oppressive cultural practices based on sexual stereotypes, however, unless they could somehow demonstrate that those practices did not originate in an emotion of care.

But the last paragraph began with an "if" clause, and it is the first part of the conditional that is false. Care theory doesn't merely advocate acting in a caring way. It also requires us to think systemically about what sorts of social systems support caregiving, and what social systems make caring difficult or impossible. Further, it notes the centrality of care to all human lives, and requires moral theorists to take seriously how that care is provided, to whom, by whom, and under what circumstances. This structural aspect of care theory is clear in the work of theorists such as Tronto and Sevenhuijsen,[6] but I think it has sometimes been overlooked in the work of other theorists. Held argues that a feminist ethic based in women's experiences of care work would have a radical effect on the structure of society.[7] Ruddick ends her discussion of mothering practices with an argument that the ways of knowing embedded in such practices would lead to a politics of peace.[8] Noddings's work on how educational systems need to be rethought indicates that her advocacy of care is not a simple situationalism but a far more structural account of how human life needs to be organized.[9] Either these central figures in care theory are confused about what they are doing, or care theory does not validate any action that arises from caring emotions.

II. Human Flourishing

To show that care theory is not a simplistic situationalism, however, and that it does not support either unjust social structures or entrenched sexism, we must return to the notion of an ideal of human flourishing. We cannot critique social structures without simultaneously advocating alternative social structures with some claim to be more conducive to good human lives. If a theorist criticizes racism while claiming to make no substantive assumptions about human flourishing, either she is making substantive assumptions, but pretending not to, or she has undercut the very possibility of making any critique at all. To see why this is the case we need to turn to specific issues that are relevant to the criticisms that are raised against care theory.

A. Situationalism

One version of the situationalist critique is generated in part by the assumption that a theory that is particularistic cannot generate or rely on generalizations about human nature or flourishing.[10] An emphasis on particularity and uniqueness seems to require the theorist to deny a common human nature and any general ideals of human flourishing. Particularity would seem to rule these out because it appears to be opposed to the universalism inherent in any endorsement of a common human nature and an ideal of flourishing. Care theorists certainly defend an ethic that focuses on particularity, so it may seem that they are required to reject any notion of human nature or ideals of human life.

This assumption, however, is based on the misconception that the notion of particularity is in conflict with the notion of universality, or a common human nature. This is a misconception because evaluations of particularity actually require the assumption of a universal human nature. Human flourishing, in a care theory account, must be agent relative. That is, the evaluation that Silvia is living a good life must be made with reference to the particular person Silvia is. But this does not mean that the evaluation cannot at the same time be objective and related to the nature of human being.[11] Particularity and uniqueness are not absolute concepts. Like categories such as "tall" and "heavy" they are inherently reliant on a field of comparison. When I focus on the particular person in front of me, trying in good Levinasian fashion to respond to her as a unique and infinite "other," I am not responding to her as unique and particular in comparison to, say, an earthworm or a field of spinach. I am responding to the unique and particular way she lives out her humanity. But I cannot even be aware of her particularity unless it appears against a background of general knowledge of the parameters of human life, of the sorts of characteristics that humans generally exhibit, and the like. If I were concerned with her particularity in comparison with an earthworm, I'd find the fact that she has limbs remarkable, but this is hardly what is usually meant by respect for particularity. When we speak of respect for particularity we have to assume a general range of background assumptions about what humans are normally like, and what sorts of characteristics count as indicators of particularity.

Most theorists would agree that there is a general background of assumptions about human existence that provides the context for our recognition of the particularity and uniqueness of an individual. But we need more than those general background assumptions. I also approach another in the context of certain assumptions about how she should or should not live her life. If the woman I'm speaking to suddenly falls to the floor and begins to convulse, I don't respond by thinking that this is an interesting example of a unique conversational style. I respond by recognizing that she's experiencing some sort of medical emergency and I move objects that might cause her harm, call for medical assistance, and so on. That is, I work with a set of operative assumptions about the desirability of certain physical and psychological attributes. In a situation in which an individual exhibits such strong deviation from a norm of behavior, we have no trouble recognizing that we make such assumptions about normal human functioning.

Both of these may seem obvious. But a recognition that we judge particularity against the background of a presumed standard of human lives reminds us that we cannot even begin to recognize and enjoy the particularity of a unique individual without universal background assumptions. The assumption that particularity is incompatible with generalizations about human nature is not only false, it is nonsensical. Judgments of particularity have to occur within the context of generalizations about human nature. But they require more than just a general account of human life. They also require a fairly substantive set of background assumptions about what sorts of characteristics are good ones for a human to have, or what sorts of characteristics to look for in evaluating a person's life. In short, they require an ideal of human flourishing.

To see this we need to imagine a slightly different situation. Imagine that I am confronted with a student who holds deeply bigoted hatred for members of other racial and ethnic groups, and is loud and expressive of her views in the classroom. How am I to think of such a student? Should I affirm her uniqueness and particularity, and encourage her to continue to espouse her views loudly and openly in a classroom in which there are members of those other racial and ethnic groups? I cannot argue that she should not be encouraged in her racism and bigotry unless I am committed to the notion that certain types of particularity and uniqueness are not to be affirmed or valued. Certain types are to be challenged, and those who exhibit them should be encouraged to conform to an ideal that holds for all humans. All humans, in this view, should learn to treat others with respect, regardless of racial or ethnic characteristics. So we find ourselves rejecting the particularity and uniqueness of this individual's beliefs in favor of an abstract ideal.

Perhaps, though, this is an unfair example. It involves a set of beliefs and attitudes, and perhaps these are not what is to be valued when we are concerned to affirm particularity. I need to respect and affirm, the proponent of particularity could argue, the unique and individual characteristics of this person. It is not her beliefs and attitudes, but rather a particular way of being, that is unique to her. This already involves a substantive move away from the affirmation of all particularity, but it still is insufficient to capture what is being affirmed in care theory. When Noddings speaks of the teacher's care for her or his students, or when Ruddick talks about a mothering person's concern for the growth and development of a child, both clearly assume that there are better and worse ways of going through life. If I find myself confronted with a student who, due to her racist beliefs, treats others with disdain and cruelty, I will be distressed at the beliefs that she holds. But I will also be distressed with the pattern her life is taking on.

Cruelty, self-aggrandizement, and an incapacity to see another person as valuable in her own right because her skin is the "wrong" color are character traits that make human life worse, for both those who have the traits and those who have to live in their vicinity. No care theorist is interested in arguing that we are required, by our care for the particularity of another, to enhance her or his racism and cruelty, nor would a Levinasian accept this as an instance of respect for the infinite otherness of another. The reason for this is that, like Augustine, care theorists and Levinasians advocate care for uniqueness against a background picture of what human life should be like. In fact, the advocacy of care requires that one think a life in which close, caring relationships are possible, both because of character traits and external circumstances, is better for humans than a life in which this cannot occur.

Bigotry requires an attitude that precludes the possibility of caring relationships with certain classes of others; it also requires an attitude of hardened self-righteousness that makes healthy reciprocity with others impossible. Care theorists, of course, reject the notion that bigotry could be a praiseworthy exhibition of uniqueness, and in so doing they demonstrate that they rely on an ideal of human life that includes general norms of respect and willingness to care for other humans.

If care theory does inherently assume an ideal of human flourishing, shouldn't care theorists give up the notion of attentiveness to uniqueness and particularity? (Shouldn't Levinasians and Augustinians do the same?) But this is a false dilemma. It arises because we have a mistaken view of what an ideal is and how it functions; namely, we think of an ideal as an absolute determinant of every characteristic of what a thing is or ought to be. Properly understood, an ideal does not determine every detail of what can count as an instance of reaching for (or even attaining) that ideal. Instead, when we hold an ideal of a characteristic or of a thing, we have in mind a set of characteristics that can be instantiated in any number of different ways.

We acknowledge this in our everyday lives on a regular basis. For a philosopher trained in the analytic tradition, for example, one ideal characteristic for philosophical writing is clarity. When I read Martha Nussbaum's philosophical writing, I find that she writes with admirable clarity. When I read Annette Baier I find that she writes with admirable clarity. When I read Jean Hampton I also find her writing lucid and clear. I could keep on enumerating models of clarity here, but I fear the list would get a bit boring.

The point is that all of these theorists can have an admirably clear style of writing without writing in identical styles. Each manages to be clear in her own way. But the diversity of styles of clarity does not imply that there is no ideal of clarity by which to judge—Luce Irigaray's writing is well worth reading, but clarity is not one of its salient virtues. We could make a very similar argument with respect to any number of other traits and characteristics. One can be a generous person in many different ways, for example. The fact that one can be generous in many different ways, however, does not negate the fact that some people are not generous, and that this is a character flaw.

Our example of clarity is instructive in another way. There is a debate among philosophers over the question of whether clarity really is a virtue in philosophical writing. Some philosophers argue that it is a central virtue. Writing that fails to attain a certain level of clarity, they argue, is unworthy of the name "philosophy." Others consider clarity a virtue, but a secondary one. In the ideal case philosophical writing exhibits clarity, but if the subject matter is too complex to be expressed clearly, then one is better off writing in a difficult style that may not be particularly clear. Still others argue that clarity is not a virtue in philosophical writing at all. Ideas that are complex enough to count as philosophy cannot be expressed clearly, and ideas that are expressed clearly fail to require the reader to engage in true philosophical enquiry.

This debate models, in a miniature way, debates among proponents of different moral visions of human flourishing. Care theorists are committed to the centrality of care, reciprocity, and interdependence as central aspects of a flourishing human life. Proponents of "rational economic man" would reject all of these as central aspects of human flourishing. Classic Aristotelians would evaluate them as secondary virtues, arguing that theoretical reasoning is the central requirement for a flourishing human life. But in all these cases, what we have is disagreement about what the ideal should be, not a debate between someone who holds an ideal and someone who does not. In fact, someone who rejected any conception of an ideal of human flourishing would be unable to participate in this debate, since one cannot argue that rational economic man is a flawed ideal unless one can simultaneously point to a better set of characteristics.

Care theorists have an important advantage over other thinkers in that the ideal that they assume is compatible with practical lived experience. Philosophical theorists sometimes give theoretical allegiance to an ideal that they clearly do not accept in their own lives—the case of rational economic man being a classic example. The notion of rational economic man carries with it a sense that ideal rationality involves purely self-interested calculations of benefits and burdens, and a rejection of actions that involve altruistic self-sacrifice. But even those who argue most strenuously for this standard of rationality at the theoretical level expect to be treated with respect and care in situations in which there is no financial reward for others to do so, in the "real world" of interpersonal relationships.

What we find, then, when we examine the care theorists' concern for uniqueness and particularity, is a concern that each individual be permitted (at a minimum), encouraged, and sometimes assisted to develop her own version of the human ideal. That is, each of us should be generous and caring, able to engage in close loving personal relationships, and able to do so in a way that is uniquely our own. How we will do that will differ from situation to situation, from life to life. Without such an ideal, however, it is impossible to articulate what it means for care theorists to advocate attentiveness to particularity.

The implicit reliance on an ideal becomes even clearer when we consider evaluations of social practices and cultural structures. To resume our use of clarity as an example of an ideal, suppose I am teaching an introductory course in philosophy to a large group of students. I will not be able to figure out how my teaching should be structured unless I have some sort of ideal or goal that can provide that structure. Suppose, further, that I am one of those philosophers who think that clarity is an absolute virtue in philosophical writing. In that case, large portions of the class will be dedicated to learning how to recognize clarity, how to achieve it in one's own writing, and so on. If clarity plays this central role, then I may have to give up on other goals a philosophy class might have, such as deeper reflectiveness or understanding of alternative worldviews. This example suggests, however, that I cannot produce any structure for the course without assuming that there are certain ideals, and using those ideals to organize what I do. Structure requires a sense of purpose, or a goal, and that implies that I have some ideal in mind. We can often reconstruct an ideal from examining the structure of, in this case, a course, or, in other cases, an ethical theory. The ideal need not be directed toward the good of the students, or the agents who are expected to obey the demands of a particular theory. I could structure a philosophy course to provide me with a decent salary at a minimum of bother, and then I would implicitly endorse a very different ideal of philosophy, one that makes it secondary to my own egoistic aims.

The philosophy class here serves as a microcosm for thinking about larger social structures. Evaluations of social structures imply some set of goals, and ethical evaluations assume an account of what constitutes human well-being. This doesn't mean that the concept of human well-being that is assumed is unchallengeable, or a timeless absolute. It does mean, however, that without a picture of what human life ought to be like we cannot organize social structures, nor can an ethical theory provide grounds for the critique of social structures. The picture may be revisable in certain respects, and open-ended in others, but it must have definite features and some sense of what is and is not a good way for humans to live. Without such a picture an ethical theory cannot function.

The claim that care is an empty situationalism depends on the assumption that there are no criteria for care, that what care theorists argue for is merely reacting in an emotionally caring way to others. But care is defined in reference to a particular account of human nature and human flourishing, and that account provides limits to what can be said to count as care. The first criticism, we can now see, is not valid. Care has an emotional component, it is true. But the emotional component alone does not determine whether a chosen action or policy is caring. Noddings frequently uses care to provide a context for educational theory, and she does not argue that as long as teachers are motivated by care they are doing what they ought. Instead she is concerned to investigate research on how children learn and how the relationship they have with a teacher affects that learning. The emotional connection between teacher and student is important, but it is not a substitute for careful study of what sorts of social structures allow all students to become people who are capable of care, reciprocity, and interdependence with others.

Noddings does argue that the emotional component of care is the most basic requirement of ethics, because without such motivation moral action cannot occur. Natural caring, then, for Noddings, is necessary, though not sufficient for an ethical response. In saying this Noddings is simply following Hume (and contemporary advocates of Humean anthropology) in arguing that without emotional engagement, there can be no motivation for action. This is very different from the claim that emotional engagement makes an action morally acceptable, a claim that no care theorist should endorse.

The same sort of response can be made in the context of larger social structures. Care theorists such as Julia Wood and Eva Feder Kittay criticize the provision of care for those with chronic needs in the United States.[12] Their criticism of the current system does rely on an empathetic understanding of the situation that both caregivers and care recipients face, generated in both writers' work by first-person experiences of giving care to dependent family members. But neither Kittay nor Wood is so naive as to think that an emotional response to the needs of dependents is sufficient, nor would either argue that simply feeling the right amount of sympathy for the situation of caregivers is sufficient for restructuring the provision of care in Western societies. The emotional response provides the impetus for calling for social change—for trying to make changes in the economic structures that leave caregivers vulnerable, for example, and providing a more responsive and secure safety net of care for those who need it. If we care about these issues, we will be motivated to work for social change. But the emotional connection is insufficient in and of itself. Caring about the provision of care for dependents generates the requirement that we think on an abstract level about the principles that structure our society, and it also requires us to think about the political actions necessary to make changes in the social system.

A theorist who claims to care because she sympathizes with the situation of dependents and caregivers, but who never moves beyond the feeling to analysis and political activism, cannot be said to truly care. Care, as Joan Tronto notes, is an activity, not simply a feeling.[13] Because of this, the charge of situationalism does not properly apply to care theory. If this is correct, then rather than conclude (as some critics have) that care and justice are in opposition to each other, we are forced to the conclusion that care and justice cannot be separated. Care requires activism to bring social structures in line with the requirements of justice that permit care to be given and received.

B. The Gender of Care Critique

The "gender of care" critique arises from a worry that care theory, in listening to what Gilligan calls a "feminine voice" in ethics, articulates women's internalized responses that are generated by, and support, patriarchal structures of oppression. Catharine MacKinnon, for example, writes that Gilligan, "achieves for moral reasoning what the special protection rule achieves in law: the affirmative rather than the negative valuation of that which has accurately distinguished women from men, by making it seem as though those attributes, with their consequences, really are somehow ours, rather than what male supremacy has attributed to us for its own use."[14] If care articulates a woman's voice, but not a man's, then it seems to pertain to women's nature, but not men's. If it is a woman's voice, then the relegation of care work to women seems justified, and care does appear to support reactionary politics.

I have already argued, however, that care is grounded in an ideal of human flourishing. At this point, then, we need to focus on the fact that it is an ideal for humans, both women and men. As I argued in the last section, we can defend particular ways of organizing human life only by making reference to a set of values and ideals that provide the structuring goals of that organizational structure. We cannot argue that denying women the right to vote is wrong unless we think that political participation is an important part of the good life for all people. We cannot argue that the images of masculinity that pervade the contemporary media, images of men as dim-witted apes driven by sexual urges, are destructive and demeaning unless we have an alternative ideal of the good life that allows us to critique those images. Without ideals we have no standard for judging practices and social structures that are damaging or demeaning. Just as a physician cannot diagnose a person's condition as pathological without a sense of what the ideal of healthy functioning is, a social critic cannot judge a practice as evil without a sense of what an ideal of social functioning is.

We still need to establish, however, that the ideal needs to be an ideal of human life, rather than an ideal of women's lives, paired with a very different ideal for men's lives, as MacKinnon argues. Should care theory incorporate an anthropological ideal for both men and women, and can it? Faced with this question, the importance of our turn to Augustine and Levinas begins to be clear. Augustine articulates the way all human lives begin, proceed, and end in the context of webs of loving relationships. It is in the context of love that we live and move and have our being. Further, love is the driving force for what we do and who we are. If Augustine is correct, the ideal articulated by care cannot be reserved only for women, because it articulates the human condition. Likewise, Levinas offers an analysis of the unavoidable and irreducible call of ethics. To exist as a human is to be called to an ethical response by others, and this way of existing is not exclusively feminine.

Neither Augustine nor Levinas articulates an ethic designed to place different moral requirements on women than on men. Augustine and Levinas have their blind spots, to be sure, but they also articulate a vision of human life that contains the resources needed to critique sexist oppression, even the oppressive practices that Augustine and Levinas themselves might have supported. The recognition that care is an essential component of all human lives, male and female, allows us to see why social practices that embody sexism and racism are deeply wrong. Sexist social structures pervert and twist care, cutting men off from participating in caring practices in ways that are destructive, and requiring care from women in ways that are destructive for them as well. When men who admit to feeling the need for care are evaluated negatively and experience social penalties, we have a pathological cultural situation.[15] When women's care is denigrated, their ability to offer care is compromised and their vulnerability exploited.[16] But we can only recognize the pathology of this situation if we begin with a recognition that Augustine and Levinas are correct in noting that all human lives are grounded in relationships of care, and that care is an essential part of any good human life.

When we recognize that care is central to the ethical life, we can also see that people who fail to develop caring abilities fail to develop part of human excellence. Social structures of domination, then, insofar as they prevent men from learning to care, cause men to lack an essential part of the good human life. Insofar as they require care from women in oppressive ways, without ensuring the reciprocal support caregivers require, they also damage women's ability to live flourishing lives. Rather than regressive social policies, then, care theory supports very progressive policies that enable men to develop characteristics such as nurturance and empathy, as well as providing a more accurate account of what is wrong with relegating an unfair amount of care to women.[17] Ethical and political explanations of why this system is flawed have tended to assume the problem is dependency. But from the perspective afforded by care we can see that dependency is part of the human condition, not a flaw to be gotten rid of. Because care theory can recognize that dependency is not the problem, but the condition for human ethical response, it can also recognize that the problem with oppression is that it is destructive for both those who oppress and those who are oppressed. An adequate ideal of care is thus necessary for generating an accurate picture of what men's character may lack in the contemporary world. But it is also an important part of developing a feminist theory that fully recognizes women's humanity. We can see this if we turn to the issue of mothering, an issue that has been as divisive as any in contemporary feminist thinking.

There is something morally fundamental about the experiences of being mothered and acting as a mother.[18] The experiences of mothering and being mothered are as universal as any human experiences. While it is true that many people are not mothers, it is simultaneously true that all people experience the care of mothering practices during their childhood, and also true that most people experience that care primarily from women. Further, that this experience is a deep and crucial part of human life should indicate that it is of moral importance.

More than this, mothering is the practice whereby children are brought into the life of a society; it is a crucial part of becoming a participating member of the moral community. One would expect, given the universality and necessity of caregiving and care receiving, that mothering practices would be central to any well-developed moral theory. They clearly are not; one has to look far and wide to find any discussion of the practices that make children's development possible in ethical theorizing, and even when children's development does appear, little mention is made of the crucial moral role played by the person who cares for the child.[19] This theoretical gap occurs because women provide the majority of the caregiving, and women are not seen as full members of the human race. This lack of full membership shows itself in two ways. First, activities from which women are routinely excluded are assumed to be fully human activities. In certain cases, in fact, it seems to be the exclusion of women from activities that mark them as fully human—think of Aristotle's exaltation of public political deliberation as constitutive of the truly good human life. The exclusion of women from activities that are constitutive of a good human life has not, historically, been seen as evidence that a theory addresses only some incomplete aspects of human life. But, as a second indicator of the fact that women are not considered fully human, activities engaged in wholly or largely by women are assumed to be women's work, not human activity. That is, while activities in which men engage (war, politics, financial transactions) have all been acceptable activities from which to derive moral theories, the practice of mothering has not been an acceptable activity from which to derive an ethical theory. Instead, the suggestion that one can gain moral insight by reflecting on mothering practice has been attacked by critics from both the antifeminist and the feminist camps. The antifeminist camp generally finds the notion that mothering is philosophically interesting ludicrous, in large part because they assume that women's work is inherently degrading, mindless, and animalistic. In one of the bizarre paradoxes that marks Western philosophy, while women's emotional responsiveness and nurturing are defined as the very basis of civilization, they are simultaneously cited as the features of women's nature that make women not fully human, incapable of political deliberation, and defective in reasoning. Such a denigration of women's work as animal labor, not human, rational activity, is perhaps not unexpected in antifeminist theorists.

Unfortunately, a similar attitude toward mothering is sometimes found in feminist writers as well. This attitude comes through clearly in discussions of the possibility of considering mothering activity a ground of ethical theory. Mothering, we are told, is not a fully human activity; Hannah Arendt thinks of it as mindless labor, necessary for species survival and little else,[20] Mary Dietz tells us that it excludes women from participation in a full human life,[21] Jeffner Allen suggests that women need to refuse to mother in order to claim their humanity,[22] and (to look for the furthest extreme) Shulamith Firestone tells us that until motherhood is abolished women will never be human.[23] It is certainly true that some of these claims are made out of sheer frustration at the difficulty of bringing about social change. I think, however, that these claims also suggest a certain denigration of the work women have traditionally done, and have found to be valuable. The abolition of motherhood suggests not the reforming of a basically valuable activity, but a complete rejection of a worthless or harmful practice.

Rejecting mothering in this way demonstrates an internalization of sexist attitudes toward women and the activities that women often find both fulfilling and morally challenging. It is true that when all women are required to act as mothers, and the role of motherhood is used to deny them access to other forms of intellectual and personal development, that situation is oppressive. But, as Fiona Mackay notes in her study of women in politics, providing care is both a burden and an important resource for those who engage in political activism. Because contemporary political roles are structured on the assumption that politicians will have a personal caregiver, women who enter politics find that their responsibilities for care are enormously costly. At the same time, Mackay finds, such women also recognize that the caring practices they engage in provide important knowledge and skills that enrich and strengthen their political participation.[24]

Respect for the work women do when they mother need not lead to the rather Victorian glorification of motherhood that crops up in Hallmark cards and Mother's Day sermons; that idealized and saccharine picture of what is involved in caregiving is no closer to the truth of mothering than are the attacks on motherhood as mind numbing and subhuman. But those theorists who use mothering practices as one resource for developing an ethical theory do not have this Victorian picture in mind. No one can read Sara Ruddick's discussion of maternal thinking (to pick an example) and come away with the belief that Ruddick is glamorizing motherhood. The truth is that many worthwhile activities have their mind-numbing and exhausting moments. That aspect of mothering no more makes it unfit as a moral resource than the dirtier aspects of political activity make it unfit for moral reflection or inappropriate for responsible moral agents.

Adequate mothering never has been and never will match the cloyingly sweet images of motherhood that are found in sitcoms from the 1950s. The odd picture of a carefully coifed white woman, wearing pearls as she vacuums, has nothing to do with the lives of mothers around the globe. In most cultures, women perform the bulk of the society's work while devoting sufficient time and energy to children to enable those children to become, in their turn, productive members of society. If the day-to-day activities of such women were seen as the valuable, essential building blocks of human life that they are; if the economic value of women's work were equitable to its value in terms of societal contribution; and if men were held accountable for contributing proportionally, social hierarchies around the world would be rather different than what they are today. So a theory that incorporates mothering into its account of human nature seems to me to hold out the promise of a more complete, less limited view of human nature.

A central and vital contribution that care theory makes to ethical and political theorizing is the recognition that care work, whether the mothering that allows children to grow into citizens, the caregiving provided to the frail elderly, and the generalized care provided by service workers of all types, is not a fundamentally subhuman activity. It can be organized in oppressive ways, and it can be demanded of people unfairly and without adequate support, but the actual practices involved are not dehumanizing. This provides the theorist with a way of thinking about the tasks and roles women often are assigned that avoids the implicit sexism of assuming women's work is not human activity, while it simultaneously avoids the reactionary sentimentality that expects women to continue to serve, unpaid and unrecognized, for the sheer love of their menfolk.

III. Ideals, Ethical Analysis, and Justice

The particular ideal of human life we find in care theory is one that stresses the needs humans have for close, supportive human relationships, and for the social structures that make it possible to have, and reflect the importance of, such relationships. It focuses on the ability for other directed care that humans should develop as they grow and mature, and on the role of practices of caregiving in developing that ability. An ethic of care offers guidelines for evaluating human lives and social structures, but it also incorporates a certain respect for indeterminacy and fluidity. It recognizes that any ethical theory needs to leave room for reflexivity, experimentation, and alternative ways of structuring human life. We need to hang on to the tension between, on the one hand, protecting and nurturing care in individuals and in social structures, and, on other hand, keeping the door open to challenges to and revisions of social structures and conceptions of human beings. The practice of mothering can provide an understanding of this tension and of the ways in which it structures reflective child rearing. Parents find that in raising children they need both to keep in view what the good for humans is, since this provides an organizing structure for their actions, and keep in mind who their particular child is, and the ways in which she will never, perhaps, achieve elements of that good, or will have to operate with a revised notion of the good in her own life. It is the constant renegotiation between these two that characterizes good parenting, and a similar renegotiation between ideals of human flourishing and the actualities of particular social and historical situations that characterizes good moral reasoning.

We don't have to use the parenting metaphor in order to see this negotiation, however. We also see it in the case of individual moral reflection. Consider for example, the difficulty we face when we think about care and love for the self or for another when the self or the other has serious defects. Here a teleological view of human nature is, I think, inescapable, since any other view leads us into deep philosophical and existential confusion. Let's start with the case of the self. When I love myself, or care for myself, what is it that I love? Do I love myself in my entirety, or do I love certain aspects of myself while not loving, perhaps even hating, other aspects? We can choose a simple example for illustration. Suppose I have enough insight into my own psychological makeup to realize that as a professor I am insufficiently generous toward and careful about the weaker students in my classes, especially in introductory classes. My natural reaction toward such students might be one of exasperation and dismissal. I don't enjoy the hard work of making concepts accessible for them, I find their papers dreary to read, and their exams to offer evidence of their generally weak intellect. One part of me wants to treat them dismissively and arrogantly.

But this is an aspect of myself of which I do not approve. Noddings speaks of having a sense of the ideal self, of the self when it is truly caring, and I can certainly use such an ideal as a measuring stick to identify where I need to make changes in my behavior and even my personality. In this case it is fairly clear that if I act arrogantly and dismissively toward my weaker students I fail to care for them as I ought. So I picture my ideal caring self, rather than my actual self, and try to act as that ideal self would act. Slowly I find I can meet my students, even the weaker ones, with an attitude of respect. I devise techniques for making the material more accessible, and develop classroom exercises that help the students grasp the point of the material we are studying.

Now we can ask our question again. When I recognize my own arrogance and resolve to change it, how should I think about my sense of self-love and self-worth? Should I see myself, warts and all, as essentially lovable, or should I say that what I love is what I could be, not what I currently am? It seems to me to be evidence of a certain level of confusion to advocate the pop psychology adage that I love myself "just the way I am" because "I deserve it" or "I'm good enough." I need to make changes precisely because there are aspects of myself that are not good enough and don't deserve to be loved. If we postulate the notion of an ideal self, we automatically must also endorse the notion that there are aspects of the self that are not deserving of love and acceptance. If I don't love myself, however, I can't wish to get rid of bad character traits and develop better ones. If I don't dislike the bad traits I cannot wish to rid myself of them. Which aspects of myself are worth loving and which are worth hating are clearly matters that require ethical judgments that rely on some picture of what a good human should be like, and cannot be derived solely from an understanding of who I am at this present time.

But if this is true of self-love, it will turn out to be true of love of others as well, so we see that a teleology is necessarily assumed in moral reasoning about both self and others. Again, let's begin with a fairly concrete example. We'll assume I am still the professor described in the preceding paragraphs, and I am faced with a student who is not, frankly, one of the brightest or best in the classroom. The young man who sits in my office is a gawky, pock-marked adolescent, more interested in sports, sex, and alcohol than he is in Plato's *Republic*. He is in my office because a paper is due tomorrow on Plato's notion of justice. Because he has not been doing the assigned readings, and has missed several classes, he really has no clue what to write in this paper. He sits in front of me hoping that I will simply give him the basic words to say in his paper so that he can get a passing grade and get out of the class. As a person who wants to respond to the young man from an attitude of care, how should I think of this situation?

In the first place, it does not seem required by care that I endorse all of this young man's characteristics and desires as good or appropriate. Professors often jokingly refer to these situations as "teachable moments," but the humor holds an element of truth. What I need to do with my student is to let him know that he screwed up and will have to face the consequences, while letting him know that I do not consider him a complete waste of my time or a failure. If I fail to send the first message I entrench in him habits and traits that are harmful. If I fail to send the second message I fail to respond to him as one caring.

What this suggests is that an adequate picture of our moral self-evaluation and our moral responses to others cannot exist without a standard of objective goodness. If I operate completely within a subjective notion of moral character, I cannot separate out who I am from who I should be. Unless I assume a standard that exists apart from my own choices and desires, I will have no standpoint from which to judge some of my character traits as good and others as bad. Likewise, if I assume that my students' subjective feelings about what they want are definitive for their own good, then I cannot challenge them to grow as persons. There are, however, two different senses in which I might recognize that I or another falls short of an objective ideal.

I might fall short because of moral failings. The examples we've looked at so far suggest that some work remains to be done to move both myself and my student toward an improvement in character that can best be described as moral. But I may also face a student with severe learning disabilities, one who can read only with great difficulty, one who can take exams only with no distractions and extra time, and one whose paper-writing skills are severely hampered. In this case, though I still recognize that the student falls short of an ideal, I do not assign moral blameworthiness to that condition, nor do I assume that the best response to such a student is to encourage him to strengthen his moral fiber. Instead, faced with a student with disabilities, I recognize that a caring response has to involve accommodation for the disabilities without compromising the goals of the class. But in both cases I recognize that there is a ideal for the student that is not being met, and though in the one case I assign moral blame and in the other I don't, in both cases the gap between actual and ideal is a cause for regret and intervention.

We cannot make sense of either the regret or the intervention, however, unless we assume that there is some standard that is not achieved, and that this standard is not determined by the subjective desires of the agents themselves. Whether or not my first student recognizes that he is acting in ways that sabotage his ability to learn, he is. Whether or not I recognize (in the first example) that arrogance and dislike are moral failings, they are. Whether or not my student with learning disabilities is willing to acknowledge them as a barrier to learning, they are. In all these cases we are faced with a gap between current reality and ideal that cannot be diminished by resorting to questions of whether the individual in question sees the gap or wants to bridge it. Hence in all three cases we are forced to the conclusion that we do have an ideal, and we assess behavior in light of that ideal.

That some ideal or other is presupposed, then, seems relatively uncontroversial, as does the claim that the ideal cannot coincide completely with how things are at the current time. There is another question that still needs to be asked, however, and that is the status of the ideal in terms of two issues. We can get at one issue in terms of the objective/subjective split mentioned above. The subjective desires of an individual at a given time will deviate from the ideal, so that we can speak of the ideal as objective, as I did above. But the term "objective" could be defined in two different ways. We could use the term to signify the considered desires an individual would have if she or he had full information and were able to view her or his desires clearly in relation to one another, a sort of "ideal observer" version of objectivity. Something like this seems to be Nodding's notion of the ideal self, since she describes the ideal self as my ideal self at a given time, and uses images of bootstrapping myself along toward an ethical ideal.

But we could mean "objective" in a stronger sense, in terms of what is good for humans as such, or good for all humans due to their nature. This notion of objectivity could be relativized to particular social and historical circumstances, or it could be intended as a timeless universal, but in either case we are speaking of an ideal that is constituted, in part, by something other than the individual's own subjective desires and choices. I think Noddings intends to reject such an external notion of the ideal, and I also think she is wrong to do so. For care to have "ethical bite," it needs the stronger, more objective sense, and some of the criticisms that have been made of Noddings's views make this clear.

I mentioned earlier Bubeck's criticism of Nodding's barricade example. Suppose we have an individual who has been raised in a close loving family, but a family with deeply racist beliefs. The individual in question has come to reject such racism, and believes that she has a moral obligation to fight against racism. There are civil rights protests going on in her town at the moment, protests that threaten to turn violent, and the individual, after consideration, realizes that she would be willing to fight to protect her bigoted family members against threats to their safety from the civil rights protesters. She also considers joining the protesters at the barricades, but doing so will cause a rift in her family relationships, a rift that may be irreparable. How should we think about such a case? Noddings considers that the individual should perhaps not go to the barricades, and Bubeck takes her to task for that conclusion. Bubeck also analyzes this as a case in which considerations of care are in conflict with considerations of justice.

What Bubeck and Noddings both assume, however, is that rejecting racism is a good thing. They differ, it seems, because Noddings believes that the family members, individuals who are bigoted and yet capable of caring, are more likely to learn to reject racism if they are not forced into confrontational relationships with our individual's actions at the barricades, while Bubeck assumes that they are largely unsalvageable and should be left to their own devices because their racist views erase any moral obligations to them. What neither theorist takes seriously is the notion that perhaps the family's racism is actually just fine, and should be commended. Stated thus baldly, of course, the view seems obvious. But if Noddings is right that the ideal caring self has to be subjective, then presumably the racist family can have an ideal of a caring self that incorporates their racism. They have no desire to give up the racism, and think of it as a proper and sensible way to view the world, and their notion of care would then incorporate that view of the world.

For this to pose a real dilemma for the individual in question, it needs to be the case that the racism is really wrong, regardless of whether the family holding the racist views can see, or wants to see, its wrongness. Noddings is able to posit the ideal caring self as subjective in part because she implicitly begins with a picture of the agent as a generally decent human being, but she does not address the issue of how to deal with human beings who are deliberately destructive, or who hold vicious views, or, in the most problematic case, deliberately reject the ideal of a caring self. In such cases there are practical solutions one can adopt, solutions Noddings mentions, such as avoiding the individual or relying on legal and police powers to limit the damage they can do. But we should not lose sight of the fact that we are also judging the individual morally, and we are relying on an objective conception of moral character in doing so.

The example of the barricades is worth thinking about for other reasons as well. Bubeck presents the case as exemplary of the failure of care to address issues of justice. She simplifies it, presenting it as a case in which Noddings advocates standing with those one cares about even when they act unjustly. But this is not exactly how Noddings deals with the issue. Noddings considers a number of different scenarios. The first is the one Bubeck discusses, in which the barricades have already been formed, and Ms. A must think about which side of the barricades she will stand on. She decides she will defend the lives of her loved ones, and so will stand with them on the wrong side of the barricades. But then she goes on to reflect on what she would do if her loved ones were to initiate racist action (starting a lynching party, for example). In such a case, she reflects, she would begin with trying to dissuade them, and if that proved impossible, she would stand against them. So now Ms. A is on the other side of the barricades, fighting against her racist relatives—the very solution Bubeck wants, and the solution she criticizes Noddings for failing to offer.

The problem here is that what Noddings is offering is a classic example of how moral reasoning functions in a practical arena. She operates with a moral ideal, an ideal that incorporates both the insight that racism is deeply wrong and that close family relationships between loving family members place moral responsibilities on agents. Her agent is engaged with trying to think through how to balance those competing moral responsibilities, and seems to be assuming that the further issue of violent aggression is important for reasoning about them. So when others threaten the lives of her relatives because they hold the beliefs that they hold, Ms. A would defend them, racist though they may be. If her relatives were to be the aggressors themselves, she would not defend them and would be willing to oppose them actively. This is no longer so clear an example of care and justice coming into conflict as Bubeck wants to make it. Rather, it reflects the complexity of acting morally in a world in which there are a number of different moral considerations to take into account.

In fact, what we see in this case is the way in which an ideal leaves room for particular moral judgments and a respect for the uniqueness of a given situation. Reasoning based on abstract principles, often called justice reasoning, sometimes glosses over complexity and offers simple answers to difficult moral situations. This is why Noddings is suspicious of principles. Economic theory offers an example here. Neither orthodox communism nor libertarian economic analyses offer satisfying accounts of how economic systems should be structured. Both theories offer simplistic answers, both framed in terms of a single principle of justice (absolute equality versus absolute property rights) that make it unnecessary to think through the complexities of economic fairness, and so both are ultimately useless. An adequate analysis of economic justice needs to respect both private property and corporate responsibility, and we all know the devils that reside in those details. In the same way, the debate between Noddings and Bubeck is not over whether racism is wrong—both would agree that racism is deeply wrong and deeply unjust. The question is whether the recognition that racism is unjust offers a simple solution to how an individual should respond to racism in another who is near and dear to her—and in that situation, it is not clear that simplicity is a virtue.

IV. Care, Augustine, and Levinas

Augustine and Levinas offer us two other, related visions of the ideal of human life structured by love or care for others as a central moral value. I return to Augustine, briefly, and then Levinas to think through how their visions might differ from that of a care theory, how they might enrich our thinking, and how they might keep us aware of alternatives to the vision of care that is operative in feminist theory.

In the case of Augustine, the differences are relatively clear and obvious. Augustine's reliance on hierarchy and order as central components of his ideal result in a picture of love, or care, that is rigidly authoritarian in some ways, and unable to take adequate account even of Augustine's own concerns. This is worth noting for several reasons. First, it reminds us that when life seems to be in wild disarray, it is tempting to fall back on orderliness, any orderliness, in an attempt to stave off the chaos. Political forces consistently play off of this desire, promising constituents orderliness as a motive for accepting morally wrong policies. As many political commentators have noted, this is a typical characteristic of fascist systems,[25] but it can be a temptation for any system of political power, including those advocated by feminist theorists. I would argue that the early white suffragette movement made precisely this error when it rejected solidarity with the liberatory aspirations of newly emancipated slaves, and I think contemporary feminists who hope to defend women's rights without entering the debate over gay/lesbian issues are doing the same. In both cases we find theorists advocating hierarchical structures that maintain social order and stave off chaos, in spite of the fact that the theorist has both theoretical and first-person experience of just how wrong such structures are. On this issue, then, Augustine serves as a horrid example—he offers us a mirror in which to see our own warts and blemishes when we settle for safety and orderliness instead of fighting for liberation.

But this is not all we find in Augustine. Other aspects of Augustine's thought offer important positive considerations for feminist theorists of care, and for thinking through what it means to live a flourishing life as a human being. Augustine's defense of love as the most central aspect of human life offers a needed corrective to the notion that care or love for the other is a feminine attribute. Care is an essential part of what makes human life human, and this is true for both men and women. This means that the ideal of absolute independence from all other humans, an ideal sharply and properly criticized in much of the care literature, is not an ideal that only women need to reject, nor is it an ideal that men automatically support. It is, rather, an ideal that gains currency in a particular historical and social context, and characterizes the thinking of certain sorts of theorists, not all of whom are men.

This is a central point for care theory. There are, as Noddings, Ruddick, and Held all note, features of many women's lives today that make an ideal of independence both unreachable and unappealing. But this does not mean that the ideal of interdependence developed in care literature is an ideal for women only. It is an ideal for all human lives, because it recognizes the deeply social nature of human existence, the embodied characteristics we all share, and the extent to which we do not determine the course of our lives, either their beginning, or their ending, or large swathes of the in-between stages. Care is a basic constituent of any adequate picture of human existence.

If we allow Augustine to serve as a gentle reminder of the nongendered nature of the centrality of care, we will avoid simple gender dichotomies of the "women are nurturing, men are aggressive" sort. The rejection of such dichotomies improves both our theorizing and our practical reasoning, since it allows us to see the individuals in front of us as individuals rather than as automatic members of a class. I've found this to be true in interesting ways when I read student papers. I grade papers blind—that is, I try to ensure that I do not know whose paper I am grading—and I have consistently found that I cannot predict from a paper whether the writer is a man or a woman. Some blood-curdlingly violent responses come from (apparently) very feminine women, while some very gentle and caring responses come from what appear to be quite macho men. If we are ever to move beyond the simplistic stereotypes (ones I've just invoked in my use of "feminine" and "macho") we need to uncouple the notion of "naturally caring" from "female" and recognize it as an essential aspect of all human lives. This allows us to affirm it when it shows up in men as well as when it shows up in women.

As a further benefit, uncoupling care from gender allows feminists to acknowledge that care/nurturance is important, and that it has been associated with women, without falling into the error of allocating care work to women. Judith Baer notes the extent to which the association of women and care is a matter of societal expectations, expectations that explain, as she puts it, "why the clerk at the convenience store unloads his personal problems on me, a total stranger; why I have such a hard time getting a morning's work's done without interruption, while my male colleague works undisturbed; why, if I 'listen with the third ear' to my students' requests and complaints, I can almost hear the refrain, 'mommy, mommy, mommy.'"[26] It isn't that women are automatically nurturing, it is that we (collectively) expect and require them to act in ways that reinforce in them the view that they are nurturers.

But an intellectual acknowledgment of that aspect of human life doesn't diminish the automatic expectations generated in us by collective social belief. It is only as we slowly begin to change the way we live and act so as to reward, encourage, and support men's nurturance, as well as their positive perception of their own ability to nurture, that we will begin to change deeply rooted social expectations. Part of changing those expectations is establishing archives of masculine examples of care, nurture, and love, so that our examples of theorists who advocate care are not automatically characterized as "Mommy" types.

Further, linking the notion of masculinity and care with the Western tradition provides a much stronger position from which to accomplish social change than does automatic rejection of the tradition. To the extent that feminist theorists can argue that their vision of a good human life draws on central and important aspects of the traditions accepted by those to whom they speak, their arguments are strengthened pragmatically.[27] Just as Martin Luther King Jr.'s calls for change were far more effective because they linked the call for civil rights to deeply held values expressed in the founding documents of the United States, so feminist political activism is strengthened when its connections to deeply held values are made explicit. Although the religious right is unlikely ever to embrace a feminist agenda, many religious believers are not members of the hard-core right wing. Feminists are concerned with the political struggle to provide structures of care, protect the weakest, and create political structures oriented toward empowerment rather than control. There are links between these goals and central values in the Western tradition. When these links are made clear, it becomes easier to create coalitions and political movements that can generate true change.

Levinas offers a slightly different set of issues for thinking about how an ideal structures the notion of care. Like Augustine, he offers a notion of human nature structured in terms of openness to the other, again an important issue, given that he is not theorizing from a feminine perspective, nor is he offering a woman's view of ethics. As I argued earlier, in the case of Augustine, this offers feminist theorists an important resource for generating social images of nonmaternal calls for care, making the need for structures of care a human one, not an exclusively feminine concern.

But Levinas offers feminist theory more in terms of his analysis of the very nature of human existence. Theoretically he offers an account of why human life should not be structured on the assumption that humans are self-interested, isolated, atomic egoists. He does so in a way that does not rely, ultimately, on religious authority. While Augustine's position within the Christian tradition makes him a valuable resource for generating coalitions for political change,

Levinas offers an analysis of the destructiveness of certain perceptions of human life that is not exclusive to a particular religion or to an acceptance of divine authority. The convergence of these two thinkers' analyses suggests that care theory is metaphysically more accurate as a picture of human existence than some rival ethical theories, and this is worth noting.

Both Levinas and Augustine also offer healthy reminders to feminist theorists that the best intentions do not make us morally infallible. Augustine's obliviousness toward the oppressive situations in which women found themselves in the church and his unthinking promulgation of a male standard of human perfection are obvious to us today. Likewise, we can easily see the problems Levinas gets himself into because of his tendency to assume that the "other" is a man like himself, as seen in his analysis of the ethical relationship as the father/son relationship. These errors are glaring when we look at them today, but were largely unremarked and invisible in their own time. A healthy notion of our own fallibility should lead us to suspect that we may have equally glaring omissions in parts of our own thinking today.

Feminist theory has wrestled with this issue in terms of racial and class bias, and although feminist theorists are far more likely to be sensitive to racial, ethnic, and class issues than many other groups of theorists, they still sometimes speak as if "race" were something only nonwhites had to worry about, or "class" something only the economically disadvantaged really experienced. The incorporation of racial and class awareness has not occurred fully in feminist circles, though it has made far more progress there than in, say, contemporary analytic philosophy. Clearly there are some known blind spots in feminist theory. But the most serious blind spots are usually invisible to those who have them, and feminist theorists are probably largely unaware of what future theorists will be able to see clearly.

This is not a reason to stop thinking, or to stop political action. It is better to try to change or diminish evils in our world than to passively accept whatever happens, and concerted political advocacy can make important and vital changes. What feminist theorists should not assume is that stance of absolute moral authority that Augustine fell into, in which the theorist has no need to listen to challenges because she knows herself to be absolutely right on everything. None of us is actually God; we are all limited and fallible, and a certain amount of humility and realism with respect to our own political views is a healthy thing.

This mention of God brings us to a final aspect of Levinas's and Augustine's thought, namely the centrality for both of their religious identity. Religious belief is difficult to accommodate in feminist theory for a number of reasons. Some of these are political: feminist activism has battled the religious right for many years now, so that both parties assume that there is a natural antipathy between religion and feminism. Further, religious forces have so frequently stood as roadblocks to basic women's rights that there is some justification for feminism to oppose traditional religion. The conflict between religious faith and feminism should not be overstated, of course. Many feminists have come to their feminism out of a religious tradition. Large numbers of the early suffragettes were Quaker, and their fight for suffrage, and, sometimes, their work as abolitionists, arose directly out of their religious belief in the inherent worth and dignity of each and every human. Large numbers of political activists who have fought for civil rights, women's rights, and economic justice in the United States have come from the Lutheran, Catholic, and Jewish traditions. Certainly many of the traditionally black churches, such the American Methodist Episcopal Church, have been at the forefront of fights for economic and racial justice. Religious affiliation does not preclude political activism. In terms of political goals, the relationship between religious faith and feminism is too complex for any single description to capture it accurately.

There is a deeper issue than the political relationship between feminism and religious traditions; it concerns the place of the transcendent in human life. Both Augustine and Levinas encourage us to recognize that human life is lived in the presence of sacredness. Some feminist theorists have articulated a similar recognition of the central role of transcendence in human lives. Mary Daly, though she has rejected the institutional church as a post-Christian feminist, continues to draw on the language of transcendence and spiritual power, and many feminists have devised quasi-religious rituals for their lives to mark significant spiritual passages. The persistence of a yearning for transcendence even in theorists who reject traditional religions suggests that human lives are impoverished when a sense of spiritual connection is lost.[28]

But the attempt to generate an adequate spirituality through individual choice and action can be unsatisfactory. During the times when we are most aware of that which transcends our existence, the times of our greatest joy and greatest suffering, we need a connection to that which we have not created ourselves. In both Augustine and Levinas we find an articulation of the immensity and awesomeness of an infinite God, and in both we also find that articulation focused on the way that God is recognized in the other person. This seems to me a better beginning point for an adequate notion of transcendence in human life. It incorporates the notion of a transcendence that is not self-created and that is not limited to the individual's own values and perspective. But at the same time the recognition of God in the other person is a notion of transcendence that refuses to be unlinked from immanence, from the concrete person I find in front of me. It is a notion of transcendence that connects religious experience to an awareness of my own limitations. If we take seriously the notion that we encounter the transcendent in the other person, then we are faced with the difficult experience of recognizing that God comes to me in the face of the hated stranger, the mentally handicapped client, the other I don't want to identify with. Both Augustine and Levinas struggle with the many ways we want to deny this experience, and we can see in their own philosophical thoughts the places in which they deny it themselves. But recognizing that they failed to live up to their own ideals is not a reason to reject the ideals they held. Because the recognition of God in the other has more transformative potential than a notion of transcendence that primarily involves private emotions, it is worth incorporating it into a feminist account of human life.

V. Conclusion

An ethic of care cannot function without an implicit account of what human life should be like, nor can it provide an adequate response to criticisms without relying on such an account. We are better served as theorists if we acknowledge what drives our reasoning and investigate the assumptions on which we are dependent. When we recognize these assumptions we can investigate their connections to the assumptions of thinkers from the past, thinkers we may want to criticize, but from whom we can also learn.

But all of this operates at the level of theoretical generality. I have argued that an ethic of care is capable of offering helpful guidance as we think about challenging ethical concerns. The best way of thinking through what it can offer is to turn to concrete ethical issues and examine how an ethic of care might offer guidance in those contexts. So in the next two chapters, I make a rather large jump from the theoretical realm to the practical, and begin to examine two issues that are directly related to the notions of human nature and ideals of human flourishing, assisted reproduction and cloning. Both issues pose challenging and ethically complex problems for us as individuals and as members of societies faced with producing effective and morally responsible legislation. I examine how an ethic of care might offer a vantage point that helps us think these issues through and preserves both our sense of moral responsibility and our concern that we not allow practices and social structures that encourage exploitation. I turn to assisted reproduction in the next chapter and cloning in the final chapter.

Notes

1. See, for example, Andrea Nye's *Feminist Theory and the Philosophies of Man* (New York: Routledge, 1988); Susan Moller Okin's *Women in Western Political Thought* (Princeton, N.J.: Princeton University Press, 1979); and Jean Bethke Elshtain's *Public Man, Private Woman: Women in Social and Political Thought*, 2nd ed. (Princeton, N.J.: Princeton University Press, 1981). Mary Briody Mahowald's *Philosophy of Woman: An Anthology of Classic to Current Concepts*, 3rd ed. (Indianapolis, Ind.: Hackett, 1978), contains representative selections of the many things philosophers have said about women's nature and human nature.

2. See, for example, Nel Noddings, *Caring: A Feminine Approach to Ethics and Moral Education* (Berkeley and Los Angeles: University of California Press, 1984), pp. 1–2, 84–85.

3. Noddings, *Caring*, pp. 109–12.

4. Diemut Bubeck, *Care, Gender, and Justice* (New York: Oxford University Press, 1995), pp. 179, 239.

5. See, for example, Patricia Ward Scaltsas, "Do Feminist Ethics Counter Feminist Aims?" in *Explorations in Feminist Ethics: Theory and Practice*, ed. Eve Browning Cole and Susan Coultrap-McQuin (Indianapolis: Indiana University Press, 1992), pp. 15–26. Related criticisms are offered by Mary Dietz, "Citizenship with a Feminist Face: The Problem with Maternal Thinking," in *Feminism, the Public, and the Private*, ed. Joan B. Landes (New York: Oxford University Press, 1998), pp. 45–64; and Catharine MacKinnon, "Difference and Dominance: On Sex Discrimination," in *Feminism Unmodified: Discourses on Life and Law* (Cambridge, Mass.: Harvard University Press, 1987), pp. 32–45.

6. Joan Tronto, *Moral Boundaries: A Political Argument for an Ethic of Care* (New York: Routledge, 1994); and Selma Sevenhuijsen, *Citizenship and the Ethics of Care: Feminist Considerations on Justice, Morality, and Politics* (New York: Routledge, 1998).

7. Virginia Held, *Feminist Morality: Transforming Culture, Society, and Politics* (Chicago: University of Chicago Press, 1993).

8. Sara Ruddick, *Maternal Thinking: Toward a Politics of Peace* (Boston: Beacon, 1989).

9. See, for example, Nel Noddings, *Educating for Intelligent Belief or Unbelief*, The John Dewey Lectures (New York: Teacher's College Press, 1993); *Educating Moral People: A Caring Alternative to Character Education* (New York: Teacher's College Press, 2002); as well as *Starting at Home: Caring and Social Policy* (Berkeley and Los Angeles: University of California Press, 2002). This last addresses structural aspects of economic orders and homelessness, drug addiction, and deviance in addition to education policy.

10. And it should be noted that this is not always offered as a critique. Susan Hekman argues that care theory generates a rejection of all theorizing about human nature, pushing us instead to celebrate radical difference and plurality. See *Moral Voices, Moral Selves: Carol Gilligan and Feminist Moral Theory* (University Park: Pennsylva-

nia State University Press, 1995). As will become clear in what follows, I do not agree with Hekman that it is a good thing for a moral theory to give up any conception of what an ideal human life should look like.

11. For a very perceptive and careful analysis of these issues, see Douglas Rasmussen's "Human Flourishing and Human Nature," in *Human Flourishing*, ed. Ellen Frankel Paul, Fred D. Miller Jr., and Jeffrey Paul (Cambridge: Cambridge University Press, 1999), pp. 1–43.

12. Julia T. Wood, *Who Cares? Women, Care, and Culture* (Carbondale: Southern Illinois University Press, 1994); and Eva Feder Kittay, *Love's Labor: Essays on Women, Equality, and Dependency* (New York: Routledge, 1999). See also Fiona Mackay, *Love and Politics: Women Politicians and an Ethic of Care* (New York: Continuum, 2001).

13. Tronto, *Moral Boundaries*, p. 103.

14. MacKinnon, "Difference and Dominance," pp. 38–39.

15. Leslie Brody, *Gender, Emotion and the Family* (Cambridge, Mass.: Harvard University Press, 1999), pp. 233–43.

16. Kittay, *Love's Labor*.

17. Mackay, *Love and Politics*, pp. 202–9. See also Carol S. Robb, *Equal Value: An Ethical Approach to Economics and Sex* (Boston: Beacon, 1995).

18. I am using the term "mothering," as Ruddick and Held do, to refer to the embodied practices of protection, training, and education that allow children to grow into human beings. While one does not have to be female to mother, as Ruddick notes, in fact it has been predominantly women who have acted as mothers, and calling the practice "mothering" is one way of respecting the work so many women have done, and done well. I don't think mothering is the only practice about which one can say it is morally fundamental. Other practices that might also be fundamental are studying and gaining understanding, political activity, and play. All of these seem to be universal in human communities, and all are central to the development of humans from childhood to adulthood.

19. There are some interesting, even paradoxical exceptions to this general rule. Rousseau, for example, does pay attention to child development. But the very people he plans to put in charge of raising children (women) are trained, under his system, to lack the traits necessary to raise good children. It is significant that Emile is raised by a male tutor—women raised on Rousseauian principles would be incompetent parents.

20. Hannah Arendt, *The Human Condition*, 2nd ed. (Chicago: University of Chicago Press, 1998), p. 30.

21. Mary Dietz, "Citizenship with a Feminine Face: The Problem with Maternal Thinking," *Political Theory* 13 (1985): 13.

22. Jeffner Allen, "Motherhood: The Annihilation of Women," in *Mothering: Essays in Feminist Theory*, ed. Joyce Trebilcott, (Savage, Md.: Rowman & Littlefield, 1983), pp. 315–30.

23. Shulamith Firestone, *The Dialectic of Sex* (New York: William Morrow, 1970), p. 233.

24. Mackay, *Love and Politics*, pp. 159–79.

25. For example, the very popular *Ten Theories of Human Nature*, now in its third edition, by Leslie Stevenson and David Haberman (New York: Oxford University Press, 1998), makes the connection between fascism and the concern for order quite explicit.

26. Judith A. Baer, "Nasty Law or Nice Ladies? Jurisprudence, Feminism, and Gender Difference," in *Feminist Legal Theories*, ed. Karen Maschke (New York: Garland, 1997), pp. 159–89. Originally published in *Women and Politics* 11, no. 1.

27. Katherine Bartlett, "Tradition, Change, and the Idea of Progress in Feminist Legal Thought" in *Feminist Legal Theories*, ed. Karen Maschke (New York: Garland, 1997), pp. 273–343.

28. See, for example, Nel Noddings, "A Skeptical Spirituality," in *Philosophy, Feminism, and Faith*, ed. Ruth Groenhout and Marya Bower (Indianapolis: Indiana University Press, 2003), pp. 213–26.

CHAPTER FIVE

⌒ᔐᔑ⌒

Care and the New Reproductive Technologies

There's a poignant irony in the coexistence at the and of the twentieth century of a massive infertility that has given rise to dizzying adventures in reproductive techniques, and the ongoing challenges to women's reproductive rights. Choosing motherhood or refusing it has proven to be more complex than seventies feminism had imagined.

—Nancy Miller[1]

Care theory has often been denigrated as appropriate only for private realms, the realms to which women are so often relegated. But the critics of care generally argue that it is inappropriate for a public sphere. Positions from which care and similar ethical accounts can be criticized run the gamut from Simone de Beauvoir's argument that until women transcend their biological femaleness they will be unable to be fully human[2] to Daryl Koehn's claim that care and trust leave women vulnerable to exploitation.[3] One of the reasons care theory has come in for criticism is that it rejects the simple dichotomies of public/private and universal/particular and tries to analyze ethical issues that fall in the gray areas between these concepts.

Care, however, does not relegate women to the private realm, nor does it advocate an emotional/private ethic for women and a rational/public ethic for men. Care theory instead offers a revision of the picture of how human life should be ordered and what sorts of lives can be evaluated as good ones or not-so-good ones for humans to live. It places at the heart of the good life a value that has been associated with women, to be sure, but it is not clear that the fact that care has often been relegated to women makes it unworthy of being central for human life. As Augustine and Levinas remind us, care need not be relegated to the feminine, nor is its articulation possible only in terms of the private. Care, instead, is best thought of as the only matrix within which human life and human flourishing are possible. Further, care theory offers an account of the ideal for both individual life and social structures, an ideal of human life structured in ways that make it possible for human connections to exist, flourish, and be reciprocal. The resources this picture of human life offers ethical reasoning can now be brought to bear on the issue of the new reproductive technologies and their place in contemporary medicine. We will need to look at these issues from several vantage points: from the vantage point of those who feel that they need such technologies, from the vantage point of those who provide the new reproductive technologies, and finally from a broader social perspective.

The conclusion of this chapter will not be a set of simple, absolute rules for when infertility treatment is and is not morally acceptable. Instead, what we will be aiming at is a general sense of what the moral issues are in this case, some cautionary notes about where and when the uses of such technology can slip into abuses, and some general guidelines for protecting the most vulnerable in various scenarios. But all through this book I have assumed, as is appropriate for a care theorist, that my own moral reasoning cannot substitute for that of the reader. The book intends to provide resources for thinking about various issues, not a set of absolute rules with which to solve every moral problem. With that in mind, I begin with a brief overview of the sorts of technologies that are at issue in this discussion.

I. The New Reproductive Technologies: A Brief Introduction

Technological advances in the field of reproductive biology have increased astronomically in the past fifty years. Some of the new issues that have been examined by the courts and various legislatures are not issues of new technology (surrogacy is as old as the Abraham narrative), but they occur in the context of new technologies that shape the way we think about the nature of reproduction, and the way we think about the most intimate relationships between humans. Jürgen Habermas argues that the new reproductive technologies require that we think through what it means to live as humans in a human community, because they change the aspects of reproduction that come under our control in essential ways. In particular, he argues, the new reproductive technologies allow us to determine aspects of future generations that they may not be able to reflectively endorse for themselves. Socially constituted aspects of future generations, he points out, are the sorts of things that future generations can reflectively endorse or reject for themselves. Inherited characteristics do not offer future generations this same freedom, and so they pose ethically problematic issues that are new.[4] This is a serious moral issue, but it is not the only one posed by the new reproductive technologies, so it is worth running through the various reproductive technologies and noting some of the ethical issues different techniques raise, before turning to a discussion of what care theory can offer in terms of thinking through the ethical dimensions of various practices.

The two least technological types of assisted reproduction have been available throughout human history: artificial insemination by donor (AID) and surrogate motherhood have both been utilized more or less officially in many cultures and over many years. Laws that define legal fatherhood in terms of the man married to a child's mother at the time of the child's birth, for example, indicate a long-standing legal recognition of the occasional lack of genetic ties between a husband and his wife's children. Likewise, many cultures have had legal codes permitting surrogacy arrangements, as the story of Sarah, Hagar, and Abraham makes clear. Both of these "techniques" have a long history, so we should not be surprised to find that the sorts of moral problems they can raise are not new either. Many men have disputed paternity over the years, and many surrogates have refused to step out of the life of the children they have given birth to. What has changed in both of these cases, however, is the degree of control offered by technology.

In the case of AID, the technology of sperm banks and both interstate and global commerce have made it possible to order sperm with a fairly high degree of anonymity for both parties. The sperm donor can avoid any legal connection to the child, and the mother of the child can avoid any ties to the sperm donor; she can also ensure that the child has no way of tracing paternal connections. This protection of anonymity has come under some criticism lately, from critics in both liberal and conservative camps. In the conservative camp, concerns about protecting the structure of the heterosexual family have led to legislation requiring identification of fathers on birth certificates and pressure to prohibit the provision of sperm to unmarried women. On the liberal side, critics have argued that children need to know the medical history of their genetic father, and should be able to contact the donor when they reach the age of maturity.[5]

In addition to these concerns about familial relationships, some critics raise concerns about health risks posed by inadequately screened sperm. Critics of AID have charged that some clinics offering sperm for anonymous donation do not screen for diseases transmitted by bodily fluids, and disease transmission by sperm donation is not tracked by any national data collection.[6] Women who use sperm from an anonymous donor may face health risks if the sperm is not adequately screened for HIV or other diseases transmitted by bodily fluids. Children begotten by sperm donation may be at risk for genetically transmitted conditions, and anonymity makes it impossible to know and deal with the conditions in advance. Finally, the legal status of anonymous sperm donation is still ambiguous. Courts have not clarified whether children of sperm donors have a right to know who their genetic father is, nor have courts ruled consistently on whether a sperm donor can legally waive all parental rights and responsibilities. Recent rulings that establish genetic paternity as definitive of a father's rights over children suggest that a donor might be able to successfully sue for custody or visitation rights.

Even the language of sperm donation has been questioned by some thinkers. In most cases, the purported "donation" is a straightforward economic transaction, with the "donor" being paid for the sperm by the recipient, and with the payment mediated by the intervening clinic(s). The language of "donation," with its connotation of a gift relationship, suggests discomfort with the notion of treating reproduction as a matter of economic contract. Some feminist theorists have been very critical of this language of altruism in the case of egg "donation," since it carries implications of self-sacrifice that are problematic. We'll return to this issue when we consider egg and embryo "donation," but it is worth noting here that if the sale of eggs and embryos should not be termed "donation," selling sperm should likewise be named accurately.

Finally, in more recent years the question of sperm retrieval from an unconscious or dying donor has become a moral and legal issue. There have been a few cases of family members requesting sperm donation from men who are comatose, or who have died from some accident or physical trauma.[7] The request may come from a wife, a fiancée, a long-term partner, or a parent. These are difficult cases because there is no possibility of donor consent, and the request indicates an intent to generate a child after the death of the donor, raising questions about the acceptability of making such a decision for the father, and of imposing this lack of relationship on a child. Family members do have the right to consent to organ donation after death in many cases, but it is unclear that sperm donation should be considered organ donation, since the sperm is used to generate a new individual, not to provide an organ needed to assist an already existent individual. Courts have generally recognized the rights of individuals to make their own reproductive decisions, and have prohibited others (parents, spouses) from making those decisions for them, but this is an issue that is new enough that it does not have clear legal standing.

Surrogacy poses even more difficult questions than does sperm donation. There are two basic types of surrogacy in use today. In some cases, a surrogate mother is hired to be artificially inseminated by a man's sperm, resulting in a child who has a genetic tie to both surrogate and father. This was the situation in the (in)famous Baby M case, and it provided the rationale for the appellate court to rule that the surrogate mother ought to have visitation rights with her daughter.[8] Again, the language used to describe these cases is problematic, since the woman termed a "surrogate" is quite simply the mother of the child in question, but has agreed to relinquish her parental rights. In other cases of surrogacy, the surrogate is hired to provide gestation for an embryo generated with another woman's egg. In these cases the surrogate has no genetic link to the child, and courts have denied that she has any claims to a continued relationship with the child after it is born. Legally, some courts treat genetic ties as though they were the sole determinant of parental rights, though other courts have recognized parental rights, particularly in the case of lesbian and gay couples, in the absence of a child's genetic link to one of the partners. Further, all cases of surrogacy raise issues of whether it is appropriate or legal to treat gestation as a service for hire, whether surrogacy arrangements are inherently exploitive of women, and whether surrogacy contracts should be legally enforceable. This is clearly an issue on which the law is in flux.[9]

In both AID and surrogacy we are faced with questions about the relevant rights of parents to protect anonymity in the face of children's desire to know their heritage. We are also faced with questions about the meaning of parenthood: whether it is primarily a biological category or a social category, and whether contracts to provide "parenting" services, such as gamete donation or gestation, should be considered a contractual matter and legally enforceable. We are confronted with questions about whether gametes and gestational services are commodities or not.

But with AID and surrogacy we only begin to brush the surface of the complexities of the new reproductive technologies. The most closely related issue is that of egg donation. Recent news stories have focused on the attempt by some parents to purchase "designer eggs." They report advertisements placed in school newspapers at Ivy League universities offering $10,000 for an egg from a woman who has certain desirable characteristics—she is blonde, tall, athletic, and smart (as measured by SAT scores). Egg donation raises, of course, all the issues mentioned above in connection with sperm donation. For example, calling it "donation" in the face of a $10,000 fee requires a rather odd set of mental gymnastics. But it also raises issues not generated by sperm donation. Acquiring eggs for gamete donation is a significantly more invasive procedure than acquiring sperm, since sperm donation is a relatively low-tech, easy procedure. To "harvest" eggs requires, first, hormonal manipulation to ensure that a number of eggs are generated at one time. Next the eggs must be "harvested," usually by laparoscopic surgery. Some critics have charged that the hormonal manipulation poses a number of risks for the woman involved, including an increase in the future risk of cancer, though studies are inconclusive on this point. The surgery is generally safe, but there have been rare cases of perforated bladders, damaged blood vessels, and pelvic inflammatory disease. This last can lead to scarring of the fallopian tubes and infertility.[10]

So in addition to all the questions about anonymity of donation, parental responsibilities, and the commodification of gamete provision, egg donation poses distinct moral issues regarding the health risks it poses due to the invasive nature of the harvesting. Many of these concerns are glossed over by the rather rosy language of "giving the gift of life" that clinics prefer to use in referring to donation. If we set aside this terminology for a moment, however, we can see that egg donation involves an invasive medical procedure performed for the benefit of others, not for the individual who undergoes the procedure. She will be paid for her willingness to risk her health, of course, but the commodification of eggs and of women's bodies involved in the procedure is morally problematic.[11] It is doubtful that this is an appropriate use of medical technology. As a society we generally prohibit undergoing nonbeneficial medical procedures for financial gain, and whether health care workers should see this as an acceptable practice is certainly worth questioning.

Many of the issues raised in the case of selling eggs arise again when we turn to the techniques that are more centrally a matter of infertility "treatment." Again, the language we use in this context is problematic. Most of the techniques that are categorized under the rubric of infertility treatment are not treatments for infertility: they do not cure the underlying conditions that cause the inability to produce embryos, fertilize them, or carry them to term. Instead they are more properly termed "assisted reproduction." They offer techniques of providing various aspects of reproduction to people who are unable, for a variety of reasons, to reproduce the traditional way. There are a few techniques that do aim at restoring lost fertility, whether by unblocking sperm ducts (as when a vasectomy is reversed), unblocking fallopian tubes, or hormonally stimulating ovaries to allow them to release eggs. These techniques, like most medical treatments, pose no serious ethical issues so long as they are performed by qualified technicians and offered with appropriate informed consent. Other aspects of assisted reproduction are not so straightforward, however. Because of this concern, we will use the term "assisted reproduction" rather than "infertility treatment" to avoid confusion.

The assisted reproduction technique (ART) most people think of first is in vitro fertilization (IVF), made famous over twenty years ago when Louise Brown, the first "test-tube baby," was born. IVF involves the removal of eggs from the potential mother and sperm from the potential father. The gametes are then brought together under laboratory conditions so that fertilization takes place outside the body, hence the nickname "test-tube babies." Some of the embryos that may result from the fertilization are then placed in the mother's uterus, where one (ideally) implants and follows a normal pattern of gestation and birth. Because implantation rates are often low, it is common for multiple embryos to be used in the procedure, leading to multiple births with all their attendant health risks for both mother and babies. Reputable clinics have improved their techniques and reduced the rates of multiple births, but this remains one of the most significant health risks associated with assisted reproduction.

Of course, once fertilization is moved outside the body, all sorts of variations on this basic technique can be used, from using eggs or sperm from a third party, to using a surrogate to carry the embryo to term. We have mentioned many of the issues that the use of acquired gametes raises, and the issues raised by surrogacy, so I will just mention that all of those complexities come into play here as well. We also find the same sort of obscurantist language, particularly in the use of words that imply that "donated" gametes or embryos are simply solutions to infertility. This is false, since a donated embryo is just as much a "genetic stranger" as a child adopted as an infant, and a child generated by donor gametes is likewise not genetically related to at least one parent. But ARTs are offered as the preferential alternative to adoption, not as a form of adoption, and donor gametes are presented as a treatment for infertility. When a practice requires us to use language to obscure rather than clarify the nature of the activities it involves, it suggests that there are morally problematic aspects of the practice.

Setting aside, however, the issues already mentioned concerning gamete "donation" and surrogacy, the use of ARTs poses a number of additional ethical concerns. One of the basic criticisms made of ARTs, most frequently encountered in arguments developed by conservative and religious critics, is that assisted reproduction changes the status of the child in fundamental ways. Children should be "begotten," not made, critics argue,[12] and ARTs treat children as objects to be manufactured to a certain set of specifications rather than treating them as beings with inherent dignity and worth. The shift from begetting to making, according to these critics, begins when parents come to think that having children is something they should be able to control and determine for themselves. (In the case of Catholic moral teaching, the rejection of assisted reproduction includes a rejection of all attempts to control fertility, including contraception.) When parents choose in vitro fertilization, they substitute scientific technology for the mystery of sexual communion, and they treat the child as something to be constructed in a laboratory rather than an individual whose advent is a surprise and a gift.

This objectification, further, carries with it the notion that parents have the right to determine what sort of child they find acceptable. So screening embryos for genetic diseases becomes not only a possibility but a right, as does parental choice of the sex of the embryo, and perhaps other aspects of the genetic heritage of the child to be: height, eye color, hair color, and so on. This marks a shift in cultural perceptions, critics argue, from understanding parents as responsible to their children to seeing the children as the property of the parent, with those parents who can afford it buying the best product they can, while less-wealthy parents settle for the cheaper versions.

Feminist critics of assisted reproduction have also raised this concern that assisted reproduction treats children as commodities and objects of sale,[13] and this represents a certain degree of overlap between feminist and conservative critics. But the more general criticism of any attempt to control reproductive processes is one that most feminists have rejected. Women's control over their own fertility is thought to be a good thing by most feminists, and to the extent that ARTs enhance women's control they are morally unproblematic. What some feminist critics have argued, however, is that ARTs do not uniformly represent female control over fertility, but sometimes represent scientific control of women's reproductive capacities, a very different issue. Feminist critics of ARTs argue that science and medicine demonstrate a clear pattern of illegitimate control over women's sexuality and reproductive capacities, a pattern that begins with the early history of medicine's attack on herbalists and midwives, as well as early medical responses to "conditions" such as independence and nonsubmissiveness in women with "treatments" such as removal of the clitoris.[14]

Those who raise this critique of medicine generally argue that ARTs do not increase women's reproductive freedom, though that is the rhetoric that often surrounds such practices. Instead, they argue, ARTs contribute to a climate of pronatalism in which women are socialized to think that their lives can be meaningful only if they bear a child for their husband, in which motherhood is exalted to the highest calling a woman can have, and in which women without children are automatically assumed to be selfish, unfulfilled, and "unwomanly."[15] There is intense pressure in our society for women to see themselves as destined for motherhood, and the presence of ARTs contributes to that pressure significantly. When infertility is treated as a shameful and life-destroying condition, and when women are expected to undergo invasive and expensive procedures to rectify it, a very strong societal message is conveyed about the nature and purpose of "true womanhood."

Other feminist critics are less concerned about the societal messages sent by the presence of, and pressure to use, ARTs. These critics argue that ARTs are offered without adequate safeguards, and pose serious health risks to the women who utilize them. I've mentioned some of the dangers of egg "donation." Women undergoing IVF face the same risks: perforated bladder, pelvic inflammatory disease, and damage to the fallopian tubes. The long-term risks of the hormone stimulation needed to produce several eggs in one cycle are unknown, and studies on them are few and inconclusive.[16] Future studies may demonstrate an increase in risks associated with hormone stimulation; risks have been demonstrated for women using hormone replacement therapy for the symptoms of menopause. If so, then the widespread use of ARTs now could contribute to a major increase in new cancer cases in the next few decades. Even if it should turn out that ARTs pose few health risks, the mere fact that these techniques are being used on humans before being tested on animals should raise red flags.[17] It is a serious breach of the professional-client relationship for health care providers to offer procedures to clients without being clear about the risks those procedures involve.

If the risks of these procedures were well understood and the women who chose to use them were completely informed and had carefully weighed the various risks against the perceived benefits of the techniques, then these criticisms would lose much of their force. We expect competent adults to make such judgments regularly in their lives. What feminist critics have charged, however, is that ARTs are provided without full disclosure of the risks involved, that long-term studies of their safety are unavailable, and that the language used to describe them suggests that these techniques are risk free and harm free. This is a difficult charge to assess, since infertility clinics are largely independent and set their own standards. The prevalence of multiple pregnancies suggest that some clinics do not adequately safeguard the health of their female clients, preferring to generate higher success numbers by using large numbers of embryos and thus putting the health of the women who try to carry triplets or quadruplets to term at risk.

In addition to pronatalism, the scientific control of women's fertility, and the health risks ARTs may pose to women, critics have argued, there is a broader social issue that should be raised concerning ARTs, and that is the proper place of such technology in the national and the global context of health care delivery. Insurance carriers in the United States face increasing pressure to provide coverage for ARTs. Again we see the importance of language in this context, since the pressure to provide coverage for "infertility treatments" implies that ARTs are needed medical treatments, rather than techniques for generating children. Noting that this language is misleading is not meant to denigrate the nature or strength of the desire people have to have children, but it is important to keep in mind that many of these techniques are not designed to restore health or functioning to organ systems.

This pressure comes at a time when the health care delivery system faces rapidly increasing medical costs, partly because of the development of more (and more expensive) high-tech interventions in health care, and decreasing funds available for covering these interventions. It also occurs at the same time that we face global crises (AIDS, antibiotic resistant tuberculosis, SARS, and the like) without the resources or the social structures to address them adequately. In this context, critics have argued, we should not direct societal resources into developing and providing assisted reproduction. There are great needs for basic care at the global level, and even within the United States basic health care needs for the underinsured go unmet. From a moral perspective it does not make sense to use limited health care dollars to provide assisted reproduction for the (comparatively) wealthy when there is insufficient health care for the poor, nor does it make sense to continue to develop high-tech interventions that are not directly health related when basic techniques such as immunizations and provision of clean water will result in far greater health benefits for the population overall.

There are, then, a number of serious moral concerns raised by ARTs. On the other hand, the use of ARTs has increased in recent years precisely because they do offer benefits to people struggling with infertility. Further, supporters argue, these techniques are freely chosen and largely paid for by individuals. Limiting access to them would represent a morally problematic limitation on individual liberty, and it would not free up funds for global health concerns in any case. The strongest argument in favor of ARTs is that of reproductive freedom, although it should be noted that the argument does not provide much support for the demand for health insurance to cover ARTs.[18]

The question then becomes how we might think about these issues from within the framework provided by care theory. In order to organize the discussion, we will consider the issues as they arise at three different levels: that of the individuals who utilize ARTs of one kind or another, that of the fertility clinics that provide ARTs, and that of government regulation and control of ARTs, infertility clinics, and insurance coverage.

II. Individual Use of the New Reproductive Technologies

For those who wish to have a child, any criticism of ARTs may seem cruel and misplaced. Whether we are thinking of a lesbian couple that chooses to use anonymous sperm donation to have a child, or of a single woman with androgen insensitivity who wants to hire a surrogate to bear a child for her, or a married couple whose infertility is due to unknown causes, but who believe that through IVF they could have the child they dream of, in all these cases there is a heartfelt longing to have a child of one's own. This is a real and significant desire, and not one that we should dismiss or treat as misguided, especially from the perspective of a theory that takes the emotions to be vital parts of the moral life, and that makes caring the center of ethical analysis. So we should start by noting that the desire to love and care for a child should be affirmed and supported.

The care theorist will not be too quick to condemn ARTs, since they are techniques designed to allow people to have and love children, and this is generally a good thing to do. But care theory does suggest that the way ARTs are understood and implemented in contemporary U.S. culture is problematic, and it is problematic because of the way it exploits this basically good desire to have and love children. One of the important additions to care theory that Augustine offered us was precisely this recognition that good desires can be misdirected and lead to evil. The basic goodness of the desire to have and love children does not make all actions generated by that desire morally acceptable. In what follows, I am critical of certain aspects of ARTs as they function in contemporary U.S. culture, but I do not denigrate the desire that people have for children. Because care should be directed at the good of the one cared for, we can propose, as a general principle, that the desire to have a child should involve a basic concern for the well-being of the child herself or himself. When the desire to have a child is expressed in ways that can be foreseen to be harmful to the child, then the concern is not for care, but for self-directed desire satisfaction. Since the well-being of the child and the desires of the parents often coincide, of course, we tend to overlook cases in which they conflict, but the distinction between concern for the good of the child and desire satisfaction on the part of parents is crucial, and we will need to draw on it as we consider these various techniques of assisted reproduction.

Sperm donation raises concerns for the care theorist because it involves, in most cases, a deliberate lack of relationship between genetic father and child. Some respond to this by choosing a known donor for sperm, but this creates its own complications, including the occasional case in which the sperm donor chooses to pursue partial custody or visitation rights. Under current conditions, further, the lack of a screening procedure to minimize possible disease transmission is also problematic. From a care perspective, these concerns are not incidental, but neither are they definitive. Individuals interested in using donor sperm should consider the risks carefully, and should also think through what it means for a child to be cut off from a relationship with a father. In some cases these concerns may be sufficient to suggest that sperm donation should not be used. In other cases there may be sufficiently weighty reasons to utilize it, with careful consideration of how the drawbacks will be addressed.

The issue of surrogacy is more complicated than sperm donation. Cases of noncontractual surrogacy, as when a family member acts as a surrogate for a woman unable to carry a pregnancy to term, are probably justifiable in many cases. But these are rare. Contractual surrogacy is more common, and there seems no way to eliminate the potential for exploitation involved in paying someone for gestational services. From the perspective of care theory, this exploitation is particularly problematic. There is a built-in contradiction in the assumption that the person who hires the surrogate properly wants to satisfy his or her desire for a "child of one's own," while the same person expects that the surrogate will (and should) be willing to give up the child, toward whom she will, at birth, have far more emotional connections than can the paying parent. In addition to this basic contradiction, many surrogacy contracts include the right of the contractor to demand that the surrogate abort on command. Some contracts do not permit the surrogate to reconsider her decision after giving birth. Both of these types of clauses make surrogacy contracts problematic in any account of ethics. They represent practices of control over another's body that are incompatible with minimal concern for the other's well-being or autonomy, and they also destroy relationships of reciprocal care that are central for decent human social organization.

Contracts that are written in less exploitive terms offer less clear-cut cases—many surrogacy contracts allow a period after the birth during which the surrogate can decide whether or not to fulfill the contract[19] (and, of course, surrender her fee), and many no longer include abortion on demand clauses. Even in these cases, there is more than a whiff of exploitation in many surrogacy cases, generated by the differential social and economic status of surrogate and contractor. Surrogates are generally drawn from lower-

and working-class environments, while contractors are generally very well-off. The fees paid for surrogacy are quite low in comparative terms. The lawyers who arrange for surrogacy usually receive fees that are many times higher than the fee the surrogate receives, for example. It is not clear that paid surrogacy contracts can be entered into with adequate safeguards for the surrogate herself, and from a care perspective this would suggest that the contractors are not treating the surrogate as a particular other toward whom they act with care, but are instead using her as a means to produce something they want.

A further ethical concern raised by surrogacy is the way that it defines legitimacy in terms of a genetic link to a father, while ignoring the genetic and gestational link the child has to the surrogate mother. The choice to use a surrogate implies that an adopted child will not do for one's purposes. The child carried by the surrogate is desired because he or she has the correct genetic link to a paternal heritage. Unlike the case of sperm donation, in which the parent who plans to have the child is the one who undergoes pregnancy and birth, surrogacy severs the gestational relationship between parent and child in favor of a paternal genetic tie. Our culture has a long history of seeing children as their father's property, produced via the medium of a woman. The view can be traced back to Aristotle's notion that sperm contains the seed that grows a child, and the mother's body is merely the soil within which the seed grows. In this context it is worth noting that the first judge in the case of Baby M noted the genetic tie between baby and father in his ruling, while ignoring the equal genetic tie the baby had with her mother.[20]

Arguably, then, those who choose to hire a surrogate enter into a relationship that cannot properly be described as a relationship of reciprocal care. The employers treat the relationship as an economic contract, a matter of paying a woman for her gestational services. The contractual nature of the relationship requires that the surrogate not develop emotional attachments to the baby, in spite of her genetic relationship and the gestational relationship that extends over nine months. She is to care deeply about any actions she might take that could harm the fetus as it develops, yet she is to be willing to give it up immediately after birth. Surrogacy creates relationships in which a woman is expected to provide services of care that will benefit others, but in which she is not to expect any care in return. For this she is paid an inadequate fee. Although her services are usually described as giving "the gift of life" to an infertile couple, or as "the most beautiful gift that one person can give another," her fees indicate that her services are valued at a level quite a bit below the market value of the lawyer who writes her contract, or the physician who delivers the baby. This is a relationship that exploits women's traditional socialization as carers in order to benefit others who are not interested in the surrogate for her own sake. It is a relationship that is exploitive, and one that contributes to the social perception that the male provider of genetic material is the only real owner of a child. From a perspective informed by an ethic of care it is almost impossible to justify such an arrangement.

The use of donor eggs and embryos occurs in the context of ARTs in general, so we will treat these issues simultaneously. The issues raised earlier are all of concern for the care theorist: the commodification of children, the entrenchment of pronatalism, the physical risks of various ART procedures, and the place of ARTs in the context of the social provision of health care. But from the perspective of people considering the use of ARTs the first three are probably the most relevant. Individual consumers don't have much say in how health care services are structured at a national level, let alone at a global level, and their choice to use or not to use the services of an infertility clinic are unlikely to have any impact on the funding of AIDS treatment in Africa.

But the other concerns are worth a mention. The language of "a child of one's own" that is so often used in the context of assisted reproduction is problematic because of the way it contributes to the perception of children as commodities. This language is used whenever a clinic wants to sell its services, and no clear distinctions are drawn between surrogacy, in which the employing parents may have a genetic link to the child, but not a gestational link, and IVF utilizing a donated embryo, in which the parents have a gestational link, but no genetic link, to the child. The fact that in both of these cases parents are encouraged to think that the child is "their own," with the implication that an adopted child would somehow not be "theirs," suggests that what makes a child the parent's own is, first, payment for services rendered, and, second, consumer selection of the child and the process whereby it is generated. From a care perspective, this is particularly problematic, since close personal relationships, such as that between parent and child, are precisely the relationships that should not be commodified. The relationship between parent and child should be one in which the child's needs and vulnerabilities create parental obligations, not one in which the child is seen as worthwhile because she or he satisfies the parent's desires and wishes. Children do not exist for the sake of satisfying adult lifestyle choices.

Now, clearly, those who choose to undergo IVF do not do so with the explicit intention of commodifying their children, nor do they consciously intend to turn the children into objects to be used for the satisfaction of their own desires. But the context within which IVF occurs does imply such a conception of children. For corroboration of the notion that the children produced via IVF are not seen as individuals deserving respect for their own sake, consider the fact that most of the techniques that fall under the rubric of IVF have not been fully tested on animals for safety. We don't know, at this point, whether techniques such as cytoplasmic sperm injection (once used only in cases of weak sperm, now used routinely in infertility clinics) may have harmful effects on the children so conceived at some future point. But the absence of clinical data does not lead the potential parents, or the clinics, to hesitate to use these techniques. When future risks to the child-to-be are ignored in order to satisfy the potential parents' desires, and the clinics' profit motive, the child is made a commodity to be used by others, whether the parents consciously intend this or not.

From the perspective of care we should criticize the implicit pronatalism of ARTs as well. Women are expected to undergo risks in the course of ARTs. These risks are not undergone for the sake of improved health or the prevention of sickness. The only justification for the risks is reproduction. The implication is that it makes sense for a woman to risk her health and well-being to bear children, that her own well-being should be subordinated to child-bearing. Testimony in favor of permitting new ARTs almost always involves an attractive woman explaining in heart-rending terms that having a child is the only thing that could make her life meaningful, and that this particular technique (whether IVF, cloning, or another technique) is the only one that will allow her to reproduce. Sometimes the meaningfulness of bearing a child is phrased in terms of providing a son for the woman's husband, while at other times the plea avoids such blatant sexism. But inevitably the implication is that a woman is made to bear babies and no woman's life is meaningful unless she does so. This desire is treated as innate, natural, and overwhelming.

From the perspective of care theory, we can note, first, that while care theorists do respect the central importance of relationships, including the mother/child relationship, in human life, they do not thereby endorse every expressed desire to initiate such relationships regardless of the cost. In particular, when the notion that women cannot live worthwhile lives without bearing babies is normalized to the degree that it is in the context of ARTs, this rhetoric impacts all women's lives. The implication that women's lives ought to be subordinated to reproduction represents a failure of care for women as valuable individuals in their own right.

In the first chapter we spoke of the notion of relational identity, that an individual's identity is constituted in part by the social relationships in which the individual stands. These relationships are partially constituted by the socially constructed images and ideals that form the context within which she understands herself and her life. Both of the issues I have raised in this section about ARTs reflect this concern about relational identities. When children are seen as commodities, we send a message to parents and children that the children exist for the parents' sake, and not the other way around. When it is commonplace to assume that women without children cannot find meaning in life, the value of individual women's accomplishments is diminished. Social practices that entrench problematic social constructions need to be challenged, not endorsed.

In this context we also need to make note of the role that racial assumptions and plain old-fashioned racism play in the choice of many parents to use ARTs. Justification for utilizing infertility clinics is often framed in terms of the shortage of "acceptable" children for adoption, and what many white or Anglo parents mean by "acceptable" is white. Elaine Tyler May quotes a woman who adopted a daughter, but after discovering that the daughter was biracial, returned her to the adoption agency. "[A]fter she was with us for two months we realized she was bi-racial," the mother writes. "We struggled with this, but after some gut-wrenching introspection came to see that we were not prepared for the challenge of raising a biracial child. We loved Sarah dearly and with all our hearts, but knew that there was another couple out there who *was* prepared for this."[21] In a similar vein, several cases of white parents receiving embryos from black couples have been in the news in the past years, and the event is reported as a dilemma for the white parents. The paradoxical nature of these "dilemmas" in a society that claims to be color-blind is obvious. Again, we see the implicit commodification of children in these practices, modified by latent racial prejudices.

This does not mean that ARTs are always morally unacceptable. What it means instead is that people considering using such techniques need to spend time critically reflecting on whether they are pursuing these goals for the sake of the child they intend to generate, or whether they want to satisfy their own desires regardless of the cost to the child. Sometimes the risks and harms of ARTs are too high, both for the child-to-be and for the mother-to-be. In these cases the desire to have and love a child could be gratified in ways that show more care and respect for the child one wants to love. As a rough rule of thumb it would seem that the more invasive and risky the proposed techniques, the more likely it is that the desire for children has become a single-minded pursuit of satisfaction at all costs.

III. Providers and Researchers

The moral issues change somewhat as we turn to the providers of ARTs, whether the aides, nurses, physicians, and technicians who provide direct services in infertility clinics, or the businesspeople and advertisers who direct the organizational and public face of the industry. As I mentioned above, ARTs are often spoken of as "treatment" for the condition of infertility, though the majority of these techniques are not aimed at the alleviation of the conditions that cause infertility. Because of this linguistic convention providers tend to conceptualize themselves as in the business of health care, offering services that are similar in nature to those provided by health clinics, family-practice physicians, and nurse practitioners. But the parallel is not exact, and too quick an identification between these leads to too quick an endorsement of their existence and practices.

ARTs are provided as services to allow consumers to acquire a desired product. As such there is nothing inherently immoral about them. Selling products or services to customers is a morally legitimate way to make a profit, so long as the products are not defective, the use of them does not cause serious health risks, and the like. But we should be clear about the difference between offering health care, which is not a commercial product, and offering ARTs, which are commercial services. In saying this I am setting myself against a number of theorists in bioethics who argue that we should see health care as one commodity among many, and who endorse a market model of health care provision. This market model of medicine assumes a simplified, atomistic individualism, one that presumes that people are primarily bundles of preferences or desires, and that they go through life as rational choosers, making decisions on the basis of the best way to satisfy the maximum number of preferences. The preferences themselves are not inherently rank ordered, and cannot be, and so there is no inherent difference between purchasing the health care needed to set one's broken leg and purchasing a new sofa. Both are simply lifestyle choices. The desire for treatment of the broken leg happens to be a very strong and immediate desire for most people, so that we would be surprised at the customer who allowed his leg to remain broken in order to purchase the sofa, but in this view there is nothing inherently irrational in preferring the sofa, nor anything immoral in letting the availability and price of either be set by the market.

I would argue, on the contrary, that basic health care is not like other commodities. Health care is one of the necessities of life, in the same category as clean water, shelter, basic citizen rights, and education.[22] Without any of these, human life is destroyed or perverted. The level at which a given society can provide these basic necessities at a given point in history will vary, but a society that fails to provide some basic minimum is unjust.[23] That society should provide access to these basic necessities is suggested by the fact that parents are not allowed much leeway in providing them for their children.

Parents can fail to provide fashionable clothing for their children without doing something morally wrong. But parents who fail to provide education, water, or food for their children are condemned, and this condemnation is as close to a moral universal as one is likely to find. Likewise, adult individuals who are unable to provide these things for themselves are taken to be incompetent and generally entrusted to some sort of guardian. While there are many cultural differences about what counts as an adequate education, or about what it means to protect basic citizenship rights, such as the right to be safe from rape and murder, disagreements about the specifics should not blind us to the fact that human cultures do treat these as issues basic to life and society, not as issues of choice and lifestyle.

Just as these other basic goods are not properly treated as commodities, the provision of basic health care should not be governed solely by market mechanisms. If we see health care as a matter of central human importance, not as a pure commodity—though it is governed by social rules that may take market forces into account—then we need to look carefully at practices, such as the provision of ARTs, that blur the boundaries between health care and market production. In particular, when thinking about how providers of ARTs present themselves and conceptualize their provision of services, it seems important to consciously recognize that what such providers are offering is not, strictly speaking, health care, but a service aimed at the provision of a child.

This is particularly important when we reflect on the risks that ARTs can pose to both the woman who undergoes various techniques and the hoped-for child. If ARTs were needed health care treatment, then it would make sense to trade off future risks for healing now. But if ARTs are a matter of providing a service that is not directly health related, then the health risks it poses need to be balanced against commercial profit and consumer desires. This is a different calculation, and while it still may be the case that, for example, some women will choose to undergo potentially risky procedures in order to attain the desired result, they should not be encouraged to undergo them as if they were necessary medical treatment. Further, techniques that are untested in mammalian species, as many ARTs currently are, and those that pose completely unknown risks for the children involved should not be engaged in as if they were justified medical treatments. Imposing unknown risks on children for the sake of commercial profit is morally unacceptable.

It is important, then, for clinics that offer ARTs to do so in a way that is open and honest about what is being offered. Any practice that misdescribes itself to obscure its real nature is morally suspect. If clinics offering ARTs cannot accurately describe what they are doing, and if they find themselves choosing to describe their services in deliberately misleading terms, then health care practitioners have a moral responsibility to refuse to be involved in such practices. Moreover, practitioners have a moral obligation to refrain from offering untested techniques to consumers under the rubric of treatment.

On a similar note, the practice of describing gamete selling as "donation" and the implication that gamete donation is simply a medical treatment that restores fertility to infertile people is clearly problematic. Clinics need to be willing to explore with clients the ramifications of using gametes from other people, in terms of the unknown risks of disease for the woman who gets pregnant, and in terms of the child's inability to know her or his genetic heritage in the future. Again, if the practices of such clinics rely on doublespeak to hide the reality of buying and selling gametes for the sake of producing a particular sort of child, then the practices are not morally justifiable.

It doesn't take deep moral insights to realize that commercial enterprises based on obscurantist language are morally problematic. But care theory offers us the resources for thinking about the wrongness of such relationships. When one party relies on misdescription to hide the problematic aspects of what it is doing to another, it demonstrates that its actions are generated by a concern not for the other's good but for its own. Care theory posits that morally acceptable relationships must never compromise the other's good for the sake of one's own benefit. This doesn't mean that all relationships must be completely altruistic, of course, as we noted in earlier discussions. But it does mean that the vulnerability of another should not be exploited for one's own benefit. Commercial transactions, for example, should be structured in terms that allow for both parties to get a fair benefit for their contribution; when a transaction would not be undergone if one party had full knowledge of the ramifications, then the transaction is morally suspect.

Practices that encourage or require a caregiver to consistently hide the nature of the practice from those involved in it are destructive of the moral integrity and sense of identity of the caregiver herself or himself. Those who choose to work in the field of ARTs need to be able to understand themselves as performing a job that does not involve consistent manipulation and dissimulation. Treating others in a manipulative way destroys one's own ability to see oneself as valuable and having moral dignity. So clinics need to structure their practices, and state their business goals, in terms that clearly state what their services are and what they can and cannot do. They also may need to provide access to genetic records for the children their techniques generate, so that those children can find out who their genetic parents are. Clinics, for the most part, do not provide such records, in part because of the expense of the record keeping involved, and in part to maintain the fiction that the gamete donors provide "infertility treatment" rather than genetic materials. But by making the commitment to provide these resources, clinics could demonstrate that they are cognizant of the nature of the services they offer and the moral responsibilities they thereby accrue. Some Canadian provinces, in fact, have explored the idea of requiring gamete donation to be a true donation, and have considered legislation that would prohibit payment for sperm and eggs. Clinics have lobbied hard against such legislation, as it will diminish the availability of sperm and eggs. But it is disingenuous to lobby against such legislation and continue to use the language of "donations." Accuracy and openness, at the very least, should be part of the moral expectations we have for clinics and those who operate them.

Clinics and researchers also need to moderate their rush to provide new techniques and procedures. There is, obviously, a heavy profit motive that drives this rush to offer new techniques, but it needs to be offset by a concern for the long-term effects of these techniques on the health and lives of those affected. Moderation, however, has not been the hallmark of clinics offering ARTs. As an example, consider the fact that the first American case of human IVF occurred in 1982, the first test of IVF in baboons was performed five years later, and the first tests of IVF in chimpanzees occurred several years after that. Many of the techniques currently being used in IVF have never been tested on animals. Women who undergo hormone stimulation and egg harvesting cannot investigate the risks involved because so few studies have been done on animals, and the record for humans is incomplete and inconclusive. Future risks to children generated by ARTs have not been investigated, and no animal studies exist for comparison. Critics of ARTs argue that ARTs are the only medical interventions that are tested on humans before they are tested on animals, and this should be a matter of moral shame for clinics and providers.

Finally, clinics and other providers of ARTs need to avoid using psychological pressure and manipulation. First-person accounts of infertility treatment have noted the intense pressure prospective parents experience to spare no expense and to undergo the most invasive treatments for the sake of having a child.[24] Psychological pressure of this sort is commercially successful, no doubt, but it is not morally acceptable, and practitioners need to be clear about their moral responsibilities in this area.

Readers at this point may be shaking their heads and arguing that I have spoken of all sorts of moral responsibilities on the part of clinics, practitioners, and researchers. This might seem hopelessly idealistic. In the face of enormous profits, what practitioner or researcher would hesitate to offer untested procedures to clients? If readers find themselves thinking this, then they should recognize that ARTs are, by this very description, recognized as services, not health care treatments. There are any number of health care treatments available that practitioners will not provide to clients, regardless of willingness to pay, unless the procedure is clearly indicated because of health risks or harms. The fact that we often assume that profit should drive the delivery of ARTs is indicative of the extent to which we accept the notion that they are a commercial service, not a health care treatment.

I do think that government regulation of these services is essential, as I argue in the next section. But in this section I have been concerned to think through what it would mean for clinics, providers, and researchers to offer these services in a morally responsible way. We should not assume that all providers are completely motivated by profit, with no concern about the moral aspects of their provision, nor should we assume that only economic factors influence the decisions people make. It is more respectful of people's moral nature to articulate the moral values at stake and assume that at least some will consider moral issues to be important in determining their actions. Those who offer ARTs are not incapable of offering them in a morally responsible way. Doing so, however, requires that we clear away some of the language that is used to obscure the moral ramifications of various practices and assess their moral status clearly and accurately.

IV. Social Structures, Legal Regulation, and ARTs

Care theory requires us to look at social structures and assess how they affect the provision of care for everyone concerned in society. Because care theory operates with a conception of human nature that involves relational identity and corporate responsibility, no care theory analysis is adequate unless it addresses issues at the level of large-scale relationships and corporate existence. When we step back and take this sort of a broad view of ARTs and the role they play in society at large, what sorts of ethical issues do we find? Several issues that have been raised in our earlier analysis—particularly the health risks of ARTs; the commodification of childbearing, with its implications for social understandings of parenthood; and the pronatalist aspects of ARTs—lend support to the claim that there should be government regulation of the provision of ARTs.

Regulation is very different from a complete ban. Because procreative decisions should not be made at the state level, it is important to preserve realms of individual decision making. But individuals have real freedom to make procreative decisions on their own only when they can make those decisions with full information and full responsibility. Thus regulation is necessary to prevent manipulation and deceit. Individual freedom also must be limited by the rights of those others who are affected by an individual's decisions. While parents should have broad liberty to make procreative decisions, they should not have the liberty to make decisions that will impose unacceptable risks and burdens on the children they generate. All family law attempts to protect parental autonomy while also protecting children's health and well-being, and the regulation of ARTs should do the same.

As has been mentioned several times in this discussion, the health risks of ARTs are not well researched. The long-term effects of hormonal stimulation with respect to women's cancer risks are not well known, nor do we have much information about how various IVF techniques may affect women's fertility. This is ironic, given the language of "infertility treatment," since some of the purported "treatments" may actually decrease women's fertility. The risks ARTs pose for the children generated by the various techniques are also unknown. Some techniques are unlikely to pose many health risks for children, of course. Sperm donation, assuming a healthy donor, offers few health risks other than those we all face due to unknown genetic inheritance. One risk that some critics have noted, however, is the risk that overuse of a single donor can represent to children who grow to maturity without knowing who their genetic parents are. In at least one case a clinic's main donor was the physician who ran the clinic.[25] Since most of the parents who used the clinic lived in the same general geographical area, the chances of children from unrelated families sharing a common parent were increased dramatically—as were the concomitant risks of those children marrying a genetic half-sibling and having children of their own with genetic anomalies. This could be dealt with by limitations on the number of donations sperm donors are allowed to make, as well as by requiring information about donors to be provided to their children when the children reach the age of maturity. Both of these regulations have been considered in Canada, and both would offer some protection to the children so generated. It is also patently obvious that sperm donation should not be permitted without testing for diseases transmitted via bodily fluids. Sperm banks in the United States are not required to test sperm donors for HIV or Hepatitus B or C—though many do so voluntarily—and this is clearly an area in which regulation is needed. In terms of the long-term dangers other ARTs may pose to children, regulation should be in place to prohibit procedures that have not been tested on animals. Clinics have strong economic reasons to provide the newest and most exciting treatments as quickly as possible, and recognition of that economic motivation provides a reason for regulation. This seems a rather minimal requirement, but it would rule out many of the treatments offered today.

This brings us to the next issue: the commodification of children. When ARTs are offered without an adequate understanding of their long-term risks for the children involved, the value of the lives of the children generated by these techniques is subordinated to the economic profitability of the technology. Even though both the prospective parents and the clinics speak the language of love for children, it is clear the interests of the children are subordinated to the economic motivations of clinics and the desire satisfaction of the prospective parents. When the interests of the children are so clearly not what is central to either deciding party, it is hard to argue that the motivating factor is love of the child to be generated. Instead this case is one in which the child is understood as existing to satisfy another's preferences, as is born out by the racial considerations mentioned earlier. The child is treated as a product that must meet certain specifications to be acceptable—racial specifications, genetic specifications, and health specifications—none of which is compatible with a concern for the child's own good.

This suggests that allowing ARTs to continue to be provided in the largely unregulated way they are currently offered will contribute to the perception that the proper relationship between parent and child is one of ownership and property rights. Children, this suggests, are properly thought of as belonging to the parents and as existing for the sake of the parents. Particularly when the children are acquired at great expense by their parents, these practices contribute to a perception of children as objects of purchase, to be held to certain standards of acceptability.

From the perspective of care ethics, an ethics that requires moral relationships to focus on the good of the other, and an ethics that emphasizes the need for familial relationships to involve attentiveness to the particularity of the other as an individually valued self, this is a situation that is morally unacceptable. If ARTs are to be offered in a morally acceptable way, they must be structured in ways that prevent the commodification of children and clearly express the proper relationship between parent and child. This will involve some limitations on the rights of parents to do as they please in generating and in raising children. Of course we already impose some limitations on what parents can do to and for their children, and we do so properly. Such limitations need not involve gross state intervention into most parents' lives. In many cases parents are the best judges of what is good for a child, and state intervention would cause more harm than good. We need not advocate totalitarian intrusion into the family simply because we recognize that some parents do not act in the best interests of their children. But we should be willing to regulate practices that can be foreseen to encourage parental abuse of children's interests, as we have done in the case of child labor laws. Parents are not allowed to hire out their ten-year-old children to work in sweatshops, and few of us consider this an unacceptable infringement on parental autonomy. In the same way, the regulation of ARTs for the sake of preventing parents from putting future children at risk and from treating children as commodities seems well within the bounds of proper social structuring.

Arguments that rest on protecting the interests of children are relatively easy to make, since we all can see the vulnerability of children and recognize that laissez-faire government policies are insufficient in their case. The issue of regulation designed to protect adult individuals is another issue, and one we need to address when we turn to the issue of pronatalism. Care theory is not a libertarian account of proper social structures. It does not assume that all regulation of adult interactions should be kept at an absolute minimum. Nel Noddings's recent discussion of issues such as homelessness and drug abuse, for example, assumes that the state does have a proper role to play in protecting and supporting individuals who cannot care for themselves.[26] At the same time feminists are very wary of government regulation of women's lives, since the history of such interventions is not one that gives a woman confidence in the profeminist abilities of the state. So there is a careful balance to be struck here.

But the fact that a careful balance must be struck is not a reason to reject any state regulation of practices that affect women, so our task is to think about how the regulation of ARTs might affect pronatalist perceptions about women. Sexism and its concomitant pronatalism function much like racism in terms of structuring people's perceptions of social realities. One of the lessons to be learned from philosophical and psychological studies of racism is that dominant groups are not the only part of society that accepts racist beliefs. When a society holds racist beliefs, those beliefs are internalized by both dominant and subordinate groups. Adequate responses to racism, then, require addressing internalized racist assumptions held by both dominant and subordinate groups. Within portions of the African American community, for example, there is a strong preference for light skin and straightened hair. While this preference is shaped by the racism of the society in which we all live, it is internalized and entrenched in the very sector of society to whom it is oppressive. We find the same dynamic in the case of sexism. Both men and women internalize sexist valuations of women's and men's lives. As a result, women are often strongly opposed to changes in women's social and political roles. Groups of women opposed female suffrage during first-wave feminism, and groups of women opposed passage of the Equal Rights Amendment to the U.S. Constitution. This is a dynamic that has complicated feminist political action from its inception.

Pronatalism is the socially entrenched view that women's primary or sole worth lies in giving birth to and mothering children. In the context of ARTs, pronatalism appears in the expectation that women should be willing to undergo almost any procedure, regardless of its invasiveness, painfulness, or risk, in order to have a child. Moreover, this willingness is not seen as supererogatory, but as the expected reaction of a properly "womanly" woman. This view of women's role has a long history. Sigmund Freud, for example, placed female masochism and the notion that women can find satisfaction only in giving birth to a son at the heart of his account of women's psychological development. Some women who describe their experiences of infertility use the language of agony, of inescapable, mind-numbing pain; others describe how their whole identity is tied up with becoming a mother and how infertility leads them to become suicidal.[27] Without diminishing the very real pain these women feel, we need to step back and think about why they would experience infertility in this way. Just as we can recognize that, when an African American sees her own dark skin as ugly, she is expressing the internalized values of a racist society, so when an infertile woman sees her life as meaningless she is expressing the internalized values of a sexist society. In both cases, we may recognize the reality and strength of the feelings and still argue that they should be challenged, not endorsed.

Now, clearly, the state has no role to play in dictating to adults what desires they can have. Mind control is no part of a properly ordered state. But the state does have a role to play in regulating what the acceptable range of activities in pursuit of those desires can be. The state cannot dictate that women and men, both, see women's value in terms of a broader range of activities than the single-minded pursuit of motherhood. But the state can properly say that the pursuit of motherhood at all costs, regardless of the physical harm it may cause, is not acceptable. To continue our analogy, consider the use of skin creams that claim to lighten one's skin. An individual who hates her dark skin might be willing to use any cream that claims to lighten skin, and she may not be concerned about long-term risks. But if a lightening cream poses a serious long-term risk of causing skin cancer, it should not be marketed, regardless of the demand for it. In the same way, ARTs that pose serious long-term health risks for women should be limited or banned. It is not the government's responsibility to try to change women's belief that their lives can be meaningful only when they experience motherhood. That would be an unacceptable infringement of freedom of speech and thought. But it is the government's responsibility to regulate practices that exploit this belief for economic gain while posing a serious risk to the health of the women involved.

Finally, the state also has a role to play in sorting out the various understandings of parenthood that are at stake in the use of ARTs. The law has traditionally assumed that biological parent status occurs in tandem with the social parenting role. Departures from the conjunction of the two require legal oversight, so that state regulation is needed for adoption procedures, custody in divorce cases, and the like. ARTs, however, separate these various aspects of parenting, allowing the provider of either gamete to be separate from the gestational mother, who may also be separate from the social parents of a child. Some feminist theorists have seen this as a situation to be celebrated, as a postmodern deconstruction of the family. But before we leap to celebrate such new practices, we should stop and think about what might get lost in a new definition of family ties as completely chosen and arbitrary.

Family relationships usually cannot be subsumed under the contract model of relationships that lies at the heart of much of contemporary political theory. Contractual relationships make sense in the context of economic transactions between roughly equal parties. But relationships between individuals with vast disparities in vulnerability and power are badly described by a simplistic contract model. Familial relationships in particular are very badly modeled by contract theories. Annette Baier's discussion of trust, for example, highlights the way vulnerability and intimacy require relationships in which neither party is completely free to negotiate for contractual advantage.[28] Given the fact that children come into the world completely vulnerable and needy, we should recognize that contractual models of familial relationships are absurdly inappropriate for capturing the moral responsibilities of such relationships.

If we were operating within the model of some contemporary ethical theories we might think that the only alternative to a contractual model is ownership. If children cannot function as rational contractors, which they patently cannot, then they must be outside the moral compact, and thus they fall under the category of things that are owned, things over which the owners have largely unregulated property rights. This view of children is even worse than the contract view. From a care perspective, however, children are neither fictional rational contractors nor property that adults can own and dispose of as they please. Children are vulnerable others whose very vulnerability places an enormous responsibility on us to arrange for their care, and to permit them to grow into full and flourishing members of a caring community. Part of that responsibility involves creating and maintaining structures that can provide adequate care for children and resources to support caregivers in their work.

Parental responsibilities, then, are not a matter of pure individual choice and preference, nor can they be avoided by merely declaring some contract null and void. But the legal structure that currently governs the provision of ARTs suggests otherwise. It allows economic incentives for people to provide gametes without requiring any responsibility for the life that will ensue. At the same time, legally permitting surrogacy undermines the notion that ties of physical support and affection create responsibility (or legal relationship) between parent and child. The widespread use of ARTs supports a view of parenthood as ownership, including the notion that children who fail to live up to certain measures of adequacy should be "returnable" or discardable.

A more robust and sustainable view of parenthood would insist that parental responsibilities cannot be treated as simple contractual matters, nor can they be treated as a matter of property ownership. A legal paradigm that focuses on the well-being of the child would produce better and more consistent legislation in terms of defining parental relationships and responsibilities. Gamete donors, for example, would be required to provide familial health histories and to limit donations in any given geographical region. The contributions of gestational mothers would be recognized as relational bonds producing legal rights to a continued relationship. While biological ties would be seen as important, they would not always be allowed to trump associational ties, so that biological parents who wanted to reverse an adoption would be required to show that the reversal would be for the benefit of the child, rather than a matter of parental property right. These changes would require a legal paradigm of children as individuals whose vulnerability and immaturity are not taken to be proof that they have no value, but are taken instead as evidence that they deserve heightened protection and care. This perspective would provide a far better conceptual basis for state regulation of ARTs than the contractual model currently in use.

V. Conclusion

Care theory provides a perspective from which to understand why ARTs and related procedures are morally problematic; it also has more explanatory power than the contractual model of ethics that structures much contemporary thought. Rather than dealing with assisted reproduction in terms of basic property rights and abstract libertarian freedoms, care theory encourages us to think about how we structure social practices and institutions to provide adequate care for the most vulnerable in society and their caregivers. Various ARTs are currently offered in the context of a system that commodifies children, treats women as of merely instrumental value, and threatens to weaken the bonds of care that should hold between parent and child. They exploit for economic purposes people's desires for loving family relationships.

It is not the case, however, that something inherent in the nature of ARTs is immoral. ARTs are techniques that can serve either good or evil, depending on the context in which they are used and the uses to which they are put. We cannot analyze their rightness or wrongness outside of the social, cultural, and historical context within which they are used. From that contextual perspective we can see how ARTs may fit into a community that values care. We live in a society that still struggles with both racism and sexism. Not surprisingly, the new reproductive technologies operate within that context in ways that reinforce both racism and sexism. We live in the context of a late-capitalist society, in which all practices are pulled toward the economic logic of profit at any cost. In that context it is very difficult to structure commercially provided assisted reproduction without falling into the commodification of children and women's bodies. But we can conceptualize a different ordering of society, one that centers on the development and provision of care in the context of relationships of trust and responsibility. The question is whether we are willing to revise our priorities to make care count for more than cash.

Notes

1. Nancy K. Miller, "Mothers, Daughters, and Autobiography: Maternal Legacies and Cultural Criticism," in *Mothers in Law: Feminist Theory and the Legal Regulation of Motherhood*, ed. Martha Albertson Fineman and Isabel Karpin (New York: Columbia University Press, 1995), p. 9.

2. Simone de Beauvoir, *The Second Sex*, trans. H. M. Parshley (New York: Knopf, 1993), pp. 33–34.

3. Daryl Koehn, *Rethinking Feminist Ethics: Care, Trust and Empathy* (New York: Routledge, 1998), p. 15.

4. Jürgen Habermas, *The Future of Human Nature* (Oxford: Blackwell, 2003), pp. 18–19.

5. Some of the complexities of this situation are discussed in Kate Harrison's "Fresh or Frozen: Lesbian Mothers, Sperm Donors, and Limited Fathers," in *Mothers in Law: Feminist Theory and the Legal Regulation of Motherhood*, ed. Martha Albertson Fineman and Isabel Karpin (New York: Columbia University Press, 1995), pp. 167–201.

6. See the *BBC News* report, October 26, 1997. Regulations differ in the United States and United Kingdom, but the wide availability of sperm, which can now be ordered over the Internet, makes regulation and the provision of adequate safeguards difficult.

7. See, for example, the *Sydney Morning Herald*, January 7, 2003, for an account of an Australian case in which the Brisbane Supreme Court turned down a woman's request for retrieval of her dead fiancé's sperm.

8. See Gregory E. Pence, "Surrogacy: Baby M," in *Classic Cases in Medical Ethics*, 2nd ed. (New York: McGraw-Hill, 1995); and Mary Briody Mahowald, *Women and Children in Health Care: An Unequal Majority* (Oxford: Oxford University Press, 1993), pp. 104–10.

9. For a discussion of the many thorny ethical and legal issues surrogacy raises, see Lawrence Kaplan and Rosemarie Tong, *Controlling Our Reproductive Destiny: A Technological and Philosophical Perspective* (Cambridge, Mass.: MIT Press, 1996), chap. 10, "Contracted Motherhood."

10. For a summary of some of the relevant literature, see Laura Shanner and Jeff Nisker, "Bioethics for Clinicians: Assisted Reproductive Technologies," *Canadian Medical Association Journal* 164 (May 2001): 1589–94.

11. Elizabeth Anderson, "Is Women's Labor a Commodity?" *Philosophy and Public Affairs* 19, no. 1 (1990): 71–87. Anderson's argument focuses primarily on surrogacy, but her articulation of why commodification is wrong provides the framework for almost all subsequent discussions.

12. The phrase is Oliver O'Donovan's. See his *Begotten or Made?* (New York: Oxford University Press, 1984). This concern is also a central aspect of the arguments made by Leon Kass against the new reproductive technologies, especially cloning. See his "The Wisdom of Repugnance," in *The Ethics of Human Cloning*, ed. Leon Kass and James Q. Wilson (Washington, D.C.: AEI Press, 1998), pp. 3–59. The concern that children be "begotten," not made, is also invoked in Catholic arguments against cloning and other assisted reproductive techniques. See, for example, John Haas, "A Catholic View of Cloning," in *The Human Cloning Debate*, ed. Glenn McGee (Berkeley, Calif.: Berkeley Hills Books, 2000), pp. 276–84.

13. Elizabeth Anderson's essay, cited in note 11, develops this argument.

14. Barbara Ehrenreich and Deidre English, *For Her Own Good* (New York: Anchor, 1979).

15. See Gena Correa et al., *Man-Made Women: How New Reproductive Technologies Affect Women* (Indianapolis: Indiana University Press, 1987); and Robyn Rowland, *Living Laboratories: Women and Reproductive Technologies* (Indianapolis: Indiana University Press, 1992).

16. An Australian study did find some long-term risks associated with hormone stimulation: *Long-Term Effects on Women from Assisted Conception* (Canberra: National Health and Medical Research Council, Commonwealth of Australia, 1995). A more recent study did not: A. Venn et al., "Risk of Cancer after Use of Fertility Drugs with In-Vitro Fertilization," *Lancet* 354 (1999): 1586–90. There are not many studies on this, and since IVF has been available for only about twenty years, long-term studies of the risks are only now becoming possible.

17. Animal studies have not been done on these techniques. The literature provides references to human studies only.

18. Mary Anne Warren, "IVF and Women's Interests: An Analysis of Feminist Concerns" in *Bioethics* 2, no. 1 (1988): 37–57.

19. These clauses are generally included not out of concern for the surrogate herself, but because of the legal requirements that prohibit baby selling. Surrogacy, in the states that permit it, is generally treated more like an open adoption than a case of producing a baby for sale, and adoptions require a certain period during which a mother can change her mind.

20. Pence, "Surrogacy: Baby M," pp. 129–30.

21. Elaine Tyler May, *Barren in the Promised Land: Childless Americans and the Pursuit of Happiness* (Cambridge, Mass.: Harvard University Press, 1995), pp. 249–50.

22. For an overview of some of these issues, see Mark Hall, *Making Medical Spending Decisions: The Law, Ethics, and Economics of Rationing Mechanisms* (Oxford: Oxford University Press, 1997).

23. Tom Beauchamp and James Childress, *Principles of Biomedical Ethics*, 4th ed. (Oxford: Oxford University Press, 1994), pp. 348–61.

24. See, for example, Rowland, *Living Laboratories*, pp. 256–60; May, *Barren*, pp. 230–41; and Renate Klein, *The Exploitation of Desire: Women's Experiences with In Vitro Fertilisation* (Geelong, Australia: Deakin University Press, 1986).

25. The case occurred in Virginia; the physician's name is Cecil Jacobson. For a discussion of the many legal and societal complications involved in various techniques of gamete "donation," see Fred Norton, "Assisted Reproduction and the Frustration of Genetic Affinity: Interest, Injury, and Damages," *New York University Law Review* 74 (1999): 793–843.

26. Nel Noddings, *Starting at Home: Caring and Social Policy* (Berkeley and Los Angeles: University of California Press, 2002), part 3, "Toward a Caring Society."

27. See, for example, May, *Barren*, pp. 222–25.

28. Annette Baier, *Moral Prejudices: Essays on Ethics* (Cambridge, Mass.: Harvard University Press, 1994), especially chaps. 1, 3, 7, and 12.

CHAPTER SIX

Care and Cloning

Care theory has generally been thought to be appropriate to familial relationships, so the various techniques of assisted reproduction might be
thought to be an unproblematic choice of topic for a care analysis. But can
care theory address more abstract, less personal questions? In particular, can
care theory offer anything as a tool of analysis in the context of issues that
are clearly social and political rather than primarily personal? When we
speak about issues of how we order our collective lives, structure our society,
and rule on disputed issues of rights and responsibilities, we have entered the
realm of justice. In the wake of Gilligan's *In a Different Voice* it has become
fairly commonplace to oppose the voice of care to the voice of justice, and
with some justification. There are certain conceptions of justice that exclude
many of the central considerations of an ethic of care. Part of the value of
Gilligan's work is her identification of these conceptions and the ideas and
considerations they exclude. But rather than oppose justice to care, in this
chapter I develop a suggestion made by Marilyn Friedman that an adequate
understanding of either care or justice is impossible without taking into consideration the concerns and moral concepts of both "voices."[1] That is, I argue that an account of justice that incorporates the picture of human nature
I have been developing as the basis of an ethic of care offers a better vantage
point from which to analyze public issues.

I call the view of justice that excludes care concerns "abstract justice"
to capture its assumption that justice is properly thought of as a matter of
abstract principles, applied by a rational process, to roughly substitutable

individuals who are themselves largely characterized by rationality and autonomy. The conception of rationality inherent in such a view is primarily a matter of logical consistency. Although this abstract conception is sometimes assumed to be *the* meaning of justice, I will argue that there are other, rival versions of the notion of justice.

If we begin, not with abstract individualism, but with the picture of human existence I have been sketching, a picture that is central to an ethic of care, we necessarily derive a very different picture of what it would mean to structure our social lives in a just way. That is, to the extent that we take seriously the notion that humans are socially constituted, embodied, finite, and affective, we need a different picture of the nature and demands of justice. Likewise, if we revise our notion of rationality to include affective and experiential components, we need to challenge the assumption that reason can deliberate about justice without taking into account the lived experience of those about whom we reason. The contrast between these two accounts of justice can be seen most clearly if we consider some concrete cases.

Two specific issues, both of which appear in discussions of the new genetic technologies, highlight the contrast between these two notions of justice. The first issue is the moral appropriateness of the goal of general improvement of the human genetic code, or eugenics. The second issue is what ethical factors should govern public policy about cloning. These two issues go to the heart of debates about the new genetic technologies, the first because it poses the most central question about the new genetic technologies,[2] and the second because it raises issues about personal identity and the meaning of human life. Both issues are dealt with in one of the most influential recent discussions of genetic technologies, *From Chance to Choice: Genetics and Justice*.[3] I use the analysis offered by this book as an exemplar of abstract justice reasoning and argue that care offers an importantly different analysis of both issues.

I. Abstract Justice, Eugenics, and Cloning

Let's begin with the abstract justice analysis of eugenics and of cloning. *From Chance to Choice* offers one of the most thorough treatments of the ethical dimensions of the new genetic technologies available today. The book was written jointly by some of the most prominent bioethicists in contemporary practice, Allen Buchanan, Dan Brock, Norman Daniels, and Daniel Wickler. It is a remarkable book in many ways, informed by the years of experience of all of its authors, offering an understanding of issues raised by genetic technologies that is sophisticated and current, and (perhaps most remarkable of all, in this day of individual achievement) produced as a unified project by four authors who are not in the same theoretical camps by any means, but who were able to reach agreement, for the most part, on a wide variety of issues. Because of the status of its authors and the nature of the book, it is clearly one of the most important contributions to the current debate.

I think this is a valuable and timely book, so, while I am somewhat critical of it in what follows, I also want to emphasize its importance. I have learned enormous amounts about the moral issues from working through them in the company of these authors, and find their work to be consistently of a high quality and thought provoking. At the same time, however, I think that the book exemplifies the tendency for an abstract account of justice to take over the public debates about the new genetic technologies in ways that are problematic.

The methodological assumptions adopted in *From Chance to Choice* offer a classic example of abstract justice reasoning. The basic reasoning pattern relies on a "wide reflective equilibrium," moving back and forth between general principles of ethics and of reasoning and specific cases that may challenge or modify those principles (372). The authors assume that such a wide reflective equilibrium will permit participation in the debate by agents from almost any perspective—communitarians (at least those of a slightly liberal bent), libertarians, religious believers, agnostics, atheists, liberals, conservatives, and so on (373–74). All these voices, it is assumed, can bring arguments and concerns to the table; these arguments and concerns will be heard and adjudicated and incorporated into the moral consensus the authors intend to construct. The agents who are to participate in the formation of this wide reflective equilibrium are assumed to be morally equal individuals capable of critical reflection (379). The authors specifically reject concern about the well-being or flourishing of collectivities except insofar as it affects the condition of individuals.

Within this general framework the authors adopt a synthesis of two basic sets of values, the first the values of a public health model that adopts a largely consequentialist methodology (11–12), and the second the values of a personal choice model that is assumed to maximize individual autonomy (12). These two value sets restrict the authors' consideration of moral factors to those of public goods and private choice. What the authors do not consider is whether these options may both be too limited right from the start, with their assumptions of the basic uniformity and substitutability of humans.

Proceeding from this basic methodology (wide reflective equilibrium) and this goal (finding a *media via* between consequentialist public policy and individual libertarianism), the authors complete their theoretical context with an analysis of the notion of justice. Justice, they write, concerns primarily two issues, equal opportunity and the morality of inclusion (16). Equal opportunity questions will generate concerns about how much society should intervene to prevent disadvantages due the "natural lottery" of genetic endowments. One of the important contributions of this book is the authors' careful analysis of the various ways in which the notion of equal opportunity can be interpreted, generating different accounts of what individuals can claim as a matter of justice. Issues of the morality of inclusion, the authors argue, have to do with questions of how society is structured, specifically how the "dominant cooperative framework" adopted by a society creates or accommodates differential abilities. There is a societal obligation, the authors contend, based on justice concerns, to work collectively toward developing cooperative frameworks that allow as many individuals as possible to fully participate in societal practices (301). That is, given a choice between structures that exclude certain classes of people (those with limited mobility, for example) and structures that include them, all things being equal, society has an obligation, based in the principle of justice, to choose those structures that enhance inclusiveness.

These are both important concerns, and the authors' development of them is perspicuous and careful. Again, however, I would like to note the limited nature of this abstract account of justice. It is a fairly contentless account of justice, one that makes procedural but not substantive assumptions about what justice demands. It fits well with the earlier analysis of the moral issues at hand here—the consequentialist concern with the public good and the individual libertarian concern with autonomy. What is missing is a clear sense of what human lives may require for flourishing in terms of situated relationships, particular identities, or the development of temperament and character. A framework of abstract justice, with its assumption of separated, largely self-defining individuals, is not entirely satisfactory from the standpoint we have been developing in this book—that of humans as necessarily connected to each other in webs of relationships and dependencies.

To see how the ethical framework developed by the authors of *From Chance to Choice* works in practice it is necessary to turn to two specific issues that they consider, eugenics and cloning. I've selected these two because they stretch the authors' framework to the breaking point, and we can see the ways in which standard theories of justice are insufficient for the purposes to which they are put in contemporary society. After detailing the authors' treatment of these two issues, I note where the strains and tensions in their thought appear, and then turn to an alternative conception of justice, one generated from the care perspective I've been developing in this book, and argue that such a perspective allows us to respond to the strains and tensions surrounding reasoning about these two issues in ways that are more satisfactory. From a perspective informed by care we can understand these issues better, and also explain why abstract accounts of justice are less capable of generating satisfactory analyses.

The first substantive issue the authors of *From Chance to Choice* address in their discussion of genetic justice is that of eugenics and the history of social interventions designed to enhance the "social genetic endowment." This is an important place to begin, since the eugenics movement casts a long and extremely dark shadow over any contemporary movements that aim at the "genetic improvement" of segments (or all) of society. The authors begin with a brief summary of the history of the various eugenics movements, noting that, although we tend to equate eugenics with the Nazi regime, it was a much more widespread movement, with proponents on both political Left and Right, and international in scope.[4] Further, the authors argue, it relied on three core assumptions. The first assumption was that of *degeneration*, the claim that society faced a widespread threat of loss of fitness due to the increase of certain traits in society. The second thesis, the *heritability of traits*, argued that the traits that posed the risk to social survival were genetically based. Finally, eugenics depended on the claim that the method by which these inherited, "degenerate" traits could be diminished was *breeding*, that by selective reproduction human society could change the frequency of such genes and so reverse the trend toward degeneration (40–42).

Each of these theses comes in for analysis in *From Chance to Choice*. The degeneration thesis, the authors note, was viciously classist and racist from its inception, as well as simply false (52). But the ethical wrongness of the thesis is attributed to the individual moral failings of its proponents, not to the very nature of such general claims about the social genetic endowment. The racism of the movement's supporters is to be condemned, but the basic concern for the "betterment of society" through genetic means is not in and of itself morally unacceptable. "In short," the authors write, "the central theses of a social movement, including its moral premises, ought not to be dismissed because of the intellectual and ethical failings of its adherents" (45). We see here one of the omissions to which an abstract account of justice can be prone. The degeneracy thesis was an integral part of the eugenics movement, and the authors note that the movement would not have been successful without it. But they do not directly address the extent to which the contemporary impetus for genetic technologies relies on either overt or implicit assumptions that too many of the "wrong sorts of humans" are coming into existence.

With respect to the heritability thesis, the authors are quite careful to note that blanket genetic improvement may be outside the bounds of genetic manipulation. They note, for example, that intelligence *simpliciter* is too complex a trait to be "improved" in some absolute sense (153), though they are willing to imagine cases in which individuals receive a "genetic enhancement treatment" that renders those individuals more resistant to respiratory diseases and depression, and able to do better on tests of memory skills than the average (4). The authors occasionally shift back and forth between analysis of specific and (relatively) identifiable genetic disorders (achondroplasia, hereditary deafness) and broader characteristics (aggression, empathy) and assume that if cures for the former are morally acceptable, then "improvements" in the latter might be morally acceptable. It is worth noting that many writers on these topics are not nearly so careful. Ethical discussions of genetic technologies are frequently shockingly unrealistic in their assumptions about the values of particular genetic endowments, suggesting that some of the assumptions that drove the eugenics movement remain strongly in force today.[5]

The third thesis of the eugenics movement, the breeding thesis, is rejected by the authors of *From Chance to Choice* because it is false. The presence of recessive genes and the complexities of human procreation doomed the early eugenics movement to failure. But with a better understanding of the human genome today, increasingly effective means for "improvement" have become available, so that this question can no longer be evaded. The authors' conclusion about the moral aspects of eugenics is, "Reprehensible as much of the eugenic program was, there is something unobjectionable and perhaps even morally required in the part of its motivation that sought to endow future generations with genes that might enable their lives to go better. We need not abandon this motivation if we can pursue it justly" (60).

In the chapter that follows their discussion of eugenics, the authors consider the importance of an account of human nature for their analysis, and argue that any substantive view of human nature is made problematic by advances in genetic technology that make possible the blurring of traditional boundaries between the human and the nonhuman. The authors do, however, consider two aspects of human nature to be relevant to the view they develop, namely the existence of inequalities among humans and a generalized obligation to prevent harm, both harm to specific individuals and harm to the human collectivity. The discussions of inequalities and harms are closely connected, since what it means to be harmed, largely, is to be made unable to compete equally in society with others. The one exception to the tendency to treat individuals as isolated units in a larger totality of society comes in an interesting subsection entitled "Pluralism and Liberalism" (176–78), in which the authors discuss the danger that smaller-scale communities pose and the way that genetic modification could exacerbate that danger.

The discussion is remarkable for its assumptions that only some people are members of such small-scale communities—people who appear to be very different from the writers and imagined readers of the volume—and that they present a danger to the liberal, tolerant, pluralistic state by existing as pockets of communal identity in a sea of pluralistic and noncommunal individuals. These community-identified "others" represent a danger, the authors think, in that they could decide to use the resources of genetic technology to modify the genetic makeup of members of their community. After extensive genetic modification, the community members might no longer recognize the common humanity of all people, which would destroy the possibility of mutual respect and toleration needed for existence in a liberal society. This threat is treated separately from the issue of eugenics and is considered largely as a problem that "we" will have to solve with respect to "them."

Eugenic concerns lie at the heart of assessments of the new genetic technologies. An author's moral assessment of eugenic concerns is a good predictor of how she or he will assess more specific genetic issues, and this is certainly the case for the authors of *From Chance to Choice*. Just as they evaluate eugenic concerns as having a moral core, but unjust implementation, so they evaluate other techniques, such as reproductive cloning, as morally acceptable, if carried out properly.

The authors discuss reproductive cloning under the general rubric of "Constraints and Permissions Allowed Parents" (181–203), as the last of a series of possible restrictions of parental rights that could be justified on the basis of the authors' moral assumptions and methodology. The presumption is that the parental right of reproduction stands as a basic factor in favor of allowing any technique of genetic modification that parents might wish to use on, or in the production of, their children, and this basic right can be overridden only by clear dangers or harms, whether to the parents, society at large, or the children who are so modified.

Cloning then comes in for fairly careful scrutiny in *From Chance to Choice*. The authors recognize that contemporary cloning techniques are not sufficiently developed to guarantee a reasonably high chance of a healthy child. This makes reproductive cloning, at the current time, an unacceptably risky technique to use on children. Until the technological prowess of experimenters increases to the point where cloning can take place without undue risk to the children so produced, permitting it is unacceptable, although the authors stress that limits on cloning due to fears about safety cannot be more stringent than those imposed on other reproductive methods (199).

But what about the other moral concerns that theorists have raised about reproductive cloning? One of the most central has been the issue of loss of identity—some opponents of cloning have argued that in cloning one predetermines the cloned individual's identity in ways that are problematic. This concern is largely dismissed by the authors. A cloned individual is not the same person as the originator of her or his genetic material, and so the concern that cloned individuals will fail to have a sufficiently "open future" is a matter of social (mis)perception. The authors refer to an individual cloned from another as a "later twin," and addressing Hans Jonas's argument that such a "later twin" would be denied the right to a fully individuated identity, they argue that, because crude genetic determinism is false (two individuals with identical genetic endowments are not ontologically identical), one cannot claim that a cloned individual has been harmed by the loss of an open-ended identity. Instead, they write,

> It seems more plausible to say that if the twin's future in reality remains open and his to freely choose, that someone's acting in a way that unintentionally leads him to believe his future is closed and determined has not violated his right to . . . an open future. Likewise, suppose you drive down the twin's street in your new car that is just like his, knowing that when he sees you he is likely to believe that you have stolen his car and, therefore, to abandon his driving plans for the day. You have not violated his property right to his car even though he may feel the same loss of opportunity to drive that day as if you had in fact stolen his car. In each case he is mistaken . . . and so no right of his . . . has been violated. (197–98)

Individuality and a unique identity, the authors seem to assume, are ontological facts about an individual, and so social perceptions about them that may be fallacious have no real bearing on their moral standing.

I believe the authors of *From Chance to Choice* dismiss the importance of the social perceptions of genetic determinism too quickly here. The impetus to produce a clone cannot, in practice, be divorced from the "crude genetic determinism" that the authors reject in this passage.[6] If one did not think that genes determined identity, then what impetus would there be for cloning? It is hard to see why parents would choose to produce a child through the complicated, expensive, and risky technique of cloning if they did not think that the cloned individual would *be*, in some sense, the individual cloned. While their perception would be logically false, its power would not be diminished, any more than the power of social perceptions of racial or gender stereotypes are diminished by their falsity.

We can see why logical falsity need not diminish the power of social perceptions if we turn to the issue of racial stereotypes. Racism is based on the assumption that racial categories are real and determinative of an individual's identity. Recent scientific studies of racial categories, however, have consistently shown that socially defined racial categories do not correlate with deep genetic divides. Racial differences are not based on deep genetic differences but on historically and culturally defined patterns of legal and social discrimination. The scientific demonstration that racial categories have no basis in biology, however, does not make race unimportant for an analysis of racism in contemporary society. Racial categories structure our experiences in fundamental ways. For example, as I noted in the last chapter, many white parents believe that they cannot parent an African American child. The lack of a biological basis for racial distinctions does not mean that racial distinctions do not affect people's lives in fundamental ways. Likewise, the social perception that a cloned individual is, in some sense, not a unique individual may be biologically false, but socially real, and may have profound effects on the person's life. Commonly held beliefs, true or false, are an important determinant of existence as a social being.

After considering the "loss of individuality" argument, the authors go on to consider other risks, harms, and benefits that might accompany cloning. Other moral theorists have argued that in using cloning techniques we illegitimately turn the process of reproduction into a technological feat—manufacturing rather than begetting new life, to use the phrase made famous by Oliver O'Donovan.[7] The authors of *From Chance to Choice* are largely dismissive of this concern. They enumerate a number of benefits that cloning could provide, such as allowing women who lack ova or men who lack sperm to produce children who are genetically related to them, or allowing parents to clone a child who dies. The authors do note that such a desire would be "based on a deep confusion" (200), since they have already argued that such a transfer of identity is not logically possible. The mistakenness of the desire is not seen as a reason to reject this benefit, however. The incongruity of the fact that they consider this benefit (based on a serious confusion) to be nonetheless legitimate, while proclaiming the parallel harm of the loss of an open future (based on precisely the same confusion) to be no harm at all should be apparent. Finally, they consider the possibility that pursuit of reproductive cloning techniques could give rise to advances in scientific knowledge.

The authors' conclusion after working through these various harms and benefits is that, while "individuals' important interests in reproductive freedom . . . do establish a moral presumption for permitting its use in some circumstances" (201), concerns about the safety of cloning, "are sufficient that human cloning should not go forward at this time, and so society has time for continuing public and professional debate to clarify and evaluate people's concerns and objections to cloning, together with the reasons to permit it" (202). It is safety concerns that should stand in the way of cloning, not concerns about how the practice of cloning might affect the way we understand ourselves and others.

II. Analysis: Seeing What Isn't There

What is left out of the analysis the authors of *From Chance to Choice* have given so far? In both the case of eugenics and the case of cloning, the authors assume that it is impossible to make substantive assumptions about human nature, and about what constitutes human flourishing or well-being. They do believe that substantive conclusions can be drawn about certain aspects of human life. For example, they do assume that an individual is better off not existing than existing with certain types of genetic defects. So certain types of harm are taken to be unquestionably incompatible with the good life for humans.

Further, the authors assume that there are only two levels of decision-making capacity—that of the individual and that of the whole society. Parents are the one exception to this, as the authors do acknowledge that parents come in pairs. But the authors' discussion of both the ethics of the eugenics movement and the ethics of cloning suggest that decisions go on only at the levels of the individual and the whole society. These are the levels at which harms and benefits can be identified and become issues in the public sphere. At the level of the whole society, or the "public good," we can speak of costs and benefits—the costs to society of children with handicaps, for example, or the benefits due to lower incidences of disease. At the level of the individual we can specify conditions that lessen a person's competitiveness in society, and so lessen her or his opportunities to succeed in the great game of life. Apart from these two levels of analysis, not much can be said in *From Chance to Choice* about how human life ought to be structured.

But there are other levels at which reflection goes on in human life. In particular we might need to think here about communities of identity that are smaller than national or state-level decision-making bodies. These groups can be religious, political, or other; they can be either voluntary or not; but they are of immense importance for thinking through how one ought to live and what sorts of lives are good ones. Further, it is not just the odd communitarian or two who exist in the contexts of such communities. As we noted while discussing Augustine's anthropology, all of us are dependent on such communities for our self-understandings and ability to live meaningful lives. If we conceptualize decisions about the new genetic technologies without taking these communities into account, we will frame issues badly.

For example, consider how differently a prenatal diagnosis of Down's syndrome would be understood in two different communities. Imagine that the first is a community that publicly values parents raising children with special needs, a community in which there are sufficient affectional ties to offer support for the parents and love for the child, and in which this family can understand itself as "normal." Imagine that the second is a community in which parents of children with special needs are criticized for spending extra time with their families, children with mental handicaps are objects of derision or dislike, and most community members treat disabilities as something shameful. Both communities might well offer education and training to children with handicaps, and so pass the test of the "morality of inclusion," but the decisions the parents face in these two communities are nonetheless very different. Framing questions about prenatal diagnosis in terms of private choice and public costs has the effect of making crucial aspects of the situation disappear.

The social context into which a child with special needs will be born is a matter of collective decision making. Sometimes this collective decision making takes place at the level of the whole society, but in many cases it arises at the level of medium-sized communities, and it can be sustained only by the allegiance of individuals to the community as a whole. Abstract accounts of justice obscure the collective aspects of human social life and the ways that such collective aspects may determine, in turn, issues that the authors of *From Chance to Choice* derogate to individual decision making, with some limitations imposed by the good of the social whole. Midlevel communities disappear on this picture, though their existence and identity are often crucial for the other levels.

The only way for abstract accounts of justice to frame ethical issues is in terms of individual rights or in terms of harms to individuals or to society as a whole. Harms to individuals are framed primarily in terms of physical disabilities, or conditions that minimize the ability to compete in society, while harms to society are framed largely in terms of economic costs (of providing care for people who are disabled, for example). Issues of collective identity are largely absent in *From Chance to Choice*, although they do come in for some attention during the authors' discussion of the morality of inclusion. Even in that section, however, the authors' main concern is whether society is structured to allow full participation by as many individuals as possible (a goal that I would endorse along with the authors). The section does not address issues of how a social group or society might choose to see itself in terms of collective identity, however. That is, there is no attention paid to the question of how local communities such as school boards, city councils, and ecumenical groups ought to understand collective identity in terms of the presence among us of those with mental handicaps.

This absence is typical of abstract accounts of justice, since one of the central features of such accounts is the ideal of neutrality with respect to individual definitions of the good human life, an ideal that also plays a central role in contemporary jurisprudence. But this neutrality, a number of critics have pointed out, is unsustainable.[8] For a society to protect its existence as an environment in which it is possible to pursue certain good lives, particularly the good life generally assumed by this abstract account of justice (a life marked by autonomous decision-making capacity and respect and toleration for others) the society must be concerned to inculcate certain virtues in its citizens, and these virtues cannot exist in the absence of communities of identity that sustain them.

From a care perspective we can make this point more strongly. For a society to be one in which differently abled individuals are respected and loved, and in which a wide variety of types of individuals can live fruitful and flourishing lives, the society must make a commitment to creating citizen members who respect and value others, regardless of levels of intelligence or mental acuity. But such a commitment requires that society limit some sorts of freedoms, for example the freedom to mock and harass individuals who are disabled, or the freedom to exclude such individuals or their families from the public sphere. More than this, a society that has such a commitment needs to strongly encourage the development of respect for individuals with disabilities. Such respect involves not only providing adequate public support for individuals with disabilities, in the form of education and care, but also requiring that others in society be educated to see such individuals as valuable and worthy of respect. An education of this sort often does go on in schools and workplaces, but it is hidden from view by the rhetoric of public neutrality.

Issues such as eugenics and cloning raise questions about the meaning of human life, questions about who and what count as human and how their lives are socially and technologically manipulated. In such contexts public neutrality about the structure of decent human lives is not an option. We cannot simply claim that any individual choice will be equally respected as long as others are not harmed; it is precisely by turning every issue into a question of individual choice that we create certain important sources of harm.

The ideal of neutrality rests on a further assumption, the assumption that individuals are largely self-defining. Public policy should be as neutral as possible with respect to individual choices, it is assumed, because individual choices reflect the ways in which autonomous individuals choose their identity. But this is a deeply falsifying notion of human identity as well. Care theory, Augustinian anthropology, and Levinasian analyses of the structure of human experience all offer important reasons to reject the notion that the self is a matter of individual definition. Humans are fundamentally social creatures, and their identity and self-understanding are not separable from that sociality. This has important ramifications for the notion of autonomy and self-worth. If I am understood by my community and social group to be subhuman, it may not be possible for me to see myself as a full moral agent.[9] Further, the emotional structure of my reasoning will be formed, at least in part, by the assumptions my community makes about appropriate emotions and values. So when I reflect on my own identity, I do not do so in a vacuum. I do so in the context of a community and a society that defines certain attributes and emotions as good, others as optional, and others as bad. Moreover, it is not simply cultural definitions and concepts that determine autonomy. The ability to act as a self-determining agent is an inherently relational property, one that can be destroyed when the relationships that constitute the self are broken or destroyed, and that must be reconstructed, in some cases, after a world-shattering experience. Anne Donchin argues that agency requires a relational context in which connections between people provide the strength and self-understandings that allow for both understanding oneself as capable of acting and the emotional resources for making choices and acting on them.[10] It is not just a matter of the social structures that permit one to see oneself as autonomous, but a matter of being in relationships that provide the emotional and relational structures without which the social self cannot act.

As both Augustine and Levinas argue, and as care theory has emphasized, humans are not independent and self-sufficient. We are finite, dependent, and limited, and this is not just a matter of physical limitations, though it includes those. It is also a matter of psychological and emotional limitations and dependencies. Rather than see our psychological dependence on others as a matter of weakness, or a matter of insufficient autonomy, then, we need to recognize that to be autonomous is to receive the right kind of support—physical, emotional, psychological, and social—to be able to see oneself as free to make choices and determine one's life.

III. Care Theory: Framing Assumptions

I have been arguing that the background assumptions of contemporary ab-stract accounts of justice make them inadequate theories for addressing some of the problems the new genetic technologies generate. An ethics of care be-gins with the assumption that humans are, first and foremost, relational be-ings, born into a world and into families and traditions that provide the con-texts of care without which no one can survive or flourish. Care theory, then, when addressing issues that are thought of as justice issues, offers important modifications to the abstract model of justice, insisting that we recognize the finite, dependent, situated, and relational nature of humans when we delib-erate about what justice demands of us. In particular, care ethics recognizes that part of what justice demands is that we analyze and construct social in-stitutions that take into account the needs and interdependencies that are a part of human life; that we recognize that humans come in a broad range of ages, social situations, and dependency conditions; and that we build these assumptions into our analysis of whether a given situation is reasonably just or not. Further, because care theory generates an account of justice based on the notion of care, it builds into the idea of justice a concern for the flour-ishing, the full development, of the individuals covered by the principles of justice, and recognizes the extent to which they are dependent on socially constituted communities.

This allows for a more adequate account of the issues raised by the new ge-netic technologies. It allows us to consider, for example, whether the genetic manipulation of embryos reflects a basic concern for the well-being of the family in which the embryo will become a person and the flourishing of the person the embryo will become. Future persons are notoriously difficult to ac-commodate in standard accounts of justice, as they cannot be accorded rights or let into the contract-making system until they reach a certain threshold of rationality. But in an ethics of care, one begins with the assumption that hu-mans exist with a wide range of capabilities and needs, and so the question becomes whether the genetic manipulation is important for maintaining the human social bonds of the community in question, and whether it also will contribute to the one manipulated being able to participate in practices of care and flourishing.

Further, if we begin with an account of care we must take into account the need that individuals have for social contexts within which they can develop and flourish. That is, we need to acknowledge in our account of justice the central importance of what I called earlier midlevel communities, or com-munities of identity in people's lives. An adequate account of justice, then, of the ways we structure our corporate lives together, needs to address the role that such communities play in our decisions and in the structuring of our identities. As Anne Donchin argues, genetic counseling decisions often do take such considerations into account, but the extent to which they do is obscured by the language of individualism in which such decisions are usually framed. She discusses, for example, cases in which the courts have been faced with families in the difficult situation of needing a bone marrow transplant from one child to be used to cure another.[11] When the child who is to donate the bone marrow is too young to understand the situation, or has a mental handicap preventing such understanding, the courts have generally been willing to endorse such donation, arguing that it is to the benefit of the donor to have her sibling survive, and to have an intact family. But the benefits in such a case go beyond the limited benefits to the individual of the continued companionship of a sibling. That the child can be a participant in such structures of care is an essential part of her existing as a member of the family. This latter consideration, however, has no place in the abstract justice language that tends to occur in court cases.

Justice, in a care account, must also recognize the relational aspect of human lives in another way. When the notion of rights is cashed out, it is essential that those rights be balanced with concomitant responsibilities, and the complex relationship between the rights and responsibilities developed. When, for example, we think of parental rights to reproduction (which I think are valuable and not to be taken lightly), we also need to articulate parental responsibilities in reproduction. We need to emphasize, for example, the irresponsibility involved in choosing to reproduce in ways that put the child-to-be at enormous risk, as happens when infertility treatments yield multiple births, and when parents volunteer to bear a cloned child in full knowledge that current techniques of cloning in higher mammals have not been tested, let alone perfected. We also need to articulate an account of responsible parenting in terms of how the choices adults make about reproduction reflect assumptions about which children are acceptable or worthy of being loved.

An ethic of care also leads to what I would call a chastened notion of justice, a conception of justice that understands itself to be fallible and always subject to revision based on new information and new challenges from those who have not yet had a chance to speak to issues. This is part of the emphasis on particularity and situatedness that is found in care theory; it is also a matter of respect for human finitude and limitations. That is, when one makes pronouncements about justice, it is also necessary to note that there may be exceptions to the principles one develops, and it is necessary to maintain internal systems of revision and revocation in the legal systems one develops.

Abstract accounts of justice attempt to include such revisability under the heading of "wide reflective equilibrium." The ideal scenario is one in which a wide range of voices is heard. But what such a notion obscures is the existence of extent to which there are gatekeepers and judges determining whose voices should be given weight, which judgments are reasonable, and which harms and benefits actually get to count as harms and benefits. In the case of cloning, as we have seen, benefits to existing adult decision makers, even when illusory, have been adjudicated as important. Harms to a child in terms of her ability to see herself as a unique individual are judged to be unimportant, on the order of making a silly mistake about car ownership. The effect of relying on wide reflective equilibrium is to include the considerations of those who have moral standing in an abstract account of justice, those who are largely self-sufficient individuals, and to exclude concerns about those whose identity is not yet formed, who are not yet (or never will be) independent agents.

In a care account of justice, concerns about the formation of identity and the particularities of the situation in which a person is born and lives move to a more central location in moral reasoning. Care does not reject some of the basic aspects of the standard accounts of justice, such as rights. Rights are an enormously important concept for any adequate account of justice, but they are not sufficient as an account of what justice requires. Care, instead, requires us to broaden the scope of our concerns about justice, so that while we continue to consider the reproductive rights of the prospective parents of an embryo, we also consider issues of what sort of community, with what sorts of values, we are becoming. Care theory provides resources for considering how parental decisions about a child's genetic destiny can form a parent's own character, for better or worse, and raises central questions about what sort of society we ought to aspire to become and what sorts of practices fit within that ideal.

IV. The Difference Care Makes: New Voices in the Public Square

Let's turn to the specific issues considered by the authors of *From Chance to Choice*, eugenics and cloning. In the case of eugenics I've noted that the authors tend to assume that there are only two levels of human interaction, the level of individual decision making and the level of social policy affecting all within, say, a nation. I've argued that a care account of justice should deal with concerns about midlevel communities, communities of identity. In the case of eugenics an emphasis on the notion of identity constituting communities allows us to see that the evil of eugenics operates at a level that is not captured by the authors' analysis, namely the level of constituting whole communities in terms of elevation of identity (in the case of those who define themselves as having desirable genes) and derogation of identity (in the case of those defined as the source of degeneration). When doctors sterilized young black women against their will and without their knowledge, the results of that action were not just a violation of the rights of the individual women, though they certainly were that. The results went much further, destroying, for example, the ability of many in the black community to trust the medical community (which is still perceived as largely white).[12] The identity-constituting effects are also visible in the white community, with its implicit assumption that white lives are more valuable than other lives, and with its tendency to define identity in terms of the denial of the full humanity of others, and in terms that justify exploitation and self-aggrandizement.

Before, then, we offer an assessment of eugenics as justifiable in theory as a matter of improvement of individual lives, we need to think through whether "genetic improvement" can ever be separated from the illegitimate assumption that some human lives are worth less than others. I would argue that we cannot assess eugenics decisions in terms of individual choice and public policy alone, but we must place such decisions in the context of communities of identity. Eugenic decisions can derive from and entrench deeply wrong notions of in-group and out-group identity.[13]

Further, accounts of eugenics that treat improvement as a legitimate goal run into the problem of ignoring finitude and embodiment. It is one thing to identify a specific genetic disorder and attempt to modify it so that an individual can participate more fully in life. It is quite another thing to countenance "genetic improvement" overall. Respect for the limitations of human existence should make us extremely skeptical about any blanket claims about the perfectibility or improvement of human beings. Given that we live in an environment that is changing more rapidly than at any time in the past, largely due to human activity, to claim that we know what intelligence is and can select the genetic endowment that produces it seems ludicrous. But this is a crucial aspect of the argument for the acceptability of the general eugenic program, and if it goes, the argument collapses. If we really cannot determine what intelligence is, let alone which genetic sequences are likely to produce more of it under rapidly changing circumstances, then we ought not base our moral conclusions on that possibility.

A care perspective offers a needed corrective to this perfectionism in standard justice thought. Care requires that we learn to value a wide variety of ways of being human, that we learn to respect the particular person for who he or she is. We need to reject what David Tracy calls "an emerging global monoculture" of human communities and lives.[14] This doesn't mean we cannot choose to fix specific genetic disorders when we learn how to do so, but it does mean that we will be wary of global fixes, of changes to genetic codes that claim to improve the whole "genetic endowment" of humanity. Changes that offer a reasonable chance for an individual to lead a normally fulfilling life are one thing; changes that offer to elevate humans in general to a new ontological status are another. In particular, with its emphasis people existing in loving and affective relationships with each other, care theory is very resistant to any simplistic notion that increasing some aspect of intelligence will lead to improvement. Care is simply not the sort of thing that can be generated by genetics. It is a matter of being socialized, loved, and made capable of caring by existing within relationships.

I would advocate, in fact, a moratorium on any blanket claims about the improvement of human nature. We are not in a position to know what exactly would be an improvement in human nature, and we should adopt a position of sufficient humility that we cease claiming to know this. In this I am drawing, of course, on Augustine's notion that we cannot take the place of God, but I am also drawing on a rather unlikely resource, a biologist and environmental writer, Wes Jackson. Jackson argues that we humans have an unfortunate tendency to assume that we know better than nature how life ought to be ordered, so our solution to environmental and agricultural processes tends to involve "fixing" nature's perceived errors.[15] Nature has the unfortunate tendency to produce weeds and insects where we want to grow crops, so we fix nature by pouring on herbicides and pesticides. We've discovered slowly that this generates a spiral of increasingly tenacious insects and the loss of natural balances, but we continue to try to apply fixes to these, generating a new set of problems.

According to Jackson the problem is that we always assume knowledge is our strong suit, that we can solve problems with increases in knowledge and understanding. But what if we rethought our approach, he asks, and started thinking of ignorance as our strong suit? We'll always be more ignorant than we are knowledgeable, and if we were to accept that fact and begin to try to work with what we find in nature, rather than control it through knowledge, we might find that there are other ways of developing agriculture, ways that respect the particular environmental and geographical constraints of particular locations, ways that require us to move more slowly and assume less control over the world.[16]

In a similar manner we may need to begin to learn what it is to be human by accepting human differences and finitudes rather than assuming that the best way to think about human nature is as something we can modify with impunity. Sara Ruddick offers the lovely image of mothering as a matter of negotiating with nature on behalf of love, a negotiation that is respectful, appreciative, and at times confrontational.[17] Her conception of nature does not require that we accept an absolute and timeless account of essential natures, but it does require an acceptance of limitations imposed by what is found in life, a willingness to work with the given rather than to seek absolute domination and control over human life. It is a willingness that is essential to parenting, and a willingness that also needs to inform public policy making in the area of wide-scale public endorsement of changes in the human genetic code.

If we turn to the issue of cloning we will also see that a care account of justice offers a very different context for analyzing the ethical considerations that are relevant. We've seen how Levinas emphasizes the uniqueness of the other and the need to refrain from turning the other into a mere copy of oneself, or into a defined set of categories. This gives us a language for thinking about why human cloning may be morally problematic that is better, I think, than the language that has become very popular in recent years of manufacturing versus begetting. As the authors of *From Chance to Choice* note, the fact that there is a high level of technological intervention involved in cloning is not sufficient, in and of itself, to show that cloning is morally problematic. Every new intervention into human biological processes tends to be greeted with concern about technology taking over the natural, a concern that seems generated more by a fear of the unknown than by any deep moral principle. But having noted that it is not simply the artificiality of the process that generates moral concern, we cannot stop there.

Reproductive cloning is attractive because it seems to offer children who are known quantities. Theorists offer lip service to the notion that genes do not determine identity, but go on to endorse parents who might want to replace a child who has died, or who undergo infertility treatment and choose to clone an embryo so that later "copies" might be made of a child who turns out well. This reveals a deep fear of difference, of children who are unpredictably and maddeningly individual. Rather than celebrating the way in which each child is uniquely a bearer of her own image of the infinite, we pursue technological fixes that will produce children who are "known quantities," whose lives are predefined as "acceptable."[18]

When reproductive cloning is envisioned we need to ask questions about what sorts of communities we have become and are becoming, and how reproductive practices fit into those communities. If we are concerned to create communities where, as Levinas has urged us, there is a social and legal structure in place that permits each of us to meet others with care for them in their particularity, then we may need to be skeptical about the claims made for reproductive cloning, for the need parents are claimed to have for a genetic relationship to their children. Before baptizing such a "need" as legitimate and overriding, we need to stop and think about what it means for us as a community to assume that parents can only truly love children who are their genetic kin.[19] The experiences of adoptive parents and stepparents suggest that it is quite within the realm of possibility for parents to have loving, mutually fulfilling relationships with children who are not their genetic kin, and we need to be a bit suspicious of the naturalizing language that hides this possibility.

Public policy questions about the uses of new genetic technologies cannot exclude questions about the meaning of these technologies for particular lives in particular historical circumstances. We cannot discuss eugenic programs without recognizing the implicit assumptions every eugenic program must make that there are certain types of humans who are unacceptable, who should be prevented from existing, or at the very least from reproducing more of the same, subpar genes. We cannot discuss cloning without recognizing the implicit assumption that it is preferable to produce a known quantity than to welcome an unpredictable stranger into one's life. Assumptions such as these structure the way we think of our identities and structure our communities, and if we do not examine them critically we are likely to become people who cannot care for others, who cannot see the beauty of the infinite in the face of one who is not like us.

V. Conclusion

No theory of justice can be truly neutral with respect to its conception of human life. Abstract theories make a claim to neutrality, but their implicit assumptions demonstrate that the ideal life is one in which an autonomous individual achieves social success in a competitive arena. Barriers to competitive participation constitute harms, and anything that facilitates competition constitutes a benefit. This ideal is an important component of the abstract conception of justice, and it is what leads proponents to claim that justice must be silent about how we ought to shape our communities and social structures, and about what sorts of people citizens ought to become. This ideal of neutrality is also what leads ethicists such as H. Tristram Engelhardt Jr. to conclude that in a secular liberal state there can be no substantive government limitations on genetic manipulations performed on embryos, other than constraints imposed by the consent of individual moral agents.[20]

But we need not adopt this ideal of human existence, and we should not adopt it. Human lives are never self-defining and self-sustaining in the ways that would be needed for neutrality to make sense. Humans have limited abilities to care for themselves, and they are dependent on the others around them to support and provide for them. Given this finitude and dependency, abstract justice, with its fiction of absolute independence, cannot offer a vision of how we should arrange our lives together to provide for the support we all need. An alternative vision of a life that respects the networks of care within which we all exist, and that revises the notion of rationality to include concerns about how we sustain and strengthen care and concern for particular others, is available to us. We've seen how it is articulated in overlapping ways by feminist theorists of care, by an Augustinian anthropology, and by Levinas's investigation into the nature of human existence.

These offer us the resources to articulate and live out a conception of human life that recognizes limitations on the range of lives that can be considered good ones, that advocates social structures that encourage care and respect for others as a basic and ineliminable component of the good human life, and that rejects social policies that allow individuals to be defined as worthwhile or not on the basis of their genetic makeup. Such a conception of human life offers resources for thinking about public policy in ways that respect the collective and communal nature of human identity. Patricia Williams offers us two metaphors for human community. We can think of human community as a jar full of marbles, she writes, in which each marble is roughly equivalent to the others and all are self-contained. When one marble is removed from the jar, the other marbles are unaffected, other than perhaps experiencing slight shifts in location.

But an alternative metaphor is available to us. We can also think of human community as a jar full of soap bubbles. When one bubble pops, the others are not unaffected. Instead, because the boundaries of each are partially dependent on the boundaries of the others, none can be changed without affecting the others' very identity.[21] It may be that we would prefer not to think of ourselves as soap bubbles, though there is a long history of philosophers trying to help us see that the human condition is one of transience and dependence—that we are but grass that withers, to invoke a very different image. But we will develop better public policy if we respect the human condition as it actually is than if we insist on seeing ourselves as we are not.

Notes

1. Marilyn Friedman, "Beyond Caring: The De-Moralization of Gender," in *An Ethic of Care: Feminist and Interdisciplinary Persepctives*, ed. Mary Jeanne Larrabee (New York: Routledge, 1993), pp. 258–73.

2. The topic of eugenics may seem irrelevant here if it is thought of as a failed policy used by the Nazi regime to justify its genocidal project. But, as recent historical studies have shown, eugenics was a worldwide movement, with adherents from various points on the political spectrum. See, for example, Diane Paul's *The Politics of Heredity: Essays on Eugenics, Biomedicine, and the Nature-Nurture Debate* (Albany: State University of New York Press, 1998); and Daniel Kevels, *In the Name of Eugenics: Genetics and Uses of Human Heredity* (Cambridge, Mass.: Harvard University Press, 1995). Further, although few are willing to use the term "eugenics" today, the issue of eugenics is central to any ethical evaluation of contemporary genetic technologies, as evidenced by its appearance in any number of recent analyses of genetic interventions. See, for example, the National Bioethics Advisory Commission's report on human cloning, which includes a lengthy section on the topic of eugenics (reprinted in Richard Sherlock and John Morrey, eds., *Ethical Issues in Biotechnology* (Lanham, Md.: Rowman & Littlefield, 2002), pp. 527–50.

3. Allen Buchanan, Dan W. Brock, Norman Daniels, and Daniel Wickler, *From Chance to Choice: Genetics and Justice* (Cambridge: Cambridge University Press, 2000). Hereafter, references to this book will be inserted in the text in parentheses.

4. An excellent discussion of the history of the eugenics movement can be found in Diane Paul's *The Politics of Heredity: Essays on Eugenics, Biomedicine, and the Nature-Nurture Debate* (Albany: State University of New York Press, 1998).

5. See, for example, Eric Posner and Richard Posner, "The Demand for Human Cloning," in *Clones and Clones*, ed. Martha Nussbaum and Cass Sunstein (New York: Norton, 1998).

6. A similar argument is developed by Leon Kass in his widely anthologized essay, "The Wisdom of Repugnance," in *The Ethics of Human Cloning* (Washington, D.C.: American Enterprise Institute, 1998), pp. 33–35.

7. Oliver O'Donovan, *Begotten or Made?* (New York: Clarendon, 1984).

8. See, for example, Charles Taylor's brief analysis of the provision of health care in "Philosophical Reflections on Caring Practices," in *The Crisis of Care: Affirming and Restoring Caring Practices in the Helping Professions*, ed. Susan Phillips and Patricia Benner (Washington, D.C.: Georgetown University Press, 1994), pp. 174–87.

9. See, for example, Paul Benson's "Feeling Crazy: Self-Worth and the Social Character of Responsibility," in *Relational Autonomy: Feminist Perspectives on Autonomy, Agency, and the Social Self*, ed. Catriona Mackenzie and Natalie Stoljar (New York: Oxford University Press, 2000), pp. 72–93.

10. Anne Donchin, "Autonomy and Interdependence: Quandaries in Genetic Decision Making," in *Relational Autonomy: Feminist Perspectives on Autonomy,*

Agency, and the Social Self, ed. Catriona Mackenzie and Natalie Stoljar (New York: Oxford University Press, 2000), pp. 236–58.

11. Donchin, "Autonomy and Interdependence," p. 242.

12. Sociologists have called this generalized mistrust of the white medical community the "Tuskegee Effect," because of the notorious Tuskegee experiment, which involved the same sorts of racialized assumptions about lives not worth living that were in evidence in the forced sterilizations of women of color.

13. The concerns raised in this paragraph are shared by others, particularly those concerned about the way "genetic improvement" will play out in a society structured in racist and classist ways. See, for example, Jonathan Beckwith's "The Genetics of Human Behavior: Lessons from the Human Genome Project," and Fatima Jackson's "The Human Genome Project and the African American Community: Race, Diversity, and American Science," both in *The Human Genome Project and Minority Communities: Ethical, Social, and Political Implications*, ed. Raymond Zilinskas and Peter Balint (Westport, Conn.: Praeger, 2001), pp. 21–34, 35–52, respectively.

14. David Tracy, "Human Cloning and the Public Realm: A Defense of Intuitions of the Good," in *Clones and Clones*, ed. Martha Nussbaum and Cass Sunstein (New York: Norton, 1998), p. 192.

15. Wes Jackson, *Becoming Native to This Place* (Lexington: University Press of Kentucky, 1994).

16. Jackson, *Becoming Native*, p. 24.

17. Sara Ruddick, *Maternal Thinking: Toward a Politics of Peace* (Boston: Beacon, 1989), p. 77.

18. See, for example, cases that are offered as reasonable scenarios for reproductive cloning in Andrea Bonnicksen's *Crafting a Cloning Policy: From Dolly to Stem Cells* (Washington, D.C.: Georgetown University Press, 2002), pp. 190–91. In each case the cloning aims at avoiding "otherness."

19. Jean Elshtain notes this in "To Clone or Not to Clone," in *Clones and Clones*, ed. Martha Nussbaum and Cass Sunstein (New York: Norton, 1998), pp. 188–89.

20. H. Tristram Engelhardt Jr., "Germ-Line Genetic Engineering and Moral Diversity: Moral Controversies in a Post-Christian World," in *Ethical Issues in Biotechnology*, ed. Richard Sherlock and John Morrey (Lanham, Md.: Rowman & Littlefield, 2002), pp. 509–11.

21. Patricia J. Williams, *The Rooster's Egg: On the Persistence of Prejudice* (Cambridge, Mass.: Harvard University Press, 1995), p. 86.

Index

abstract justice, 165–67, 178, 184. *See also* justice and care
abstraction and idealization, 26–27
adoption, 141
alterity, 81
animals, 57–58
Aristotle, 7–8, 25, 56
artificial insemination by donor, 137, 139
assisted reproduction, 140–45, 149, 165; and adoption, 141; commodity, not treatment, 151–52, 153; and donated gametes, 148–49; government regulation of, 155–61; morality of, 145–50, 150–55, 162; and parent/child relationship, 157
Augustine, 18, 23, 48–49, 79–81, 83, 97, 99, 100, 110, 115–16, 136, 175; contrasted with care theory, 65–74; and desires, 145; on embodiment, 58–62; and feminist theory, 52–54; on finitude, 62–63; on hierarchy, 70–74, 126; on human nature, 54–65, 126–28, 129–31; on love, 54–58; and place of God in human life, 129–31; and Platonism, 58–63; and relational identity, 56, 63–65, 177
authority, 72, 97
autonomy, 45, 50n21, 64, 126–27; and isolation, 128; and state regulation, 155–56, 158–59. *See also* reproductive freedom

Baer, Judith, 127
Baier, Annette, 88, 160
Benson, Paul, 47, 64–65
bias, 129
Brock, Dan W., 166
brotherhood, 94, 96
Bubeck, Diemut, 106–7, 123–25
Buber, Martin, 88
Buchanan, Allen, 166

Caputo, John, 91
care, 24–29; and embodiment, 30–33; and family relationships, 160–61, 165; and gender, 115–19, 126–27; and interdependence, 33–35; and justice, 14, 18, 29, 87–88, 106–7, 114–15, 124–25, 165–66, 178–80,

184–85; and love, 54–58; and
masculinity, 128; origins of, 34,
74–75; other-directed, 121–23, 145;
providers of, 12–13; and proximity,
57; and relational self, 35–40; and
social structures, 33, 41, 86–88,
105–6, 111–13, 116, 161, 176–77;
social value of, 2, 12
care theory, 153; and Augustine, 65–74;
definition of care, 24–29; and
enjoyment, 83; and eugenics,
182–84; and evil, 68–69; and
hierarchy, 70–74; history of, 14–17;
ideal of human nature, 9–10, 21–23,
40–48, 52, 104–5, 115–16, 119–23,
131; and Levinas, 91, 92–98; and
public/private, 135–36; and
relativism, 105–6
Caring, 14–15, 88, 99
chaos, 71–74, 126
citizenship, 35, 41
City of God, 59, 71, 72
cloning: abstract justice analysis, 166,
168, 171–74; and communities of
identity, 184; health risks of, 171–72;
and loss of identity, 172; and public
neutrality, 176–77
Code, Lorraine, 16
commodification, 140, 147–49, 157, 161
communication, 85
community, 56; of identity, 170–71,
174–76, 178–79, 181, 184. *See also*
relational self
Confessions, 54, 56, 59, 60, 62, 65, 70
contract ethics, 31, 83, 89; and
parent/child relation, 160–61
creational ontology, 54–55, 57, 59,
65–66, 73, 74–75

Damasio, Antonio, 47
Daniels, Norman, 166
delight, 83
democracy, 33

dependency, 116
Descartes, Rene, 85
Descartes' Error, 47
Dietz, Mary, 15
difference: and cloning, 183; gender
difference, 100, 117
discipline of the body, 32
donation of gametes, 138–40, 153; of
eggs, 139–40; of sperm, 137–38, 146,
156–57
Donchin, Anne, 177, 179
dualism, 83
duty to self and other, 86–90

Elshtain, Jean B., 15, 16
embodiment, 10, 30–33, 40–41; in
Augustine, 58–62; control of, 61;
emotions, 24–27, 42–43; and
flourishing, 43–45; in Levinas, 81,
82–85; as origin of care, 114; and
particularity, 58–62; and reason, 47;
and reproductive decisions, 145
empathy, and understanding, 32, 42–43
essentialism, 15. *See also* gender
difference and mothering
ethical responsibility, 81
ethical theory, 7–8, 89; and fact/value
distinction, 3–6, 11; and mothering,
117–19; and physical harm, 31–32;
and practice, 1–3; and principles,
105; and relational self, 36
ethics, and communication, 85
ethics of care. *See* care theory
eugenics: abstract justice analysis of,
166, 168–70; and community
identity, 181; and perfectionism,
181–82; and public neutrality,
176–77; and racism, 187n13
evil, 59–60, 68–69

the face, 82, 91
fact/value distinction, 3–6, 11
fallibility, 129

family relationships, 45–46. *See also* mothering; paternity; reproductive freedom

feminine: in Levinas, 95–98; voice, 115

Feminist Morality, 16

feminist theory: and Augustine, 52–54; equality and difference, 8–9; and fact/value distinction, 4–6; and human nature, 104–5; and Levinas, 97–98; and loyalty, 66–67; and mothering, 15, 118–19; and religion, 129–30; and transcendence, 130–31

finitude, 33–35, 62–63; and flourishing, 46–47

flesh and spirit, 58–62

flourishing, 2–3, 21–22, 43–48, 174; and genetic manipulation, 176–77; and health, 43–45; and justice, 178; and social self, 37

freedom, and social self, 38. *See also* autonomy; reproductive freedom

Friedman, Marilyn, 45, 165

friendship, 55–57, 59

From Chance to Choice, 166, 180, 183; analysis of cloning, 171–74; analysis of eugenics, 169–71; critique of, 174–77; methodology of, 168

future persons, 178

gender difference, 17; and care theory, 107; and ethical theory, 95; and mothering, 117

Gilligan, Carol, 14–17, 55–56, 114, 165

God: in Augustine, 129–31; and domination, 72; and evil, 54–55; image of, 57–58, 66, 70, 74–75, 80, 98; in Levinas, 129–31; love of, 55, 57–58, 60; and properly ordered love, 54–55; relationship to, 65–68, 80–81, 84

Habermas, Jürgen, 17, 136–37

Halpern, Jodi, 42–43

health, 21–22; and human flourishing, 43–45

health care: and assisted reproduction, 151; as commodity, 151–52

health risks: of assisted reproduction, 143, 152, 155–56; of harvesting eggs, 140

Held, Virginia, 16, 35, 41, 72, 94, 107, 127

hierarchy, 65, 70–74, 126

Hobbes, Thomas, 25–26, 55

human nature: and abstraction, 81–82; for Augustine, 54–74; and care, 14, 24–29, 40–43, 52; and cloning, 170–71; criticisms of, 104–5; and embodiment, 30, 82–85; exclusion of women, 104–5; and fact/value distinction, 5–6, 11; and finitude, 33–35; and genetic manipulation, 176–77; ideal of, 43–48; ideal as subjective or objective, 123–24; improvement of, 182–83; and justice, 184–85; masculine model of, 8–9; and particularity, 85, 108–13; relational, 16–17, 27, 35–40, 80–82; teleological account, 6–7; and theory, 2

Hume, David, 26

ideal of human nature, 131; and cultural critique, 115; and ethical reasoning, 119–23; as objective or subjective, 123–24; and particularity, 111–12, 125

idealization and abstraction, 26–27

identity: and cloning, 172–73, 183; and community, 170–71, 174–76, 178–79, 181

idolatry, 67

ignorance, 182–83

In a Different Voice, 14–15, 55–56, 165

in vitro fertilization, 141

individualism, 34–35, 80, 83, 166, 174, 176–77, 180

infinite, 85; demands of morality, 86–90
infinity, 81, 91–92
interdependence, 12, 33–35, 40; in
    Augustine, 62–63; and flourishing,
    45–46

Jackson, Wes, 13, 182
Jonas, Hans, 172
justice: abstract, 178, 184; and care, 29,
    87–88, 106–7, 114–15, 124–25,
    165–66; ideal of, 93; and self-
    sacrifice, 86–90

Kant, Immanuel, 84, 86
Kittay, Eva Feder, 24, 114
knowledge, 22; and love, 63; and
    particularity, 53, 85; relational nature
    of, 63–64; of the self, 63–64; and sin,
    68; and trust, 62; and women's
    experience, 15, 16. See also reason
Koehn, Darryl, 135

Levinas, Emmanuel, 18, 23, 48–49, 75,
    110, 115–16, 136; and care theory,
    91, 92–98; and cloning, 183; and
    embodiment, 82–85; and feminist
    theory, 79, 97–98; and gender,
    95–98; on God, 129–31; on human
    nature, 126, 128–31; and
    particularity, 85; and relational
    identity, 80–82, 177; and social
    structures, 184
love: in Augustine, 74–75; and care,
    54–58; and conflict, 60–61; of God,
    55, 57, 58, 60; and knowledge, 63; of
    neighbor, 57; properly ordered,
    66–67; for the self, 120–21
loyalty, absolute versus limited, 66–67

Mackay, Fiona, 118
MacKinnon, Catharine, 115
masculinity and care, 128
Maternal Thinking, 15

May, Elaine Tyler, 150
methodology, of abstract justice
    reasoning, 167–68
moral reasoning, 125
moral responsibility and social self, 64–65
mothering, 28, 38, 107, 117–19, 120;
    and assisted reproduction, 158

naturalistic fallacy, 3–6
nature: state of, 25–26; teleological or
    descriptive meaning, 6–7, 10, 21;
    wisdom of, 13
Noddings, Nel, 14–16, 24, 29, 34–35,
    57–58, 68, 75, 80, 83, 86, 88, 93, 94,
    99, 105–7, 110, 113–14, 127;
    barricades example, 123–25; ideal
    self, 120–21; on role of state, 158
nurturing, 127–28. See also mothering
Nussbaum, Martha, 47

objective ideal of human nature,
    123–24
O'Donovan, Oliver, 173
O'Neil, Onora, 26, 43
order and chaos, 71–74, 126

parental rights: and cloning, 171–73.
    See also reproductive freedom
partiality, 29
particularity, 30–33, 36–37, 43, 99, 135;
    and assisted reproduction, 156; and
    care, 58; and embodiment, 58–62;
    and flourishing, 105, 108–13; for
    Levinas, 85; and reason, 62–63;
paternity, 95, 147
physical desire, 65, 67
political: activism, 126, 130; for
    Levinas, 92–95
power, 25, 72
principles, 16, 105, 125
private, 135
profit motive, and assisted reproduction,
    154–55, 162

pronatalism, 142–43, 149, 158–59
proximity, 81; and care, 57–58
public, 135

racism, 37, 41, 124, 173; and assisted
    reproduction, 150, 162; and
    eugenics, 169, 187n13; and medical
    practice, 181; and social structures,
    158
reason, 9–10, 25; abstract and
    particular, 125; and dependence,
    62–63; and embodiment, 30–31, 33;
    and emotion, 42, 47; and human
    nature, 81, 82, 92; and lived
    experience, 15, 16, 166; and love,
    74–75; and morality, 84; and rational
    economic man, 111; and sex
    difference, 27, 70–71; situated, 16,
    41; social nature, 63–64; and trust,
    75; and violence, 93
reciprocity, 57
reflective equilibrium, 167, 180
Relational Autonomy, 64
relational self, 10, 35–40, 41, 74–75,
    177; in Augustine, 63–65; and
    demands of multiple others, 87; and
    justice, 178; and new reproductive
    technologies, 137, 149–50. See also
    community of identity
relationships, 84; asymmetrical, 97; of
    care or commodification, 148–49;
    moral evaluation of, 149
reproductive freedom, 142, 144,
    155–56, 179; and cloning, 171–73
reproductive technologies, 136–45
Ruddick, Sara, 15, 16, 34, 38, 83, 85,
    107, 110, 119, 127, 183

Schlabach, Gerald, 58
self, moral ideal of, 120–23
self determination. See autonomy
self-sacrifice, 86–90
separation, 55. See also individualism

Sevenhuijsen, Selma, 88, 107
sex differences, 100; and hierarchy,
    70–71; and reason, 70–71
sin, 68–69, 72; and bodily desires,
    58–59
situationalism, 108–13
social contract, 25–26, 27. See also
    contract ethics
social criticism, 41–42
social self. See relational self
social structures, 43–44; and assisted
    reproduction, 155–61; and authority,
    70–71; and autonomy, 64–65; and
    care, 87–88, 107, 111–13; and
    emotional health, 47–48; and
    finitude, 46–47; and moral
    responsibility, 90; and political
    change, 73–74; and scarce medical
    resources, 144
sperm donation, 137–38, 146, 156–57;
    post-mortem, 138–39
Starting at Home, 94–95
surrogacy, 136–37, 139, 146–48

Taylor, Charles, 34
The Trinity, 70
theory: and practice, 1–3, 44; and
    relativism, 42; and social context, 39
transcendence, 65–67, 74–75, 80,
    91–92; and feminist theory, 130–31;
    and hierarchy, 71–72
teleology, 6–7; and moral reasoning,
    121
Totality and Infinity, 94, 95
trinity, 57, 73
Tronto, Joan, 16, 28, 33, 35, 46, 83,
    87–88, 94, 107, 114
trust, 75, 160; and knowledge, 62

universals, 105, 135; and human nature,
    24, 39; and particulars, 108–13; and
    relativism, 62–63
utopian thought, 69, 95

What Can She Know? 16
Wickler, Daniel, 166
will, as source of evil for Augustine, 59,
    68–69
Willett, Cynthia, 91, 97
Williams, Patricia, 185

women, 30; and care theory, 79; and
    ethical theory, 14–15, 17; and love,
    126–27; social expectations, 127–28,
    159
women's voice, 53, 128
Wood, Julia, 114

About the Author

Ruth E. Groenhout is associate professor of philosophy at Calvin College. She is coeditor (with Marya Bower) of *Philosophy, Feminism, and Faith* (Indiana University Press, 2003).